ADVENTURES IN GENEALOGY

Case Studies in the Unusual

by Norman Edgar Wright
Professor Emeritus, Family and Local History
Brigham Young University

CLEARFIELD

Printed for
Clearfield Company, Inc. by
Genealogical Publishing Co., Inc.
Baltimore, Maryland
1994

Reprinted for
Clearfield Company, Inc. by
Genealogical Publishing Co., Inc.
Baltimore, Maryland
2003

International Standard Book Number: 0-8063-4500-4

Made in the United States of America

PREFACE AND ACKNOWLEDGMENTS

This book contains case studies of some unusual genealogical experiences I have had, and it has been written primarily for those interested in genealogy and family history. These experiences have been motivating as well as educational to me, and I hope they might be the same to you. Each study has been documented so that the approaches taken and the sources investigated might serve as guides for your own research, or for use in a classroom setting.

Most of my working hours during the past thirty-six years have been spent studying, researching, and teaching American genealogy. This has included applied research on my own lines as well as those of others, and it has encompassed my work as an instructor and director of the subject at Brigham Young University, where thousands of student pedigrees have been personally analyzed and evaluated. I have been excited and consumed with the work over this long period, and the case studies outlined here represent a few of my most interesting experiences.

Special appreciation is expressed to Ronald Anderson, the Jesse E. Taylor family, Clyde M. Lunceford, and all of the students who have taken genealogical courses at Brigham Young University. They have strengthened my faith in divine guidance, and without knowing it, they have given me strength and determination to continue in the work when discouragement might have dictated otherwise. Appreciation is also expressed to my wonderful family, both living and dead, because they have been the real motivation for my interest in the subject. Special gratitude and love are also expressed to my lovely wife, Daniele, who suggested I write this book; she said: "If you'll write it, they'll read it.!"

NORMAN EDGAR WRIGHT
Pleasant Grove, Utah
June 30, 1994

CONTENTS

ILLUSTRATIONS AND PHOTOGRAPHS

INTRODUCTION

The study of genealogy and family history is one of the most interesting and rewarding activities you will ever engage in; it is detective work at its best, and it challenges your mental as well as your physical resources. The satisfaction of personal accomplishment is a reward you can obtain from the work; whether it be strengthening family ties, creating new and lasting friendships, locating living and deceased relatives, or solving some other problem.

Genealogists and family historians are a peculiar breed and are usually consumed with their work; but don't ever get one started talking about his experiences, or if you do, prepare yourself for a long and one-sided conversation. They are eternal optimists and are always looking for new avenues and approaches to their problems, and they are very determined in their quests. They are usually generous in sharing their findings with others, and they are always willing to give free advice, but unfortunately there are a few who would take advantage of others; beware of them!

It is interesting to know that most genealogists and family historians believe they are guided by some special force; whether it be physical or spiritual, luck or fate, providence or inspiration, they are convinced others are helping them find information. I consider myself one among them and feel personally rewarded for my association with them. I have had many unusual genealogical experiences, and I truly believe that others have helped me in my quests, both seen and unseen.

My interest has not always been with the subject, and perhaps a brief review of some personal history leading up to full involvement in the work will help you understand where I am coming from in this book.

If you were to poll my high school friends and associates, they would very probably vote me last to succeed in such activities as genealogy and family history. In fact, I had no academic skills nor interests in such work during my youth and young adulthood; girls, cars, and sports were my social interests, and livestock farming was my primary occupational interest.

After military service during the latter part of World War II, a two-year LDS missionary experience in New Zealand, then another military tour of duty during the Korean War, my interests were finally directed toward additional schooling; primarily because of the "GI Bill," but my occupational interests still remained in the field of Livestock production and management. Degrees were obtained from Brigham Young University in Provo, Utah and Utah State University in Logan, Utah in Animal Husbandry and Agricultural Economics, then I entered my chosen profession, working for a "prosperous" Uncle and dreaming of a partnership with him. He had assisted me financially with my schooling and had provided me with a checkbook and management experience after graduation, but that tour of duty lasted less than three months, and my earlier dreams of partnership became nothing more than romantic imagination.

With a young growing family to provide for, I found work as a carpenter, a cement finisher, and as a general construction worker, but none of these jobs were what I really wanted, so I began "beating the bushes" for more satisfying possibilities.

Frank Smith, well known genealogical author, lecturer, and researcher (now deceased) was a neighbor and close friend of mine at that time (fall of 1957). And while attending one of his classes at our local church, he suggested that I apply for work at the LDS Genealogical Society's Research Department (where he was employed), because they were expanding and looking for new researchers. He suggested the pay wasn't the best, but he said it was interesting work and I might enjoy it. I hadn't thought of that type of work as a profession before, but now it seemed alright, so I applied. I also applied for a job as an "Insurance Adjuster" at the same time, but I continued working as a carpenter while awaiting their responses.

As it happened, the insurance job became available first, and after a personal interview, the company accepted me and sent me home with books to study for the new job. When I returned home that same day, my wife said Phil Cederlof had just called from the LDS Church

Employment Office, and they had accepted my application; directing me to report for work the following day. What a dilemma! Now I had three jobs and would have to make some fast decisions or I would be in real difficulty. My carpentry job was only temporary, and I wasn't really worried about it, but which of these other two jobs should I accept? I had already accepted the insurance job, but my feelings were now leaning toward the Job at the Genealogical Society.

At this point, I would like to take you back to 1948 and relate an experience I had shortly before leaving on an LDS mission to New Zealand. In the LDS Church, it is a common and recommended practice for members to obtain a "Patriarchal Blessing" (father's blessing) from a local church official who has received a special calling as "Patriarch." The member usually receives the blessing as a young adult, but that is not a requisite, and it is accepted as a guide and promise for blessings throughout one's life, based of course upon righteous living. My sweet mother had encouraged me to obtain my patriarchal blessing on several previous occasions, but for one reason or another, I had procrastinated and not obtained one.

One beautiful morning in September of 1948, while in Salt Lake City receiving training before our departure to New Zealand, my friend, Lewis John Winter, and I were walking along South Temple Street, just east of the Hotel Utah. The subject of patriarchal blessings had been discussed in class the previous day, and we were talking about the new "Church Patriarch" Eldred G. Smith, who had just been appointed. I mentioned to Lew that I hadn't received a patriarchal blessing and probably wouldn't receive mine until after my mission. He turned to me and said: "Why don't you go into the Church Office Building and see if you can get one from the new Church Patriarch?" This was not the authorized procedure, because a member was supposed to receive a recommend from his Bishop and get his blessing from the local Patriarch, but I accepted his suggestion and we walked right into Church Headquarters (47 East South Temple); we were standing in front of the building while we were talking about the subject.

We entered the main foyer and were questioned by a receptionist, and when we told him what we wanted, he directed us to Eldred G. Smith's office, which was immediately across the hall on the main floor. We enter the office and another receptionist asked us how she could help us. I responded and told her that we were missionaries, about ready to depart for New Zealand, and I didn't yet have my patriarchal blessing: "Would it be possible to receive one from the Church Patriarch?" She was very polite and said: "Please have a seat. I'll ask Elder Smith." She was gone only a moment or two, then returned, saying: "Elder Smith with see you now!" We were somewhat shocked, but very pleased, and entered his office which was immediately to the West.

Elder Smith was most cordial, asking us our names and suggesting this was an unusual procedure, but he would be happy to give me a blessing. He asked me my name and birthdate, my parent's names, and one or two other general questions, then he placed his hands on my head and gave me a patriarchal blessing. The blessing was recorded electronically and would be sent to me some time later; I was actually in the mission field when my parents sent it to me about a month later. As I read it over and over, I was somewhat astounded with the promises and challenges I had received; also, I was fascinated with the many things the Patriarch had told me about myself, both in the past and in the future; he had not known me nor my family before this short encounter, and I wondered how he could say the many things he did. I had not remembered each of these points as he was giving me the blessing, but it was a pleasure to read them after, and I reviewed the blessing from time to time after receiving it.

Now, back to our main story. My wife and I were trying to decide which job I should accept in 1957; should it be the insurance job (which I had already accepted but hadn't yet appeared for work) or should it be the genealogical research job which Frank Smith had recommended? At that moment, my patriarchal blessing came to mind, and I recalled some of the promises Patriarch Smith had given me nearly a decade earlier. I mentioned it to my wife, and she said: "Go get your blessing and let's read it together!" After reading the entire document carefully, there was no question in either of our minds as to which job I should accept, and the very next day (11 December 1957), I became an employee of the Research Department of the LDS Genealogical Society in Salt Lake City; to work full time in the most fascinating subject I had ever studied, and to enjoy the work without major interruption for over thirty-five years. It was almost a shame to be paid for such interesting and pleasant work, but I did have to support my young growing family; to eat and make the house payment, so I happily receive my monthly paycheck and readily spent it.

Four selected paragraphs from my patriarchal blessing are copied below; they were partially responsible for my entry into this fascinating field of genealogy.

CHURCH OF JESUS CHRIST OF LATTER-DAY SAINTS
Office of the Patriarch to the Church
Salt Lake City 1, Utah

Date: September 20, 1948
A BLESSING given by ELDRED G. SMITH, Patriarch, upon the head of
NORMAN EDGAR WRIGHT
Son of Cleeo Datell Wright and Mary Musser Wright, Born January 9, 1927 in Murray, Utah.

....The blessing of the Lord shall be with thee, that his providing care shall be over thee, that thou shalt not be in need for the necessities of life and none shall need leave they gates in want, for the Lord shall bless thee in thy righteous endeavors that thou shalt have success therein and shall have sufficient means to assist thee in accomplishing the duties and responsibilities placed upon thee and enable thee to fulfill thy mission upon the earth to a good measure, for much may be required of thee and of they time and talents and abilities and means. And as thou shalt be generous in the use thereof the Lord shall reward thee richly for thy efforts and generosity and they desire to progress the work of the Lord on the Earth.

As thou are not preparing to depart to fulfill a foreign mission, the Lord shall bless thee therein, that thou shalt have success in thy labors and it shall be an experience unto thee to assist thee in preparing thee for thy life's work. And the Lord shall open up the way before thee that thou shalt have success in thy labors...

....Thou shalt be as a saviour upon Mt. Zion and many shall bless thee for thy efforts in their behalf. As thou shalt endeavor to seek out the records of thy people, many of whom have not been so fortunate as thee, many of the records shall be made available to thee.

From time to time as thou shalt seek the guidance of the Lord and His assistance, He shall be mindful of thee and give unto thee those blessings which shall be for thy good as thou shalt seek them...

(signed) ELDRED G. SMITH Patriarch.

Extract of Norman Edgar Wright Patriachal Blessing

Donald Ristich

born: About 1906
where: Chicago, Illinois
married: 1930
died: about 1932
where: Chicago, Illinois

Ronald Anderson

born: 21 Dec 1930
where: Chicago, Illinois
married:
died:

Lillian Elaine Gustafson

born: 30 Nov 1907
where: Menahga, Becker, Minnesota
died:
where:

4 Oct 1962
Ronald Eugene Anderson
571 Heineman Blvd
Mansfield, Ohio

CHAPTER 1

RONALD ANDERSON

WHO AM I?

During 1962, I was an employee of the Research Department of the LDS Genealogical Society in Salt Lake City, but by assignment, I was teaching genealogical courses at Brigham Young University on a part-time basis. Archibald F. Bennett, former head librarian of the Genealogical Society, had begun some regional genealogical courses at the University, and Research Department personnel were assigned to teach them. David E. Gardner had been teaching the English courses and Vincent L. Jones had been teaching those in the American area, but when Vincent became heavily involved in computer work, I was invited to take over his assignment teaching the America courses. We were also teaching introductory courses in genealogy, which were offered through the Department of Religious Instruction. At the time, David Gardner and I were commuting to Provo three days a week to fill our teaching assignments, but we were also conducting applied research at the Genealogical Society during the remainder of the week.

On the first day of classes during the Fall Semester of that year, a young man came into one of my introductory classes, which had just begun, and without any other comment called out: "Is this the right class to find out who you are?" I was a little puzzled with his question and asked him to explain himself. Then he said: "I'm an adopted child and don't know who my real father is; I figured this course might help me." With that, I said: "You're in the right class; take a seat!" And then I continued my lecture without further interruptions.

Immediately after class, this same student came forward, and after waiting a few minutes while I answered questions from other students, he began to explain his problem. He said his name was Ronald Anderson; that his home was in Mansfield, Ohio, but he had recently joined the LDS Church and had registered at Brigham Young University to obtain a degree in Sociology. He was single, but it was obvious he was older than the ordinary freshman (Ron was born 21 Dec 1930), and to me, he also seemed more mature in his thinking than the other students. He said he was an adopted child; that his mother (Lillian Gustafson Anderson) was his real mother, but he said his father (Mr. Anderson) was his foster father. He said he loved and respected his foster father, who had raised him from childhood, and he certainly loved his mother, but he wanted to know more about his "real" father. I immediately responded by saying: "Why don't you ask your mother about him; she surely must have known something about him?" After that remark, Ron said: "I have asked her, several times, but it's a sore spot with her, and she would only tell me his name (Donald Ristich). Evidently his father had died shortly after Ron's birth, then his mother married Mr. Anderson and the family moved from Chicago, Illinois (Ron's birthplace) to Ohio where Ron had spent his childhood.

It was apparent that Ron was serious in his quest and was determined to find more details about his natural father, so I made a few suggestions as to how he might proceed. My first recommendation was to get a copy of his own birth record from the State of Illinois, because it should include the names of his parents as well as other important facts. He said he had already done that, but it listed his foster father (Mr. Anderson) as his real father and said nothing about Donald Ristich. Next, I suggested he write the Illinois Bureau of Vital Statistics and explain that Mr. Anderson is a "foster father" and request a copy of the "original" birth record. Ron agreed to do this, and after determining the appropriate fee and address, he mailed his request to the State of Illinois. He continued to attend class regularly and participated with the other students.

About two weeks later, Ron walked into my office and said: "Look what I've got!" He showed me a letter from the State of Illinois; they were responding to his earlier request for a photocopy of his "original" birth record, but they hadn't sent him a copy. The letter indicated an original birth record for Ron did exist, but it had been "sealed by court order" and a court order would have to be obtained to get a copy. They didn't give any instructions or details as to how that might be done, and neither of us were knowledgeable about such procedures, so we did some checking with a local attorney. We learned that a court order to open such a record could be obtained, in as much as Ron was the party of interest and was of legal age; but it would cost well over $100 to accomplish the task through this attorney. Neither Ron nor I had that kind of money at the time, so we would have to take another approach.

We did know the name of his father (Donald Ristich), and according to Ron's mother, the father died after Ron's birth (21 Dec 1930); very probably in Chicago, so why not try to obtain a copy of Donald's death record. It should include his birth date and birthplace, certainly his date and place of death, and it might include other important facts. Ron sent a request for the death record the very next day, and in less than two-week's time, he had a reply from the State of Illinois indicating they had been unable to find such a record. Ron was a little discouraged, but he continued the quest.

LOOK WHAT I'VE GOT!

At this very time, some of my students were conducting a survey of morticians and funeral homes, in their respective home towns, to determine what types of records were typically being kept. We had been pleasantly surprised with the wide time periods covered, the content of typical records, and their availability. The students had been using a National Morticians Directory, obtained from a local Provo funeral director, so I suggested that Ron check the directory and write to morticians in Chicago, asking if they had buried Donald Ristich. I didn't realize how many establishments were listed for Chicago, or I probably wouldn't have suggested it, but Ron eagerly took up the task and wrote to every one of them.

It was about a month later that he came into class one morning waving a document in his hand and saying, loudly: "Look what I've got!" The class had just begun, and his loudness was a little disturbing, but I stopped my introductory remarks and looked at the document he held. It was a record from a Chicago mortician who had "received" and "buried" the body of one "Donald Ristich" alias "Donald Rylich" in a specified Chicago cemetery. Most interestingly, the record listed Donald's place of death as "New Orleans, Louisiana." By this time, the whole class was involved and everyone was excited. Ron's basic information was correct, in that his father had died shortly after Ron's birth, and he was buried in Chicago, but Donald didn't die there. The New Orleans place of death was the reason Illinois couldn't locate a death record for Donald, because the death record is normally filed in the state of death; not necessarily where a person might have been buried.

With this new information, Ron wrote to Louisiana for a photocopy of the death record of his father, and it was but a short two weeks later that he burst into the class again waving another document and saying: "Look what I've got today!" This time Ron had a copy of his natural father's actual death record. He handed it to me to read, but as I read the document, I gulped and hesitated after reading the top few lines. The record listed the name of the deceased as "Donald Ristich alias Donald Rylich" and gave the date and place of death. The date of death was okey, but the place and cause of death were what shocked me. Donald's place of death was listed as the "Parish Prison" and the cause of death was listed as "fracture of the cervical disc." Written in parenthesis immediately after the cause of death were the words "legal hanging."

Wow! This was a real shocker; something that I had never experienced before, and I didn't really know how to respond. This is the time when most of us would drop our genealogical pursuits and take up some other hobby or activity, but not Ron. After asking him what he was going to do now, he said: "I'm going to find out why he was hung in the parish prison!" I suggested he might be uncovering something which would hurt him, or perhaps embarrass his family, but he was as determined as ever and wanted to go forward with the

search. We could see why this had been a "sore spot" with Ron's mother, and why she hesitated to tell him about his natural father. But I wondered if any good could come from further pursuit of the case, but Ron was convinced something good would come from it. Letters were written to the appropriate Louisiana Parish Courts, and to the actual Prison where Donald had died. The results were astounding and the information was most interesting.

Evidently Donald Ristich and two companions, all from Chicago, were in the City of New Orleans looking for work. These were the great depression years and work was hard to find, and Donald had a new young family to support, so he was traveling from city to city trying to find employment. These three young men, one of whom was a young Black American, had tried desperately to find work, but they had been unsuccessful and resorted to even more desperate means to get money. They "held up" a grocery store in the suburbs of the city, but the proprietor wasn't about to give in; he pulled a gun from under the counter and threatened the would-be robbers. Several shots were fired, and after the skirmish was over, the store owner lay dying and the would-be robbers were in flight. The attempted robbery had been witnessed by others, and the police were soon on the scene. It was a very short time before the three young men had been captured and incarcerated, and a later trial convicted all three of "Murder in the First Degree." One might imagine the concern of a southern jury in the 1930's, when a murder had been committed in their city by three persons from Chicago; and one of them being Black.

Ron had some consolation, however, in that court records proved his father was not the person who pulled the trigger of the killing weapon; but nevertheless, he was an accomplis and was considered just as guilty as the person who did pulled the trigger. The trial and appeals carried forward for nearly two years before conviction and execution, and the events were covered in great detail by local newspapers. It was here that Ron obtained some of his best information; he even located a photograph of his father in one of the newspapers. In another, he determined that a "Nick Ristich" and "Marie Medindorp" had visited Donald while he was on death row. He also learned they had petitioned the Governor of Louisiana for commutation of Donald's death sentence, because he did not actually pull the trigger of the weapon used; but their efforts were in vain, and the sentence was finally carried out.

A TRIP TO CHICAGO AND NICK RISTICH

But now, back to BYU. It was spring semester of 1963, the Winter Semester was over and my introductory course had ended, but Ron continued his genealogical pursuits and even registered in a more advanced genealogical course which I was teaching. We had become the best of friends and continued to work together, trying to extend his pedigree and gain additional information about his family. At this same time, I was a member of the LDS Priesthood Genealogical Committee and was traveling four out of five weekends to various local LDS Church units, promoting genealogical research among the members. It was my practice to tell my students where I would be going each week, and I would naturally report interesting experiences to them on my return.

One day in May, Ron came to my office and asked me if I would help him with a special project. My immediate response was: "Why yes, of course!" He then handed me a list of names and telephone numbers and asked me to call each one of them and see if they knew anything about his father Donald Ristich; he understood that I would be traveling to the Virginia LDS Stake the next weekend and would probably be changing planes in Chicago (all the numbers he handed me were Chicago, Illinois phone numbers). After looking at the list, I said: "Why don't you call the numbers yourself? You could do it as easily as I could, and they don't have to be called from Chicago!" His response was: "I'm short on money, and you could make local calls from the airport as you're changing planes."

Ron had made a special trip to Salt Lake City earlier in the week, and had copied every "Ristich" and "Medindorp" entry from the Chicago directories at Mountain Bell's Headquarters

(there were more than fifteen names on the list he handed me). What could I say? It had to be a positive response, because this young man was not to be thwarted in his family history pursuit.

Bye the way, on that particular conference assignment I was privileged to accompany Elder Howard W. Hunter, now President of the Council of Twelve Apostles for the LDS Church, and Elder William H. Walsh, then a member of the LDS Church Welfare Committee. It was a most interesting and educational experience for me; we were able to visit Colonial Williamsburg, Yorktown, and the U.S. Naval Shipyards at Norfolk, Virginia.

On that particular trip, we did have a lay-over in Chicago, at O'Hare Field, and I did have time to begin calling the numbers Ron had given me. I remember well the first number called and the response received. It was for "Anna Ristich," and as she answered, I asked her if she was related to a Donald Ristich who had lived in Chicago during the 1930's. She was an older lady and had a definite foreign accent. Her tart response was: "No! I no related to no one no how!" then she hung up in apparent disgust. Several other numbers were called without success, but then I dialed the number of an "August Ristich." A young lady answered the telephone. By this time, I was simply asking: "Does the name Donald Ristich mean anything to you?" When I asked that question, she said: "No! That name means nothing....(then she paused and said)..Oh, Donnie! We don't talk about him!" I was so excited I nearly fell from my seat. But at that instant, Elder Hunter tapped me on the shoulder and said: "Come on! Come on! Our plane is leaving; We've got to go!" He had no idea what I was up to, and insisted that we must leave to catch our plane. This young lady was the daughter-in-law of August Ristich, also known as "Nick Ristich" (brother of Donald), but Nick wasn't home at the time, and now I must go. I quickly explained my interest in Donald to her, then asked if I might call back on Sunday evening when we would be in Chicago on our return flight to Salt Lake City. She happily agreed and suggested her father-in-law would probably be home at that time.

Needless to say, I was anxious to make the call-back on our return to O'Hare on Sunday evening. This time I was able to speak with August (Nick) Ristich in person. I told him that I was a friend of Ron Anderson who was, in fact, the son of Donald Ristich. At this point, Nick became very excited and said: "Where is he! What's he doing? Is he Okey! How is his mother? Where is she! We haven't seen or heard of them for thirty years!" I told him what I knew about the family, and asked him if he would object to Ron getting in touch with him personally. I had mentioned that Ron was attending Brigham Young University in Provo, Utah, and he said: "Why, I'll pay his way out here, if he'll come and see us!" Nick was anxious to learn about his long lost nephew, and he seemed to be a very nice fellow. He told me that Marie Medindorp was his sister (and of course sister to Donald) and that she was doing family history searching herself. She and Nick had been the two family members who had gone to New Orleans, when Donald Ristich was on death row, and who petitioned the Governor of Louisiana to commute Donald's death sentence, but without success. That must have been a trying experience for both of them, but now to learn that Donald's son and mother were happy and well must have been a heart-warming event in Nick's life.

After my return and report to Ron, he got in touch with his uncle August Ristich and also initiated successful correspondence with his Aunt Marie. She gave him additional information about his father as well as the family in general, and a warm and lasting friendship was established.

From information Marie provided, and from his own research, Ron learned that his father (Donald Ristich) was born on the 27th of August 1906 in Chicago, Illinois; that he married Lillian Elaine Gustafson on the 23rd of December 1929 in Chicago, and that he died on the 1st of June 1932 in New Orleans, Louisiana. Donald's father (Ron's grandfather) was Stephen Ristich; born in Turkey in the 1870's, and who died unexpectedly in Turkey while visiting family members. Donald's mother (Ron's grandmother) was Jennie (Vukosavlevich) Ristich, who died in Chicago in 1936. She was born on the 19th of June 1878 in Cetza,

1910 CENSUS EXTRACT OF STEVE RISTICH FAMILY

U.S. Department of Commerce
Bureau of the Census
Washington 25, D.C.

Re: Stephen Ristich

May 10 1963

Donald Ristich
c/o Genealogical Society
80 North Main Street
Salt Lake City 11, Utah

The following information, including spelling of name, relationship, age, etc., is an EXACT COPY of the census record as reported by the census taker on the original schedule

Census of 1910, taken as of April 15
2010 Hastings Street, Chicago; County of Cook; State of Illinois

Ristich, Steve	(Head)
Ristich, Jennie	(Wife)
Ristich, Mary	(Daughter)
Ristich, Gusta	(Daughter)
Ristich, Nick	(Son)
Ristich, Theodore	(Son)
Ristich, Donny	(Son)
Voka, Olla	(Mother-in-law)

Yugoslavia, the daughter of Theodore and Elena (Yelich) Vukosavlevich; both natives of cetza, Yugoslavia.

Ron's genealogical efforts didn't stop with the searches on his natural father's lines; he also conducted successful searches on his mother's ancestral lines, which were from Finland. With the help of a young Finnish student at BYU, Ron was able to extend his mother's ancestry four generations through microfilmed records at the Family History Library in Salt Lake City. While other students were escorting their lady friends to dances and the theater, Ron was taking his to the genealogical library in Salt Lake City, and having her translate his Finnish Finnish genealogy.

PERSONAL SATISFACTION AND A NEW HAPPINESS

Through Ron's strong desire to learn the truth about his family, and though his undaunted determination to accomplish a difficult task, he has gained considerable personal satisfaction and a new happiness which cannot easily be measured. He has reconnected long severed family ties and opened an excitingly new era for his family. True, the family has experienced some difficult and trying times, but what family hasn't? Ron did not quit when unpleasant and possibly embarrassing information was located about his father, but rather, he persisted and learned the whole story, and was able to deal with it in a healthy and rewarding manner.

As a happy postscript, Ron received a degree in Sociology from Brigham Young University and was working in his chosen profession in Dade County, Florida when I last heard from him (1984). He was also happily married and had a young son of his own, who, by this time, has probably learned the story of his grandfather Donald Ristich as well as other relatives who carry a different surname than his.

Ron Anderson and wife, with his in-laws and son

DONALD RISTICH PEDIGREE (RON'S FATHER)

Stephan Ristich
born: About 1883
where: Turkey
married: About 1901
died: About 1935
where: Turkey

Donald Ristich
born: 27 Aug 1906
where: Chicago, Cook, Illinois
married: 23 Dec 1939
died: 1 June 1932
where: New Orleans, Louisiana

Theodore Vukosavlevich
born: About 1850
where: Cetza, Yugoslavia
married: About 1875
died:
where: Cetza, Yugoslavia

Jennie Vukosavlevich
born: 19 Jun 1878
where: Cetza, Yugoslavia
died: 8 Sep 1936
where: Chicago, Cook, Illinois

Olla Voka
born: About 1860
where: Cetza, Yugoslavia
died: After 1910
where: Chicago, Cook, Illinois

6 Mar 1963
Ronald Eugene Anderson
215 Helaman Halls
BYU Provo, Utah

LILLIAN GUSTAFSON PEDIGREE (RON'S MOTHER)

Gustav Fredrik Eriksson (Kaars)
born: 24 Mar 1830
where: Kaars, Sideby, Vaasa, Finland
married: 2 Dec 1859
died: 8 June 1873
where: Kaars, Sideby, Vaasa, Finland

Karl Erik Gustafson
born: 22 Apr 1870
where: Sastmola, Finland
married: 7 Jul 1894
died: 26 Jan 1945
where: Menahga, Becker, Minnesota

Lillian Elaine Gustafson
born: 30 Nov 1907
where: Menahga, Beker, Minnesota
married: 23 Dec 1929
died:
where:

Greta Stina Thomasdotter
born: 14 Oct 1833
where: Hogbacka, Flada, Sideby, Finland
died: 31 Dec 1930
where: Hogbeacka, Fada, Sideby, Finland

Pahl Alexander Kastreeni
born: 14 Feb 1848
where: Kylmajarvi, Oula, Finland
married:
died: 26 May 1900
where: Menahga, Becker, Minnesota

Johanna Castren
born: 22 Jul 1875
where: Kattermo, Oulo, Finland
died: 7 Dec 1927
where: Menahga, Becker, Minnesota

Anna Lisa Ryberg
born: 11 Feb 1850
where: Kajaani, Oulu, Finland
died: 29 Apr 1926
where: Menahga, Becker, Minnesota

6 Mar 1963
Ronald Eugene Anderson
215 Helaman Halls BYU
Provo, Utah

CHAPTER 2

TAYLOR/TRAYLOR

During the spring of 1962, while working as an American Research Specialist for the Research Department of the LDS Genealogical Society (now the LDS Family History Library), one of my patrons, Mrs. Jesse E. Taylor of Mansfield Avenue in Salt Lake City, came into our offices and requested an audience with me. I had done some research for her family on their Harris line of Carroll County, Maryland and supposed she wanted to continue that work, but I soon found out she had other things on her mind. She seemed troubled and was hesitant to explain exactly what she wanted at first, but finally, she said: "We have spent over $400 through the Research Department on our Taylor line, and we're not pleased with the results!" Continuing, she said: "Your Department told my husband he's a Traylor rather than a Taylor, but he doesn't believe it. He says he's still a Taylor, regardless of the documents you have found!" I really didn't know what she was talking about, because I hadn't worked on her Taylor line, and I told her so. With that she said: "Oh, I know you didn't have anything to do with it; we liked what you did on our Amos Harris line, and that's why we've come to you. Another researcher worked on our Taylor line, and we'd like you to review it and see if you think it's correct." Then she took a hand-written family group record from her purse and began to explain it to me.

YOU'RE A TRAYLOR; NOT A TAYLOR!

The family had evidently employed the Research Department to extend their Taylor line, which ended with Jesse W. Taylor who was supposedly born in Pike County, Indiana on the 6th of June 1821. According to family information, he married Mary Ellen Hardin in Winslow, Indiana (Pike County) on the 27th of February 1842. Mary Ellen had died the 9th of February 1908 at Rulo, Richardson, Nebraska, and Jesse W. had died less than a month later at the same place. Family records listed Mary Ellen's father as John Hardin and her mother as Mary (surname unknown), but they didn't know the parentage of Jesse W. and that seemed to be the concentration of search. A researcher had been assigned the problem (initials "BL" but no longer employed by the Department), and correspondence had been exchanged. The assigned researcher had concluded that Jesse W. Taylor was actually Jesse Traylor the son of Joel and Catharine (Bomar) Traylor of Pike County, Indiana.

Mrs. Taylor asked if I would be kind enough to review the Department's files and see if I thought their conclusions were correct. She emphasized that her husband was distraught and upset with the Department's previous findings, as well as with the charges which were levied (over $400). Then she informed me she had but $40 left to spend on the problem. Actually, the Research Department was responsible to review such requests without charge, so I assured her that a thorough review would be made and a report would be forthcoming. It was apparent she was a very frugal person and didn't have money to waste.

In that day, the Research Department accepted genealogical requests from interested patrons for a fee and assigned them to employed researchers under a managed program. The Department was subsidized by the LDS Church, but researchers were expected to charge their time against the accounts of their respective patrons, and strict accounting procedures were in force. At that time, each researcher had from fifty to one hundred active accounts, primarily because of the small fee charged ($1.50 per hour in 1962), and each researcher found it necessary to rotate work on his accounts from time to time. File folders were maintained for each patron, which included all research correspondence and reports as well as all research notes and documents created by the researcher. Sufficient secretarial help was available to handle filing requirements, and a typing pool existed to take care of the necessary correspondence. Each researcher dictated his own letters and reports, but a Research

Superintendent signed all outgoing correspondence and reviewed incoming requests and reports.

After Mrs. Taylor's visit, I approached the Research Superintendent, then Frank Smith (the person responsible for my employment at the Society), explaining Mrs. Taylor's concern. He authorized me time to review the problem at Departmental expense and also requested that I report back to him personally when the work was finished.

It didn't take me long to find the original file and begin reviewing the previous researcher's work, but after a thorough examination, I too was convinced that Jesse W. Taylor was really Jesse Traylor; and he was, according to certain documents located, the son of Joel and Catharine (Bomar) Traylor of Pike County, Indiana. From notes and documents in the file, it appeared that the assigned researcher had followed sound research methods and procedures; he had checked general references first and had done some preliminary work to determine whether or not the basic dates and places were correct, then he moved to original records of Pike County, Indiana. At that time, the Genealogical Library in Salt Lake City didn't have many original sources from Indiana, so the researcher had corresponded with county officials and had employed agents to reach his conclusions.

FAMILY GROUP RECORD

(Husband): JESSE W. TAYLOR
Born: 6 Jun 1821 in Pike Co, Indiana
Married: 27 Feb 1842 in Winslow, Indiana
Died: 1 Apr 1908 in Rulo, Nebraska
(Wife): MARY ELLEN HARDIN
Born: 13 Mar 1824 in Pike Co, Indiana
Died: 9 Feb 1908 in Rulo, Nebraska
(Children):
GEORGE E. TAYLOR
Born: 28 Feb 1843 in Monroe, Indiana
JOHN TAYLOR
Born: 25 Sep 1844 in Monroe, Indiana
MATTHEW TAYLOR
Born: 5 apr 1846 in Monroe, Indiana
NICHOLAS TAYLOR
Born: 2 Mar 1848 in Monroe, Indiana
MARY CAL TAYLOR
Born: 14 Feb 1850 in Monroe, Indiana
JACKSON TAYLOR
Born: 25 Jul 1853 in Mason City, Illinois
SARAH JANE TAYLOR
Born: 5 Dec 1855 in Mason City, Illinois
JAMES PERRY TAYLOR
Born: 26 Jan 1858 in Mason City, Illinois
FRANK TAYLOR
Born: 7 Jun 1861 in Mason City, Illinois
FANNIE TAYLOR
Born: 29 Nov 1864 in Mason City, Illinois

Jesse W. Taylor family

MARRIAGE RECORD

#1107
(Groom): Jesse Traylor
(Bride): Mary Ellen Hardin
(Married): 27 February 1842
(Place): Winslow, Indiana

Pike County, Indiana Marriage Record

The most convincing information located was a report from the Pike County Clerk showing a marriage entry for Jesse Traylor (not Taylor) and Mary Ellen Hardin, dated the 27th of February 1842 in Winslow, Indiana. The researcher had written back to the County Clerk, asking him if he had made a transcription error in writing "Traylor" rather than "Taylor," but the Clerk assured him it was a correct transcription from a bound volume in the Court House; and furthermore, the Clerk said there were many people by the name of "Traylor" resident in Pike County. Another bit of convincing information in the file was a probate record for Catherine (Bomar) Traylor, naming a son Jesse in the right time period to be our Jesse.

After receiving the marriage and probate information, the researcher had apparently concentrated on the Traylor family of Pike County, Indiana. Through the work of an agent, he had determined the family was earlier of Spartanburg County, South Carolina and Chesterfield County, Virginia; the earliest known ancestor being one Edward Traylor. Though I was not able to talk with "BL" myself, because he was then in Europe and no longer an employee of the Research Department, it was obvious he was pleased with his findings; He must have reasoned the Taylor family would be happy with his efforts, extending their line that far, but such was not the case. As a matter of fact, they were actually very disappointed with his research findings and conclusions.

The evidence found in the patron's file was quite convincing on the Traylor theme, but there were a few inconsistencies which weren't easily reconciled. The very fact that the Salt Lake City family was using the surname Taylor and understood it to be ancestral must carry some weight, and all records in their possession, which dated to the 1820's, included the Taylor spelling with no indication of a Traylor spelling. Also, and more important in my thinking, were the census listings in Nebraska and Illinois, where their Jesse was known to have been resident, which each listed the surname as Taylor and not Traylor. The researcher did not record any searches in Pike County, Indiana census records, though he reported searching them to the patron. Another bit of interesting information, which had evidently been overlooked or disregarded, was on entry on a family group record from one of the agents indicating Joel Traylor (the supposed father of Jesse) had died in South Carolina in 1809. If that was correct, he certainly couldn't be the father of our Jesse who was born in 1821. It was evident that "BL" had done nothing toward checking out that information.

1860 Federal Census
Mason County, Illinois
FHL Film #803,210

#513/513 Mason City		
Jesse TAYLOR	38 M	Indiana
Mary Taylor	35 F	Indiana
George Taylor	18 M	Indiana
John Taylor	16 M	Indiana
Mathew Taylor	14 M	Indiana
Nicholas Taylor	12 M	Indiana
Caroline Taylor	10 F	Indiana
Jackson Taylor	7 M	Illinois
Sarah J. Taylor	5 F	Illinois
James C. Taylor	2 M	Illinois

1860 Census Extract

A TRIP TO KOKOMO

Even though there was convincing information from original records that Jesse W. Taylor was really Jesse Traylor, there was sufficient evidence to question the conclusions reached by the previous researcher, and that was my report to Mrs. Taylor when she returned to our offices a few weeks later. The only problem now, was the fact she didn't have enough money to initiate indepth research, and the Department couldn't continue work without additional funds. After reviewing my findings and conclusions with her, she thanked me kindly for my work, saying they would just have to let things drop for now, because they didn't have additional funds. A tear came to her eye as she said it, and I was very empathetic with her circumstances. As she was preparing to leave, an idea struck me which might possibly help, so I asked her to wait while I explained it to her. As it happened, my wife and I had been planning a trip to Kokomo, Indiana the coming summer, to visit a sister who had moved there with her husband and small family for business purposes. I suggested that perhaps we could visit Pike County and try to "dig something up." We had just purchased a new car and were looking forward to a ten-day vacation through middle America; our first formal family vacation, and we could certainly spend a day or two on the Taylor/Traylor problem. When I mentioned this possibility to her, she really became excited and said: "Oh, Brother Wright! Would you do that for us?" I responded in the affirmative, but emphasized that we would only be able to spend a day or two in Pike County, and I wouldn't guarantee anything; only that I would give it a try. She thanked me several times over, then our conversation ended and she left; both of us feeling much happier than before.

Time soon passed, and come June, our little family was on the road to Indiana. I took the back seat out of our car and placed sleeping bags, blankets, and pillows in its place, and we had our own little "mini-van." Our family then consisted of my wife Carolyn and me; our four sons Preston age 7, Craig age 6, Joel age 4, Jerry age 2, and our baby daughter Diane who was 8 months old. We also had an Indian placement student living with us at the time, named Verlina Billigoadie, but she returned to her home in Arizona for the summer just before we departed.

Our new 1962 Chevy

It rained hard the day we left, and our first night was spent in a Laramie, Wyoming motel; tired, wet, and wondering what the next day might bring. A good motel room in that day was only $15, and gasoline was only $.25 per gallon; but then too, my monthly salary was only $300. The second day was beautiful and we were soon passing through Scotts Bluff, Nebraska; but I hit a pheasant going about 80 miles per hour, and it wrecked the front grill of our new car. I was very upset, but the boys got a real kick out of it and wanted to keep the pheasant which had been lodged in the grill. After that, it was on to Missouri Valley, Iowa (Harrison County), where I did some research for my old High School Science Teacher, Howard H. Hale. We located a probate record and some land records for his ancestor (Moses Marion Arnold) in the court house, and my son Preston located the tombstone for Moses in a weed-covered township cemetery near Modale, Iowa. We were happy with our first genealogical findings and were soon on the road again to Indiana.

On the third day, we arrived at my sister's home in Kokomo and continued a most enjoyable vacation with her family; my wife and I taking periodic trips to Indianapolis (only 50 miles south) for research at the State Library, and our children having a great time playing with their cousins on the farm at Kokomo. We saw greenery that we had never before imagined, and the farmland was really something to behold, for a Utahan. The most exciting time for the children, but frightening, was an evening of heavy wind and rain (which only midwesterners would understand) and a small tornado which uprooted one of the larger trees in my sister's front yard. My wife and I had success at the Indiana State Library, but our efforts were concentrated primarily on our own lines; not yet on the Taylor/Traylor problem, which would come later.

Wright Family at Scott's Bluff, Nebraska

Four "Cowboys" in Southeastern Nebraska

SOUTH TO PETERSBURG

With only two days left on our ten-day vacation, we said goodbye to our kin in Kokomo and headed south for Petersburg, Indiana (Pike County). The trip south through the state was enjoyable, but very hot and humid; both temperature and humidity reaching the 90's. We were further amazed with the lush greenery and beauty of the country side, and we were very impressed with the hospitality of the people. By late afternoon we had arrived in Petersburg, and in a very short time, I was searching records in the county court house while my wife and children were entertaining themselves in a local park.

The deputy county clerk, a congenial and considerate young lady, was very helpful, and after asking her a few questions about the records, she directed me to a large bank of bound volumes along the south wall; the county marriage records, dating back to 1817. It only took a few minutes to locate the entry for "Jesse Traylor" and "Mary Ellen Hardin" who were married at Winslow, Indiana in 1842, and I was convinced the surname was spelled "Traylor" and not "Taylor." There were many Traylor entries but no Taylor names listed in the period of interest, so I soon moved to other records, realizing the hour was getting late and the court house would soon be closing.

TAYLORS, TRAYLORS, AND HARDINS

A quick search of county land records disclosed two entries for a Jesse "Traylor" (not Taylor); the first listing a wife Mary, but the second naming only a Jesse Traylor. Separate extracts of the two deeds follow:

> Book H page 17 - Deed dated 1 January 1849 between Jessee Trailer and Mary Trayler his wife of Pike County and Polly Bager of same place...for $130...SE 1/4 NE 1/4 Sec. 18 Twp 1N $7W 39.55 acres...Bought of General Government by George Hendricks who willed the same to Mary his wife...said Mary Trayler wife of said Jessee Trayler agrees to relinquish all her right title and interest of dower in the premises aforesaid...Recorded 2 May 1849..." (Signed) Jesse "X" (his mark)
>
> Book J page 189 - Deed dated 15 april 1848 between Jesse Traylor of Pike County and James Gray of same place...for $200...Southside of NW 1/4 Sec. 19 Twp 1N $6W 62 acres...Recorded 3 May 1854..." (signed) Jesse Traylor (seal)

Pike County, Indiana Deed Extracts

These two deed entries were very interesting, but I didn't realize their important differences immediately, and moved to other collections. Interestingly, in the civil/criminal court records, I found that a subpoena had been issued for the arrest of one Benjamin Taylor (not Traylor) in 1849, but he could not be found and the subpoena was not served. This was the only Taylor entry I was able to locate before the court house closed, but it did give me some encouragement.

After leaving the court house at closing time, there was still considerable daylight left before nightfall, so after getting a motel and having something to eat, we began to drive around the area looking for cemeteries; that's a favorite pastime of genealogists, and I had some good help with me to locate and read tombstones. We had no luck at the city cemetery in Petersburg, so we drove south and east along the main road, checking a small private cemetery and a larger township cemetery, but finding nothing of interest. We continued in a southeasterly direction, and just before reaching the small town of Otwell, we came upon the "Traylor Union Church Cemetery." An older church building stood at the side of the cemetery, but it didn't look like it had been used for some time. The boys and I got out of the car and immediately began checking tombstones, but we were unable to locate a tombstone for a Jesse Traylor, though we did located stones for a Joel

Pike County, Indiana Court House at Petersburg

Pike County, Indiana Marriage Records

and a Catherine Traylor, who could well be, judging from the dates on their stones, the parents of Jesse. Finding a tombstone for Joel Traylor, the possible parent of Jesse Traylor was of particular interest, because this would rule out his (Joel's) dying in South Carolina. We took pictures of several interesting Traylor tombstones, then left the cemetery and drove a short distance to the small town of Otwell. There were only two major buildings in the town, a farm implement store and a post office, but both were closed. There was, however, a gentleman standing in front of the post office, so we stopped and asked him for directions; wanting to know if there were other cemeteries in the immediate area. In a joking manner, he asked us what we wanted to do in a cemetery, remarking: "You ain't dead yet! We laughed and told him we were trying to solve a genealogical problem. and with that, he said: "Oh, you should talk to my wife; She does that sort of thing!" He was Mr. Thomas Gray, the local Postmaster, and his wife did genealogy as a hobby. He directed us to his house, which was only a block away, and we drove there immediately, finding his wife at home.

Mrs. Gray was a middle aged lady with a very warm and personable manner, and she had done considerable genealogical research as a hobbyist. After explaining my Traylor/Taylor problem to her, she mentioned that her husband was a Traylor, and she was a Taylor. I thought to myself: "What a small World!" She then asked me to be seated while going into another room to get her records. She soon returned with her "Book of Remembrance" and a small notebook in which she had recorded inscriptions from several local cemeteries. I was quite shocked, because her book of remembrance had a picture of an LDS Temple on it, and it was the popular style which most LDS members used, yet I knew she was not a Mormon. As she opened the book to show me her records, there was an additional shock, because she was using standard LDS pedigree charts and family group records. My curiosity got the best of me, so I asked her where she got the charts and forms she was using. She answered: "Oh, I buy them from Everton Publishers in Logan, Utah; as soon as I get some extra money, I'm going to buy one of those deluxe binders." I explained to her that we were Mormons from Utah and knew the Everton Publishers personally. She seemed delighted to know that, then she began explaining her connection to the Traylor line.

Her husband's Traylor line proved to be that of Joel and Catharine (Bomar) Traylor; the same line "BL" had done so much work on for the Taylor family of Salt Lake City, and her records corroborated what we had reasoned earlier; showing Jesse Traylor, who was born in 1820 and died in 1902, to be the son of Joel and Catharine (Bomar) Traylor. Her records listed both Joel and Catharine Traylor as early residents of Pike County, Indiana and confirmed they were formerly of Spartanburg, South Carolina. But according to her records, they both died in Pike County, which knocked the theory that Joel Traylor had died in South Carolina in 1809.

Jesse Traylor Tombstone

Mrs. Gray's records also showed her to be a descendant of a Peter Taylor (not Traylor), of Warrick County, Indiana, whom she said was Irish and worked on the canals in an early day. I asked her if she knew anything about a Jesse or a Benjamin Taylor, but she replied in the negative. After checking her cemetery lists and finding no pertinent Taylor entries, we exchanged our Traylor information with her, then drove back to Petersburg and retired for the evening in our motel.

Early the following morning, I was in the County Clerk's office searching records with renewed determination, hoping to locate more Taylor information. I felt like a bird dog who was onto the scent of a pheasant, but I couldn't quite flush it out. I did an exhaustive job in the marriage records, the land records (deeds, mortgages, and leases), and in the civil/criminal court records; finding nothing really pertinent, other than the subpoena for Benjamin Taylor and the two land entries for Jesse which I had located the day before. There were many Traylor entries in the records I searched, and persons interested in that surname could spent many profitable hours in the Pike County court house, but my concentration turned to the Taylor and Hardin surnames.

The Deputy Clerk had been most gracious to me throughout the morning and early afternoon, directing me to specific record collections, and even allowing me to use her desk and typewriter to copy material. There were less than half a dozen people who used the County Clerk's records that day, so I had things pretty much to myself. My wife and children had spent the morning in our motel, but at lunch time, I returned and checked us out of the motel, because we would have to be on the road heading west by evening time. Carolyn and the children spent the afternoon playing in a local park and resting on the court house lawn in 95 degree heat and humidity.

After lunch, I returned to the Clerk's office and continued searching the county records but didn't have much success; there was very little information to be found on the Taylor surname. As afternoon approached, I became a little discouraged and thought of quitting and heading west, but after pondering my situation for awhile, I decided to spend another hour in the records and then leave; but I changed my approach and began investigating entries for the Hardin surname.

Searching the general probate index, I noted an entry for "John Hardin" in 1848 and another for "Nicholas Hardin" in 1852. My excitement returned, because Mary Ellen's father was known to be John and the given name Nicholas had appeared in the Taylor family of Nebraska. I pulled both files, taking them over to the desk where I was working, and began checking documents in them. I checked the Nicholas Hardin folder first, and the very first document I looked at had the names "Jesse Taylor" (not Traylor) and "Mary E. Taylor his wife" listed at the bottom. The document was a "Petition for the Sale of Real Estate." My heartbeat increased rapidly and I couldn't believe what I was seeing. Here was a Hardin probate with the name of Jesse Taylor included; what a find!

STAN NELSON AND OLD WILLARD HARDIN

At that very moment, a man tapped me on the shoulder, and in a very stern voice, said: "Say, I understand you're a Mormon!" It was the County Clerk. I had observed him watching me from time to time, as I had been searching the records during the past two days, but we had never spoken; my contact had been solely with the deputy clerk. But evidently, she had spoken to him about me. I was somewhat startled by his tap on my shoulder and his question, and I actually became quite worried, because I supposed he didn't like Mormons and would probably eject me from the court house. The deputy clerk had undoubtedly told him I was a Mormon, and from Utah, but I didn't know what else she had told him. What would you have done under those circumstances?

Well, I stood up from the chair I was sitting in, and looking him right in the eye, said: "I surely am!" Then, in a much softer tone, he said: "Is it true you people don't laugh, or dance, or sing?" My heart skipped a beat, but this time in joy, because it was apparent he was not mad at Mormons; he was a friendly fellow seeking some very simple answers; and being a very simple Mormon, I could answer them. I responded happily, saying: "You see me smiling don't

1850 Census of Warrick County, Indiana (BYU Film #442,957; NEW 23 Nov 92)

#122/122 Campbell Township

PETER TAYLOR	44 M Farmer	Kentucky
Rebecca Taylor	44 F	Kentucky
Polly Taylor	16 F	Indiana
Andrew J. Taylor	15 M	Indiana
Washington Taylor	11 M	Indiana
Samuel Taylor	9 M	Indiana
Nathaniel Taylor	8 M	Indiana
Hezekiah Taylor	4 M	Indiana
Moses Taylor	2 M	Indiana

Wright children playing in Petersburg Park

Pike County, Indiana Probate Court Records

you?" Also, "We certainly laugh and dance, and we probably do a lot of other things you might wonder about!" Following my response, he said: "Do you know that I'm alive because of a Mormon? See that leg!" Pointing to his left leg and striking it several times with his hand, he said: "That's a wooden leg!" I could see that it was, indeed. He continued by telling me that he had been wounded during the Korean War, in the front lines, and that a Mormon had helped save his life; that was the best news I had heard all day.

He (Stanley Nelson was his name), hadn't been able to locate the Mormon soldier after the incident, but he had followed newspaper accounts of the Mormon people and had wondered about them from time to time; I was the first Mormon he had met since his Korean experience. I learned further that he was an avid basketball fan, and he knew that the Mormons (BYU) had recently won the National Invitational Tournament in New York City (1961). He continued asking me questions and telling me about himself, but my interest was focused on the probate information I had just found, and I really wanted to get back to my searching; it was then about 4:00 o'clock p.m. and the court house would soon be closing.

After a few more questions, he changed the subject and said, abruptly: "What are you doing here, anyway?" I told him I was trying to solve a genealogical problem and briefly explained our Taylor/Traylor dilemma, then poinped out to him that I had just located a probate document which might possibly solve the case. His immediate response was: "Why don't you let us help you!" Then he beckoned the deputy clerk to come over and assist us; she had already helped me locate records and had provided me with a desk and typewriter. While I sat and copied the records, those two kind people located and pulled the files for all pertinent Hardin/Taylor probate entries, and even helped copy some of them.

The John and Nicholas Hardin probate files proved extremely valuable. John Hardin had died Intestate (without a will) in 1848, and his estate had been duly probated, several interesting documents being created in the process; some naming surviving heirs, and others showing he had been twice married. Nicholas Hardin, the father of John, outlived his son and died in 1852 (also intestate) and his file likewise included several interesting documents. Both estates apparently had limited resources, and when it came to probating the estate of Nicholas, there weren't sufficient funds to accomplish the probating requirements, so the court sold a parcel of real estate in order to raise the necessary moneys. In the process, they had to get "Quit Claims" from the surviving heirs. John Hardin, the father of Mary Ellen, was a legitimate heir to the estate of his father Nicholas, but had preceded him in death, so John's children became heirs to the estate of their grandfather, and that's why Mary Ellen (Hardin) Taylor and her husband Jesse Taylor were signatories on the Petition for the Sale of Real Estate.

Equally, if not more important, was the fact Jesse Taylor and Mary his wife had signed the petition with their "mark" (their X); not by their "seal" (written signature). This brought to mind a startling fact which had nearly been overlooked in the land records copied the previous day (see page 5). Notice that the deed recorded in Book H, Page 17, dated 1 January 1849, includes the "mark" (X) of "Jessee Trailer" and "Mary Trayler" his wife; not their 'seal" (written signature) Now, notice the deed recorded in Book J, Page 189, dated 15 April 1848, between "Jesse "Traylor" and James Gray. Jesse's "seal" (written signature) was made. I became convinced these two Jesse's were different people; and, might not the first Jesse be our Jesse Taylor and not Jesse Traylor? The second land entry could well be Jesse Traylor, the son of Joel and Catharine. Perhaps a clerk had simply made a transcription error in writing the surnames Trailer, Trayler, and Traylor; it was obviously a popular surname in the county.

Boxed Hardin probate documents

After Stan and his clerk had pulled the pertinent probate files and laid them on the desk, Stan commented: "You're not going to be able to copy all of these records before the building closes. Why don't we just put the documents you select in a box and let you take them home to copy, and then you can return them when your finished." I was flabbergasted with his suggestion. I'm sure this was not an authorized procedure, but feeling the pressure of the moment, and my predicament, I said to myself: "If he's foolish enough to make that offer, I'm foolish enough to take him up on it!" And I readily agreed. The Deputy Clerk located a box and we packed the selected documents neatly in it; an inventory list was typed which I did sign.

I can here and at this time confirm that those probate documents were safely transported to Salt Lake City, where they were reviewed and evaluated by me, then microfilmed by officials of the LDS Genealogical Society, and finally returned to the Pike County Court House by registered mail.

But back to our story. As we were boxing the documents, Stan turned to me and said: "Say, We'uns would sure like to have you'uns come to our house for a bite a vittles if you've a mind to!" I knew we must soon be on the road heading west, because my vacation was over, but I thought of my poor wife and children who had spent all afternoon in the park and on the court house lawn, without the benefit of personal facilities and conveniences, so I agreed to take him up on this second offer. Again, I said to myself: "If he's foolish enough to make that offer, I'm foolish enough to take him up on it!" And we did!

The court house soon closed and we were on our way to Stanley Nelson's home for refreshments. He gave me directions to follow him. We would drive east on Main Street to the first red light, then turn south and follow a county road nine miles to Winslow. "Winslow!" I thought, why that's where our Jesse Taylor and Mary Ellen Hardin were married in 1842. In the mean time, Stan had called his wife and told her to expect visitors, then we were happily on our way.

After a short drive south from Petersburg, we arrived at the Nelson residence in Winslow, Indiana. This was a very rural area with heavy tree cover and dense foliage, but it was beautiful and very peaceful to drive through. I was a little concerned with what we might find at his home, but on arrival, I could see there was no need to be alarmed. The home was modest but quite modern and clean, and Stan's wife was a very lovely person. They had three young children whose ages were the same as our three youngest, and it was obvious that "Southern Hospitality" reached to that part of Indiana.

Stanley Nelson and his family at Winslow, Indiana

After we had met his wife and family, Stan turned to me and said: "Say, I know and old Willard Hardin who lives just a couple of miles from here!" He continued: "I know everybody in this county; I've knock on every door! That's how I got elected! Why don't you and I go visit Willard while the wife's fixin vittles?" I agreed and we drove, in his car, to Willard Hardin's place, just two miles south on an old winding dirt road. I took my camera and small tape recorder, hoping to capture some valuable information, and I was not disappointed.

It is not my purpose to offend nor insult anyone, especially the wonderful people of southern Indiana, but if I had every seen the home of a Hillbilly, Willard Hardin's home filled the bill. It was nothing more than a "clapboard shack," never having seen a coat of paint nor experienced a carpenters hammer, at least during the past fifty years; it was truly dilapidated, but it was the revered home of Willard Hardin, who proved to be a living nephew of the Mary Ellen Hardin who married Jesse W. Taylor (not Traylor).

We drove right up to the back of Willard's house, and Stan walked in without even knocking, directing me to follow. As he entered, he called out, loudly: "Willard! Willard! Where are you? Some of your kin's here to see you!" We heard a shrill voice responding: "Come in! Come in! I'm in the kitchen!" There was no door to the porch opening, and the door to the kitchen, such as it was, lay ajar, so we walked right in. Willard was shaving at the time, even though it was after 5:00 o'clock in the afternoon. A small wash basin sat on the kitchen table, and Willard was swishing his double edged Gillette razor in the water, attempting to clean it. He had shaving cream over part of his face, and I could see he had nicked himself in a spot or two with the razor. It was really quite a hilarious picture, but I didn't laugh.

We exchanged greetings, and after Willard finished shaving, we sat down and had a good chat. I perceived Willard to be a kindly old gentleman in his 80's. He stood about five foot seven or eight inches tall and was very slim, weighing not more than 140 pounds. He seemed intelligent and was very mentally alert; he was more than willing to discuss family history with us. I had a pencil and notebook with me and recorded the genealogical facts he told us.

Willard said he was born on the 26th of November 1885 in Patoka Township, Pike County, Indiana. He said he was the son of Alvin T. Hardin who was born in Pike County on the 2nd of October 1841. He indicated his father Alvin was the son of John Hardin by a second wife, whose name was Mary Elizabeth Thompson. He couldn't give me the name of John's first wife, but he "reckoned" they were married in 1824. He said there were four boys and one girl by the first marriage; Mary, John, William, and Lewis; that there were three boys by the second marriage; Alvin T., Burrell (who was killed at Vicksburg), and Thomas.

Willard continued by saying he was married to Bessie Alexander on the 28th of January 1910 and they had three children; John Heber, Raymond (who died in 1914 and was buried in Oak Hills), and Virgil L. (who was living in LaGrange, Indiana). He said he married secondly,

1850 Census of Pike County, Indiana (BYU Film #442,943; 23 Nov 92)

#222/222 Petersburg		
HENRY HARDIN	45 M Farmer	Kentucky
Mary Hardin	45 F	Georgia
Elizabeth Hardin	22 F	Indiana
Emiley Hardin	16 F	Indiana
George Hardin	15 M Labor	Indiana
Minerva Hardin	13 F	Indiana
Malinda Hardin	9 F	Indiana
John Hardin	6 M	Indiana
#114/114 Monroe Township		
SALEY HAUCHINS	30 F Farmer	Kentucky
Nancy Taylor	66 F	Georgia
Jesse Hauchins	27 M	Indiana
George Hauchins	21 M	Indiana
#150/150 Monroe Township		
JESSE HAUCHINS	52 M Farmer	Kentucky
Elizabeth Hauchins	57 F	Kentucky
#159/159 Monroe Township		
JOHN HARDIN	22 M Farmer	Indiana
Sarah Hardin	20 F	Indiana
Mathew Hardin	6/12 M	Indiana
#171/171 Monroe Township		
Mathew Thompson	25 M Farmer	Indiana
Matilda Thompson	23 F	Indiana
MAREY Thompson	66 F	Virginia
James HARDIN	14 M	Indiana
John HARDIN	11 M	Indiana
Jasper Thompson	3 M	Indiana
James Thompson	7/12 M	Indiana

1850 Census of Dubois County, Indiana (BYU Film #7756; 9 December 1992)

#30/30 Harrison Township

JESSE TRAYLOR	29 M Farmer	Indiana
Jane Tryalor	25 F	Indiana
William H. Traylor	8 M	Indiana
Joel Benton Traylor	5 M	Indiana
Washington C. Traylor	6 mo. M	Indiana
Maria J. Noble	10 F	Indiana

#64/64 Patoka Township

JONATHAN WALKER	60 M Farmer	Kentucky
Mary Walker	55 F	Kentucky
Sampson Walker	22 M	Indiana
Derrick Walker	18 M	Indiana
Bloomfield Walker	16 M	Indiana
Charlotte Walker	13 F	Indiana
Lurena Walker	11 F	Indiana
Indiana Walker	8 F	Indiana

#713/713 Patoka Township

OBEDIAH TAYLOR	69 M Farmer	Kentucky
Deba Taylor	50 F	Penn.
Lewis Taylor	22 M	Indiana
Isaac Taylor	18 M	Indiana
Margaret Taylor	15 F	Indiana
Lucinda Taylor	12 F	Indiana
Daniel Taylor	10 M	Indiana

on the 20th of July 1918, Elsie Furgason, by whom he had Floyd, Leonard, Elizabeth (who married a Houchins), Issebelle (who married a White), Charles Herbert, Alvin D., and Evelen Ann (who married a Mount).

Willard said he had three brothers and three sisters; Francis, John, Lewis, Alice, Matilda, and Alvin (who died 31 May 1922 in a train/car wreck). All this was from his memory and at no time did he consult any written record.

When I asked him about Mary Ellen Hardin, he said she married Benjamin Taylor (not Jesse Taylor), and certainly not Jesse Traylor. Then without my asking, he said Jonathan Walker and Benjamin Taylor killed a man in Dubois County in 1841 and left the country. He said that Mary Ellen and her brother John went to "near Springfield, Illinois." I asked him if he was sure about Mary Ellen marrying Benjamin rather than Jesse, and he said: "That's my understanding." Willard certainly didn't have personal knowledge of this, and he may have been confused about Jesse and Benjamin, but it is interesting that his information about Benjamin being in trouble with the law was corroborated by my findings in the court records of Pike County; perhaps Benjamin and Jesse were brothers. It could also be possible, but heaven forbid, that Benjamin changed his name to Jesse after the altercation in Dubois County in 1841.

Willard could tell me nothing about the parentage of old John Hardin, his grandfather, but he said he knew where John was buried and would be happy to show us the place. When I suggested that old John was the son of Nicholas Hardin, Willard merely shrugged his shoulders and said that might be possible. He said the Hardin family of Pike County, Indiana was from Kentucky, but he could give me no further details. Nevertheless, his information was fantastic, as far as I was concerned, and in my thinking, he had provided the final proof that the Jesse who married Mary Ellen Hardin in Winslow, Indiana in 1842 was our Jesse Taylor, who went west and died in Nebraska in 1908; he was definately not Jesse Traylor the son of Joel and Catharine (Bomar) Traylor.

After we had talked in Willard's home for half an hour or so, Willard invited us to go see the spot where old John Hardin was buried. It was no more than a block from his house, but Stan insisted that we drive there in his car. The burial spot was on the east side of a small stream, in a heavily wooded area, but there was no tombstone nor sign of a grave. An old road had traversed the stream and crossed just north of the burial spot, but the road hadn't been used for a long time. Willard said that old John died suddenly and unexpectedly, and was buried secretly because of the smallpox. He said certain people would put a small American flag on the grave each year, but he said "John was not a veteran of the war." (meaning the Civil War). We readily agreed, because John had died in 1848, but he might have served in an early conflict. I took a picture of Willard standing near the burial spot, and I also recorded his voice as he told us about the event. Then we returned to his home, said our goodbye's, and drove to Stan's place for supper.

Old Willard Hardin of Pike County, Indiana

1850 Census of Pike County, Indiana (BYU Film #442,943 - 23 Nov 1992)

#165/165 Monroe Township

JESSE TAYLOR	29 M Farmer	Indiana
Mary Taylor	24 F	Indiana
George Taylor	8 M	Indiana
John Taylor	5 M	Indiana
Mathew Taylor	4 M	Indiana
Nicholas Taylor	2 M	Indiana
Caroline Taylor	6/12 F	Indiana
William Hardin	20 M Labor	Indiana

1850 Census of Dubois County, Indiana (BYU Film #7756 - 9 December 1992)

#30/30 Harrison Township

JESSE TRAYLOR	29 M Farmer	Indiana
Jane Traylor	25 F	Indiana
William H. Traylor	8 M	Indiana
Joel Benton Traylor	5 M	Indiana
Washington C. Traylor	6 mo. M	Indiana
Maria J. Noble	10 F	Indiana

I took photographs of Stan and his family and offered them the same hospitality which they had shown to us, if they ever found their way west. We took a southern route home; sad, in a way, about leaving the beautiful heartland of America and her wonderful people, but happy with our experiences. We were equally happy to greet our family and friends at home, and to tell them about our many interesting experiences.

When I returned to my office and reported for work, I noticed, with great interest, a report sitting on my desk from the Nebraska State Historical Society. It was dated June 14, 1962 and included copies of the obituary notices for Jesse and Mary Ellen. Shortly before we left on the Indiana trip, I had sent a request to the Nebraska State Historical Society for them, because the former researcher had not obtained them.

"Jesse W. Taylor was born in Warrick County, Indiana, June 6, 1821 (and died) aged 86 years, 9 months, and 19 days, was married to Mary Harding(sic) February 27, 1842 at Ninslow(sic), Indiana. He was married to Mary Harding(sic) just 67 years and one month to the day he was buried. Just one month and 16 days ago we buried our dear old mother and grandmother. To this union were born ten children, Gregor Taylor of Rulo, Nebraska; John Taylor of Mason City, Illinois; Matthew Taylor of Mesena, Iowa; Nicholas Taylor of Phillipsburg, Kansas; Mrs. Carrie Bouslog, New Castle, Indiana; Jackson Taylor, Bloomington, Nebraska; Mrs. Sarah DeMoss, Omaha, Nebraska; Frank Taylor, Rulo, Nebraska; Fanny Taylor, Mason City, Illinois, who died in infancy. All the children were present except three; Mrs. Bouslog, James Taylor, and John Taylor. He had many good qualifications. Grandpa Taylor will long be remembered by his dear old friends and neighbors. He was a true christian at heart. His last hours were peacefully passed away. His last words were 'Lay me down and I will rest.' Grandpa was called Uncle Jesse by the boys who knew him. He always had a smile and a good word for everybody. He had a light stroke of paralysis on Monday morning which confined him to his bed until he passed to the great beyond on Wednesday at 9 o'clock. There were 25 grandchildren and 21 great-grandchildren. Two of the former are Mrs. Martin Konaly and Mrs. Henry Gagnon of this city. He has lived in Rulo for over 30 years. The remains were interred in the Rulo cemetery. Funeral was held from the Church on the 27th of March on Friday. The service was rendered by Rev. Martin of Falls City which was a beautiful sermon."

The Falls City Journal. Falls, City, Nebraska, Friday, April 3, 1908 (As reported by the Nebraska State Historical Society, June 14, 1962; Donald F. Danker, Archivist)

Jesse W. Taylor Obituary

Of all things, Jesse's obituary said he was born in Warrick County, Indiana in 1821, not in Pike County as the family had supposed. My thoughts immediately returned to Indiana and the visit to Mrs. Gray of Otwell, Indiana. Her Peter Taylor was "of Warrick County" and very probably was a relative of our Jesse; perhaps a brother, or possibly even Jesse's father, but further research would have to confirm that.

Jesse E. Taylor after my return; confirming her husband's belief that he was a Taylor and not a Traylor, and providing her with documentary proof of my findings. I also sent her the addresses of Willard Hardin of Winslow, Indiana and Mrs. Thomas Gray of Otwell, Indiana, suggesting she should contact them at her earliest convenience. Unfortuntely, neither Mrs. Taylor nor any member of her family responded to that report. It was never returned by postal authorities, so I must assume it was received, and I hope the family was happy with the results.

1900 Census of Richardson Co, Nebr. (BYU Film #1,240.938 - 3 Nov 1992)

#128/128 Rulo City
TAYLOR, JESSE (Head) WM June 1821; age 78
married 58 years; born: Indiana
father born: Kentucky
mother born: Kentucky
TAYLOR, MARY (Wife) WF Mar 1824; age 76
married 58 years; mother of 11 children; 9 living
born: Indiana
father born: Indiana
mother born: Indiana

1900 Census of Dubois County, Indiana (BYU Film #1,240,368 - 12 Dec 1992)

#273/282
TRAYLOR, JESSE (Head) WM Jan 1820; age 80
married 38 years (Capatilist); born: Indiana
father born: South Carolina
mother born: South Carolina
TRAYLOR, MARGARET (Wife) WF May 1844;
age 56; born Indiana
father born: Pennsylvania
mother born: Indiana

One year later, I left the Genealogical Society and began teaching full time at Brigham Young

> "Mrs. Jesse Taylor was born March 13, 1827, in Indiana, died in Rulo, February 9th, 1908, aged 81 years, 10 months, and 26 days. The funeral was preached from the Holiness Church in Rulo, Rev. Bennett Maze officiating; burial in Rulo Cemetery. She leaves a husband and seven sons and three daughters, besides several grandchildren and some great-grandchildren to mourn her death. Deceased has been a faithful member of the Methodist Church for 35 years; they were among the oldest settlers in Rulo and are well known and loved and respected by all who know them. Mr. Taylor, the aged husband and father, is in delicate health. All of the bereaved have the sympathy of a host of friends."
>
> The Falls City Journal. Falls City, Nebraska, Friday February 14, 1908, page 2 (as reported by the Nebraska State Historical Society June 14, 1962; Donald F. Danker, Archivist)

Obituary of Mary Ellen (Hardin) Taylor

University, loosing all contact with the Taylor family.

Thirty five years have passed since that report, and a lot of water has passed under the bridge. I have had no contact with any of the Salt Lake Taylor family nor with any of the Indiana Traylor family in all those years, but I have told their story many times in classroom situations and it has always captured the interest of my listeners. While preparing this problem for publication, it became apparent that certain research steps could easily be taken to confirm some of our previous findings, and with that in mind, selective census and biographical searches were made which produced additional revealing information. Mrs. Thomas Gray, of Otwell, Indiana, whom we visited in 1962, was contacted by telephone in 1992 and also provided additional confirming information. She remembered our visit to her home thirty years earlier and confirmed to me that the Taylor family of Salt Lake City had never contacted her. She was also kind enough to recheck the Traylor Union Church cemetery for selected inscriptions which had long since been forgotten, and I was able to send her new and interesting information about her Peter Taylor of Warrick County.

YOU'RE A TAYLOR; NOT A TRAYLOR!

It was Jesse Taylor and not Jesse Traylor who married Mary Ellen Hardin on the 27th of February 1842 in Winslow, Pike County, Indiana; suggesting that a clerk made a transcription error in recording the surname as Traylor rather than Taylor in Pike County marriage records.

Willard Hardin, a living nephew of Mary Ellen Hardin in 1962, gave personal testimony of the Hardin/Taylor connection and gave corroborating evidence to Hardin/Taylor information known by the Jesse E. Taylor family of Salt Lake City, Utah.

Jesse Taylor was listed in the 1850 Federal Census of Pike County, Indiana and the 1860 Federal census of Mason County, Illinois with his known wife and children; both records including the Taylor spelling; he was also listed in the 1900 Federal census of Richardson County, Nebraska with the Taylor spelling.

Jesse Traylor was listed in the 1850 and 1900 Federal Censuses of Dubois County, Indiana with his known wives and children.

JESSE TRAYLOR, one of a large family of children born to Joel and Catherine (Bomar) Traylor, was born January 9, 1820. The parents were natives of South Carolina, where they followed farming till their removal to Pike County, Ind. Here Joel bought a farm of 160 acres, on which he and wife lived until their deaths. In 1841, Jesse came to Dubois County and purchased 200 acres of land. By hard work and good management, he succeeded in clearing about 125 acres. In 1841, he married Jane McDonald, born in Dubois County, in 1822. To them were born these children: William A., Joel, Lockhart, Perry G., Louis, Ellis, Edward S., Albert and Basil. In 1861 Mrs. Traylor died and a year later Mr. Traylor married Margaret Drinkhouse. They are the parents of three children: George, Kerr and Hugh. In politics Jesse is a Democrat, never having voted any other ticket.

History of Pike and Dubois Counties, Indiana.
From the earliest time to the present; with biographical sketches... Chicago: Goodspeed Bros. & Co., 1885; pages 713-714 - micropublished as publication no. 147 on reel 42 of "County Histories of the 'Old Northwest': Series III, Indiana." New Haven, Conn.: Research Publications, Inc., 1973. (BYU Film #900 Pt. 147 reel 42)

A biographical sketch of Jesse Traylor was located in "The History of Pike and Dubois Counties, Indiana" (q.v.) and it included personal and family information which distinguished him from Jesse Taylor.

Obituary notices for Jesse Taylor and Mary Ellen (Hardin) Taylor also distinguish the Taylor family of Richardson County, Nebraska.

The tombstone for Jesse Traylor (born 1820; died 1902) in the Traylor Union Church of Pike County, Indiana show that he could not possibly be the Jesse who died in Rulo, Richardson County, Nebraska in 1908.

The fact that Jesse Taylor signed legal documents in Pike County, Indiana in 1849 by his "X" (mark); and the fact Jesse Traylor signed legal documents in the same place and in the same time period by his "seal" (signature) also distinguishes the two as distinct and separate personages

With the new information which has recently been located on this problem, an exhaustive reinvestigation of Pike and Dubois County, Indiana probate and land records would undoubtedly further clarify the issue

It is also likely that Jesse Taylor's parents and several brothers and sisters have been located in Warrick County, Indiana census records (q.v.), and further searches in probate and land records of that county would undoubtedly reveal further helpful information.

History of Pike and Dubois Counties, Indiana. From the earliest time to the present; with biographical sketches... Chicago, Goodspeed Bros. & Co., 1885. Micropublished as publication no. 147 on reel 42 of "County Histories of the 'Old Northwest': Series III, Indiana." New Haven, Conn.: Research Publications, Inc., 1973.
(Page 713-714)

JESSE TRAYLOR, one of a large family of children born to Joel and Catherine (Bomar) Traylor, was born January 9, 1820. The parents were natives of South Carolina, where they followed farming till their removal to Pike County, Ind. Here Joel bought a farm of 160 acres, on which he and wife lived until their deaths. In 1841, Jesse came to Dubois County and purchased 200 acres of land. By hard work and good management, he succeeded in clearing about 125 acres. In 1841, he married Jane McDonald, born in Dubois County, in 1822. To them were born these children: William a., Joel, Lockhart, Perry G., Louis, Ellis, Edward S., Albert and Basil. In 1861 Mrs. Traylor died and a year later Mr. Traylor married Margaret Drinkhouse. They are the parents of three children: George, Kerr and Hugh. In politics Jesse is a Democrat, never having voted any other ticket.
(Page 714)

ALBERT H. TRAYLOR, and enterprising young farmer of Dubois County, Ind., is a son of Jesse and Jane McDonald Traylor. Albert was born April 5, 1854, in Dubois County. He received a practical business education in the common schools and at the age of seventeen, began working for wages on the farm: he was married to Frances A. Chattin, March 14, 1875. She was born April 10, 1856, and is a daughter of Nathaniel and Susan (Allen) Chattin. To Mr. and Mrs. Traylor were born five children: Charlotte J., Flora M. (deceased), Lola, Floyd and Bertha. Both husband and wife are members of the Cumberland Presbyterian Church, in which Mr. Traylor is an elder. He is a warm Democrat and cast his first vote for Tilden; he is a wide-awake and enterprising young man and is sure to make a success of life.

History of Warrick, Spencer and Perry Counties, Indiana: From the Earliest Time to the Present; Together with Interesting Biographical Sketches, Reminiscences, Notes, Etc. Illustrated.
Chicago: Goodspeed, Bros. & Co., Publishers, 1885.
(BYU Ref. F526 .X1 B63 Reel Index to Microfilmed Collections of County Histories of the Old North West; Series III, Indiana; Film 900 #156 Reel 44)
Page 179

GURLEY TAYLOR, a prominent citizen of Warrick County, is a son of the old pioneer, Lewis Taylor, who immigrated with a wife and child to what is now Anderson Township, Warrick Co., Ind., in 1813 or 1814, where they entered a quarter-section of land from the Government, and where they made their home during the rest of their days. Lewis Taylor was a North Carolinian by birth, but when twelve years of age became a resident of Kentucky by the removal of his parents to near Bowling Green. He was then reared on a farm and when thirty years old went to Columbia, Tenn., where he was married, in 1811, to Rachel T. Baker, the mother of our subject. He died February 14, 1874 preceded by his wife May 31, 1850. Gurley Taylor was born December 28, 1836, in Anderson Township, this county, and Warrick County has always been his home. At seventeen years of age he began clerking at Newburgh, remaining there between five and six years, when he removed to Lynnville to take charge of a branch store at that place. In October 1874, he was elected, by the Democratic part, Sheriff of the county, and removing to Boonville began serving in that capacity in August, 1875. He was re-elected to the same position and in all served four years. Since then he has been engaged in farming, stock-raising and dealing in agricultural implements. He is a member of the Commandery in Masonry, the Encampment in Odd Fellowship and is the owner of 700 acres of land in Warrick County besides other valuable property. Mr. Taylor was united in marriage March 24, 1858, to Lucinda Shaul, and to their union six children have been born, as follows: Mary (deceased), Edward N., William W. Jacob L., Hendricks G. and Pine J. Mr. and Mrs. Taylor are members of the General Baptist Church.

Page 180

HON. JOHN L. TAYLOR, a native of this county, was born in Anderson Township August 30, 1850, being the eldest of eight children of Peter and Margaret J. (Perigo) Taylor, both natives of Warrick County. He was raised on his parents farm, receiving a fair education and in his seventeenth year moved with his parents to Boonville, where he attended the graded school during the winters and followed farming during the summers. He prepared himself for teaching, which occupation he followed until 1871, when he entered the State University at Bloomington and completed his junior year. He then returned to this county and engaged again in teaching. He was Principal of the Lynnville Graded School in 1874-75 and Assistant Principal of the Boonville School in 1875-76. At the latter date he began studying law with Judge Handy, continuing one year. In the fall of 1877 he entered the Cincinnati Law School, from which institution he graduated in May, 1878. He was Deputy Prosecutor under Judge Reinhard one year before entering the law school. In June, 1878, he was nominated by the Democracy for the Legislature and was elected, serving one term, being the youngest member of the House but one. Since then he has practiced his profession of law at Boonville. He served three years as Town Attorney and County Attorney two years, and is at present filling both offices. He is a Mason, an Odd Fellow, a K. of P. and has been Chairman of the Democratic Central Committee of Warrick County through three campaigns. He was married January 5, 1879, and his child died aged ten months.

PETER TAYLOR, a native of Warrick County, Ind., and one of the leading farmers of Boon Township, was born August 31, 1829, and is a son of Lewis and Rachel T. (Baker) Taylor, appropriate mention of whom is made elsewhere in this volume. Until eighteen years of age he remained at home with his parents, receiving only a limited education. October 11, 1849, he was married to Margaret J. Perigo, and in 1850 he contracted the gold fever and with the tide of immigration was swept to California. He then met with an accident in the mines that caused him to return to Indiana in less than a year, depleted in purse and reduced physically by disease. Up to 1859 he farmed, then in connection with four brothers embarked in mercantile pursuits at Newburgh, but only continued with them about one year when he re-embarked in farming, at which he has continued to the present time. He also is extensively engated in rearing fine stock, making a specialty of Norman horses and Durham cattle. To his first marriage eight children were born, all living but one. The mother died December 4, 1866. January 5, 1868, he wedded Margaret J. Hart, his present wife. Mr. Taylor owns about 700 acres of land in Warrick County, is a Prohibitionist and a member of the Methodist Episcopal Church. The names of his children are John l., Theodore H., Union T., Albert, Francis, Virgil and Lillie J."

CENSUS EXTRACTS

1840 Federal Census of Pike County, Indiana
(BYU Film #1840 Pt 27; NEW 23 Nov 1992)

Page#3 **BENJAMIN TAYLOR**
MALES: 1-under 5; 1-20/30
FEMALES: 1-20/30

JOSEPH TAYLOR
MALES: 1-20/30
FEMALES: 1-15/20

Page#5 **FRANCIS TAYLOR**
MALES: 1-5/10; 2-20/30
FEMALES: NONE LISTED

JOSEPH S. TAYLOR
MALES: 2-under 5; 1-20/30
FEMALES: 2-5/10; 1-20/30

JOHN HARDEN
MALES: 2-under 5; 1-5/10; 1-10/15; 1-30/40
FEMALES: 1-under 5; 1-15/20; 1-20/30

Page#18 **JESSE TRAYLOR**
MALES: 1-60/70
FEMALES: 1-50/60

Page#20 **THOMAS TRAYLOR**
MALES: 2-10/15; 1-15/20; 1-40/50
FEMALES: 1-5/10; 1-40/50

SPARTAN TRAYLOR
MALES: 1-under 5; 1-20/30
FEMALES: 1-under 5; 1-20/30

Page#21 **SILAS TAYLOR**
MALES: 1-20/30
FEMALES: 1/15/20

LEWIS TRAYLOR
MALES: 1-5/10; 1-10/15; 3-15/20; 1-40/50
FEMALES: 1-under 5; 1-20/30

Page#22 **E.D. TRAYLOR**
MALES: 1-under 5; 1-15/20
FEMALES: 1-20/30

Page#23 **JOHN TAYLOR**
MALES: 1-50/60
FEMALES: 1-50/60

Page#23 **JOSEPH A. GRAY**
MALES: 1-40/50
FEMALES: 1-10/15; 1-20/30

Page#24 **EBANEZER TAYLOR**
MALES: 2-under 5; 2-5/10; 1-15/20
FEMALES: 1-15/20

CATHARINE TRAYLOR
MALES: 2-10/15; 1-15/20; 1-20/30
FEMALES: 1-10/15; 1-40/50

MATHEW TRAYLOR
MALES: 3-UNDER 5; 1-30/40
FEMALES: 1-20/30

Page#25 **NICHOLSON HARDEN**
MALES: 1-70/80; FEMALES: 1-70/80

1850 Federal Census of Pike County, Indiana
(BYU Film #442,943; NEW 23 Nov 1992)

#222/222 Petersburg		
Henry Hardin	45 M Farmer	Kentucky
Mary Hardin	45 F	Georgia
Elizabeth Hardin	22 F	Indiana
Emiley Hardin	16 F	Indiana
George Hardin	15 M Labor	Indiana
Minerva Hardin	13 F	Indiana
Malinda Hardin	9 F	Indiana
John Hardin	6 M	Indiana
#411/411 Petersburg		
Louis Trayler	50 M Farmer	S.C.
Margaret Traylor	30 F	Ohio
Emery Trayler	18 M	Indiana
Gibson Trayler	16 M	Indiana
Artimasay Trayler	8 F	Indiana
William Trayler	2 M	Indiana
#63/63 Clay Township		
Philip Traylor	20 M Labor	Indiana
Nancy Traylor	52 F Farmer	Indiana
Poley Traylor	18 F	Indiana
Joseph Traylor	16 M	Indiana
George Traylor	7 M	Indiana
#137/137 Jefferson Township		
Elizabeth Trayler	37 F Farmer	Indiana
Lafayette Trayler	10 M	Indiana
Winney Trayler	8 F	Indiana
Virginia Trayler	6 M(sic)	Indiana
Terry Trayler	4 M	Indiana
Parris Trayler	2 M(sic)	Indiana
Tennessee Trayler	1 M(sic)	Indiana
#146/146 Jefferson Township		
Spencer Gray	29 M Farmer	Indiana
Alissia Gray	29 F	Indiana
Houston Gray	2 M	Indiana
Meerillas Gray	1 M(sic)	Indiana
Jane **Trayler**	11 F	Indiana
#147/147 Jefferson Township		
JESSE TRAYLER	84 M Farmer	**Virginia**
Mary Trayler	70 f	**Germany**
#159/159 Jefferson Township		
David Trayler	29 M Farmer	Indiana
Hannah Trayler	29 F	Indiana
Emaley Trayler	6 F	Indiana
Margaret Trayler	5 F	Indiana
Cintha Trayler	4 F	Indiana
Amandia Trayler	3 F	Indiana
Thomas Trayler 6/12 M	Indiana	

#160/160 Jefferson Township		
Mathew Trayler	43 M Farmer	**S.C.**
Lucinda Trayler	37 F	Ohio
Amanda Trayler	5 F	Indiana
Cathrine Trayler	3 F	Indiana
Elizabeth Trayler	1 F	Indiana
Alvin Trayler 6/12 M	Indiana	
#176/176 Jefferson Township		
Madison Traylor	28 M Farmer	Indiana
Mary Traylor	26 F	Indiana
Elizabeth Traylor	6 F	Indiana
Thomas Traylor	5 M	Indiana
John Traylor	3 M	Indiana
#177/177 Jefferson Township		
Thomas Traylor	68 M Farmer	Virginia
Cathrine Traylor	64 F	N.C.
Cathrine Traylor	20 F	N.C.
Sanford Traylor	21 M	Indiana
#279/279 Jefferson Township		
CATHRINE TRAYLOR	60 F Farmer	S.C.
Mary Gray	33 F	S.C.
Booker Gray	11 M	S.C.
Elisia Gray	7 F	S.C.
#101/101 Monroe Township		
Joseph Taylor	30 M Farmer	**Kentucky**
Lucinda Taylor	28 F	Kentucky
Benjamin Huchins	17 M	Kentucky
Benjamin Taylor	9 M	Kentucky
John Taylor	8 M	Indiana
Malinda Taylor	6 F	Indiana
Lucey Taylor	4 F	Indiana
Joseph Taylor	2 M	Indiana
#105/105 Monroe Township		
BENJAMIN TAYLOR	37 M Farmer	**Kentucky**
Marey Taylor	37 F	Indiana
John Done	15 M	Indiana
John Taylor	13 M	Indiana
Elenor Taylor	11 F	Indiana
Benjamin Taylor	4 M	Indiana
#114/114 Monroe Township		
Saley Hauchins	30 F Farmer	Kentucky
Nancy Taylor	66 F	**Georgia**
Jesse Hauchins	27 M	Indiana
George Hauchins	21 M	Indiana
#150/150 Monroe Township		
JESSE HAUCHINS	52 M Farmer	Kentucky
Elizabeth Hauchins	57 F	Kentucky
#159/159 Monroe Township		
John Hardin	22 M Farmer	Indiana
Sarah Hardin	20 F	Indiana
Mathew Hardin 6/12 M	Indiana	

#165/165 Monroe Township

JESSE TAYLOR	29 M Farmer	Indiana
Mary Taylor	24 F	Indiana
Georg(sic) Taylor	8 M	Indiana
John Taylor	5 M	Indiana
Mathew Taylor	4 M	Indiana
Nicholas Taylor	2 M	Indiana
Caroline Taylor	6/12 F	Indiana
william Harain(sic)	20 M Labor	Indiana

#171/171 Monroe Township

Mathew Thompson	25 M Farmer	Indiana
Matilda Thompson	23 F	Indiana
Marey Thompson	66 F	**Virginia**
James Hardin	14 M	Indiana
John Hardin	12 M	Indiana
Jasper Thompson	3 M	Indiana
James Thompson	7/12 M	Indiana

1850 Federal Census of Warrick County, Indiana
(BYU Film #442,957 NEW 23 Nov 1992)
#122/122 Campbell Township

PETER TAYLOR	44 m Farmer	**Kentucky**
Rebecca Taylor	44 F	Kentucky
Polly Taylor	16 F	Indiana
Andrew J. Taylor	15 M	Indiana
Washington Taylor	11 M	Indiana
Samuel Taylor	9 M	Indiana
Nathaniel Taylor	8 M	Indiana
Hezekiah Taylor	4 M	Indiana
Moses Taylor	2 M	Indiana

1860 Federal Census of Mason County, Illinois
(BYU Film #803,210 NEW 30 Nov 1992)
#513/513 Mason City

JESSE TAYLOR	38 M Farmer	Indiana
Mary Taylor	35 F	Indiana
George Taylor	18 M	Indiana
John Taylor	16 M	Indiana
Mathew Taylor	14 M	Indiana
Nicholas Taylor	12 M	Indiana
Caroline Taylor	10 F	Indiana
Jackson Taylor	7 M	Illinois
Sarah J. Taylor	5 F	Illinois
James C. Taylor	2 M	Illinois

1870 Federal Census of Mason County, Illinois
(BYU Film #545,754 NEW 30 Nov 1992)
#178/178 Mason City

Taylor, Joseph	51 M Assessor	Kentucky
Lucinda	48 F	Kentucky
Melissa	17 F	Illinois
Conklin, Lucy	24 F	Indiana
Conklin, Lucinda	4 F	Illinois
Conklin, Philamena 4/12 F Illinois		

1880 Federal Census of Richardson County, Nebraska
(BYU Film #1,254,754 NEW 25 Nov 1992)
#7/7 Rulo Village, page 447

Demoss, Charles	28 M Works Eleva.	Ill. Ky. Ind.
Demoss, Jennie 23 F (wife)		Ill. Ind. Ind.
Demoss, Carrie	3 F (dau)	Ill. Ill. Ill.
Demoss, Josie	2 F (dau)	Ill. Ill. Ill.
Demoss, Fannie 3/12 F (dau)		Ill. Ill. Ill.
TAYLOR, MARY	50 F (mother in law)Ind. Va. Va.	

1880 Federal Census of Richardson County, Nebraska
(BYU Film #1.254,754 NEW 30 Nov 1992)
#94/160 Rulo Village

Taylor, George E.	35 M Runs Tow Busn.	Ind. Ind. Ind.
Taylor, Sephrone	26 F (wife)	Ind. Ind. Ind.
Taylor, Bertha	8 F (dau)	Nebr. Ind. Ind.
Taylor, Gurta	7 F (dau)	Nebr. Ind. Ind.
Taylor, Jesse	5 F (dau)	Nebr. Ind. Ind.
Taylor, Edward	2 M (son)	Nebr. Ind. Ind.
Carter, Frank	21 M (boarder)	Iowa N.H. Iowa

1900 Federal Census of Richardson County, Nebraska
(BYU Film #1,240,938 NEW 30 Nov 1992)
#128 Rulo City
TAYLOR, JESSE (HEAD) WM born:June 1821; age 78;
married: 58
born: Indiana
father born: Kentucky; mother born: Kentucky
TAYLOR, MARY (WIFE) WF born: Mar 1824; age 76;
married: 58; mother of: 11 children; 9 living
born: Indiana
father born: Indiana; mother born: Indiana

Clyde M. Lunceford Pedigree

John (Jack) Fitzgerald
Born:
Where:
Married: 14 Aug 1889
Died: about 1901
Where: Park City, Utah

Joseph Alvin Lunceford
Born: 6 January 1890
Where: Lakeview, Utah, Utah
Married: 2 October 1912
Died:
Where:

Martha Eleanor Lunceford
Born: 21 october 1869
Where: Provo, Utah, Utah
Died: 24 April 1950
Where: Sandy, S.L., Utah

Clyde Martin Lunceford
Born: 12 Mar ch 1918
Where: Magna, Salt Lake, Utah
Married: 4 September 1941

Thelda Moss
Born: 8 July 1919
Where: Ririe, Jefferson, Idaho
Died: 16 Oct 1979
Where: Provo, Utah, Utah

6 December 1957
Clyde M. Lunceford
232 East 20th South
Orem, Utah

CHAPTER 3

JACK FITZGERALD
"Miner at the Silver King"

GETTING STARTED WITH RESEARCH

On the 16th of December 1957, only two weeks after I had been hired as a research trainee by the LDS Genealogical Society, Thelda Moss Lunceford of Orem, Utah came to the Research Department and requested genealogical assistance. She wanted to find more information about Jack (John) Fitzgerald who married Martha Eleanor Lunceford in Park City, Utah in 1889. She established an account with us and made a ten dollar deposit; the Department was charging $1.50 per hour for research at the time. Her account was assigned to "NEW" (me) and we consulted about her request while it was being processed. Thelda's husband Clyde was a successful Orchardist and Businessman in Orem and was the grandson of Jack and Martha. Clyde's father, Joseph Alvin Lunceford, was born Joseph Alvin Fitzgerald on the 6th of January 1890 in Lake View, Utah, but he was given the maiden surname of his mother after she divorced Jack in 1895.

Mrs Lunceford explained that Jack had married Martha in Park City, Utah on the 14th of August 1889; he was a miner at the Silver King Mine and she was a waitress at a local restaurant. Evidently Jack was a drinker and became unduly severe in his habits, so Martha divorced him in 1895, giving up the Fitzgerald name and assuming her maiden surname. The family understood that Jack died and was buried in Park City, but Mrs. Lunceford said they knew little else about him, other than he had a close friend named Charlie Ford. Mrs Lunceford left a hand written pedigree showing the known information and asked that we begin research as soon as possible, but because of the holiday season and other account priorities it was two weeks before I began work on the order.

Naomi Harker, a kind middle aged lady with long and successful experience in genealogical research, was my trainer and reviewed the Lunceford account before any work was done on it. She outlined the research steps I should take and checked my work when it was completed. She had me repeat certain searches, and in some instances, she personally rechecked the sources I had investigated to make sure the findings were correct. She also reviewed and edited my reports before they were sent; I have the greatest respect and admiration for her and appreciate the many things she taught me.

> **PARK CITY, UTAH**
> **CEMETERY RECORDS**
> **(GS Utah P2a)**
>
> FITZGERALD, John F.
> b. Rossie, New York
> son of John Fitzgerald
> b. Ireland, and
> Margaret born Ireland;
> died 25 Aug 1901,
> age 44 years;
> buried City Cemetery
> Park City, Utah

Burial record for John F. Fitzgerald

Searches were first made in general ordinance collections where information was located on Clyde, his father Joseph, and on his mother Martha Eleanor Lunceford, but nothing was found on Jack. There were plenty of John Fitzgeralds noted in the records investigated, but none of them fit the description of our man. There were also several published Fitzgerald genealogies cataloged at the library, but a check of them revealed no apparent connections to him. The search was next moved to locality sources, and it was here that I found a possible reference to Jack. A general collection of Utah cemetery records included an entry for "John F. Fitzgerald," who died in 1901 and was buried in Park City, Utah.

If this was our Jack, we had his place of birth, his parentage, and his date of death, which would help in further searches. Unfortunately, the State of Utah didn't begin recording vital statistics until 1905, so an official death record couldn't be obtain, but a church record or newspaper obituary might possibly be located for him. No church records were listed in the catalog for the Park City area, other than LDS, and it was unlikely that he would be listed in them, because he was Catholic, so I attempted to locate a newspaper obituary for him. According to "Gregory's American Newspapers" (a Union List for the United States and Canada) the "Park Record," a weekly newspaper, was published in Park City when Jack died, and copies for the years 1899-1903 were supposedly on file with the University of Colorado at Boulder. I sent a request to Colorado for a search of that newspaper and then directed my efforts toward other available sources at the library.

The town of Rossie proved to be in St. Lawrence County, New York; about 50 miles south of Ogdensburg and about 75 miles directly north of Watertown. Knowing the county made a census search possible and the 1860 was chosen, because Jack, who was born about 1857, would likely be a young child in the household of his parents. In those days census indexes were few and far between, and I could locate none for New York, so a search of the entire county was conducted. I found no Fitzgeralds living in the town of Rossie, and not one household listing a John and Margaret was found in the rest of the county. There were, however, five Fitzgerald families located which included young children named John, but only one of them was near the approximate age of Jack; and in that instance the possible mother was named Mary and not Margaret. Also, that family was living in the town of Canton and not Rossie; but then people do move from time to time, and census takers are known to make mistakes, so I accepted this household as the best possible candidate to be Jack's family.

CENSUS EXTRACT
ST. LAWRENCE COUNTY NEW YORK
1860

#158/158 - Canton		
John Fitzgerald	45 M Lab.	Ireland
Mary	35 F	Ireland
James	7 M	New York
John	4 M	New York

1860 census extract of John Fitzgerald Family

After the census search was completed, funds in the account were exhausted, so I sent a report to the patron explaining the searches made and the information found. I recommended that additional searches be made in St. Lawrence county records, which would have to be done by correspondence, because few New York records were held by our the library at that time. I also suggested an additional deposit of $25.00 would be necessary to continue the work. The report was sent on the 21st of January 1958, and in less than a week a response was received from Mrs Lunceford instructing us to continue research on Jack.

For the next eight years, from 1957 until 1965, the Department conducted regular research on the Jack Fitzgerald problem without any real success, other than locating the burial record in Park City and possible finds in the 1870 and 1880 censuses. It wasn't for a lack of funds, however, because the Lunceford family made regular deposits in their account; and it wasn't for a lack of effort on my part, because I did everything I knew how to do; and, the researchers who followed me did everything they knew how to do. From December 1957 until February 1959 "NEW" and his trainer "NMH" worked on the account; then from 1960 until 1964 "CBT" and "RCG" handled it; then finally, in 1965, "JBP" took it over and recommended the account be closed; he concluded nothing more could be done.

Vital, church, cemetery, census, land, court, and military records had been investigated by researchers, by county and state officials, and by private agents without finding the wanted Fitzgerald information. Compiled genealogies, family histories, biographical collections, and quarterly magazines were also investigated. The University of Colorado at Boulder, whose library supposedly had copies of the Park Record, responded to our request, but they were unable to help us. I made a personal trip to Park City, Utah where the Park Record was still being published, but the publisher didn't have copies of the weekly prior to 1940, and he didn't know who did. I personally searched the city cemetery and two other local cemeteries adjoining the town, but without success. A personal visit to the Catholic church revealed an entry of Jack's name in the death index, but information had not been carried forward to the body of the record; both the Priest and I searched every page of the original book without finding the entry; neither Jack's nor Martha's names appeared in any of the marriage or christening records for that church. Other searches were conducted by various researchers over that eight-year period, but nothing was found which pertained to Jack.

ACCOUNT CLOSED

On the 29th of July 1965, "JBP" (the last researcher to handle the Lunceford account at the Research Department) made his final report and suggested the account be closed "because nothing more could be done." A refund of $10.45 was sent to Clyde M. Lunceford on the 13th of December 1965, almost eight years to the day the account was first opened (16 December 1957), and research for information about Jack Fitzgerald ended for good--or did it?

During the Fall of 1967, two years after the Lunceford account had been closed at the Research Department, and four years after I had left their employ for a teaching position at Brigham Young University, I was assigned to visit the West Sharon Stake of the LDS Church as a priesthood genealogical committee representative. Committee members were visiting local units of the church trying to promote genealogical research among members, and as it happened, Clyde Martin Lunceford was the President of that Stake. When I visited his stake, President Lunceford had no idea that I had been his researcher (NEW) at the Genealogical Society several years earlier, and I didn't reveal that fact to him, even though we had personal conversations and discussed the conference agenda. Meetings were held on Saturday and Sunday, and after the conference a report was dutifully submitted to the committee chairman, then N. Eldon Tanner, and the West Sharon Stake became nothing more than a memory--or did it?

Call it what you would like; a coincidence, fate, good luck, bad luck, or just plain chance, but six months later, I was reassigned to the same Stake for the same purpose. Having been a member of the Committee since 1958, I had never before been assigned to the same Stake twice, but here in 1968, my last year with the Committee, I was returning to the West Sharon Stake, and Clyde M. Lunceford was still the Stake President. There was no small concern on my part, and I wondered how things would work out this time. Would President Lunceford remember me from the last conference? Would he recognize that Norman Edgar Wright was really "NEW" the researcher who had spent a lot of his money without producing any positive results? What would I say to his people; they had already heard my genealogical presentation a few months earlier? A great deal of anxiety and apprehension accompanied me on that visit, to say the least, but after arriving at the Stake and meeting with President Lunceford, it was apparent my concerns were entirely unjustified.

Interestingly enough, at this conference, President Lunceford did recognize that his genealogical visitor was "NEW" his former researcher at the Genealogical Society, but this time he was unusually kind; almost laudatory of the research work which had been done by the Society, and before we ever got to the real business of the conference, he said: "I want you to continue research on my Jack Fitzgerald line!" My immediate response was: "I'm sorry, President Lunceford, but I don't do private research anymore; I'm teaching full time at Brigham Young University." He responded by saying: "I don't care what you're doing, I want you to continue research on my Fitzgerald line!" Anyone who knew President Lunceford understood that he had a very powerful personality and usually got what he wanted; he could also be quite intimidating. After he had made his last remark, my tone changed a little and I said: "To be honest with you President Lunceford, I've done everything I know how to do on that line; and the researchers who took over after I left did everything they could think of, but without success!" He laughed and said: "That doesn't really matter; if we keep working on this problem it can be solved." Then he said: "Money means nothing to me on this Fitzgerald line; I want it solved!"

Well, with that remark my interests did an about face, and I began to ponder what additional searches might be made to find more about Jack Fitzgerald; perhaps there was something else which could be done to solve the problem. I had never heard a patron say 'money means nothing to me on this problem" before, and it would be interesting to work under such circumstances. President Lunceford wanted to write me a check for continued research immediately, but to show some discretion in my sudden change of attitude, I told him further searches would be made, and if something new was found I'd be happy to send him a bill. He was amenable to that, and without further reference to the Fitzgerald problem the conference continued with great success.

Clyde Martin Lunceford

A TRIP TO ROSSIE UNLOCKS THE DOOR

On the 4th of July 1968, after attending genealogical seminars in Indiana and Ohio, my wife Carolyn and I, along with our youngest son Nathan, found ourselves in Rome, New York visiting a younger brother who was serving in the military at Griffiss, Air Force Base. After an enjoyable three-day visit with him and his young family, we drove north through Watertown to Hammond, New York where we visited St Peter's church and received directions in finding the town of Rossie. It was late Sunday afternoon and the Priest at St. Peter's, who was also in charge of St. Patrick's church at Rossie, was kind enough to recheck his records for possible Fitzgerald entries, but his efforts revealed nothing new; he had been contacted by us previously but had found nothing on our family.

A small winding road north of Hammond led east and south from the main highway to the small village of Rossie. An older vacant framed building, formerly a motel, stood to the south as we entered the village, and the shell of a larger stone structure stood on the north side by a large stream. An older wooden building housed the local grocery store where inquiry was made about local residents and the location of the town cemetery. St. Patrick's Catholic church was situated on the south side of the town road, east of the grocery store, and St. Patrick's cemetery (known also as the Riverside cemetery) was positioned a few blocks further east along the same road. The grocer knew of no persons by the name of Fitzgerald presently resident in the village, and after we purchased some bread, milk, and cheese, he gave us directions to the local cemetery.

The hour was getting late, but there was sufficient light to read tombstone inscriptions, and that was our activity for the next hour or so. The cemetery was divided into two distinct sections with the Catholic area lying to the south and east. We bypassed the Protestant part and began reading each of the tombstones in the Catholic section, proceeding along each row from the front to the back of the cemetery. And, wouldn't you know it, there on the very last row, at the most distant point from the road, stood a Fitzgerald tombstone identifying John

Entering the town of Rossie, New York - 7 July 1968

Looking northwest in Rossie, New York - 1968

Fitzgerald (1815-1891); Margaret Fitzgerald (1831-1911); and Lottie Fitzgerald, daughter (1875-1885). Could this be the tombstone of Jack's parents (and a sister)? The time period and place were right, and we were convinced it was.

After the earlier failures to locate pertinent information about the Fitzgerald family, this find brought excitement which can't be explained in words. Upon finding it, I let out a yell, which almost frightened my wife out of her shoes, and our young son began to cry thinking something terrible had happened to his father. The stone was relatively modern, of a red and white granite formation, and it must have been fairly expensive to purchase. I wondered who might have been there to take such interest in John and Margaret? If we had only known, we might have been able to contact them and find out much more about Jack, but that was evidently not to be; not yet at least. My memory took me back nearly eight years earlier, to 1959, when we had employed an agent to search this same cemetery; he reported having searched it without finding any Fitzgerald headstones. How could he have missed this beautiful large stone?

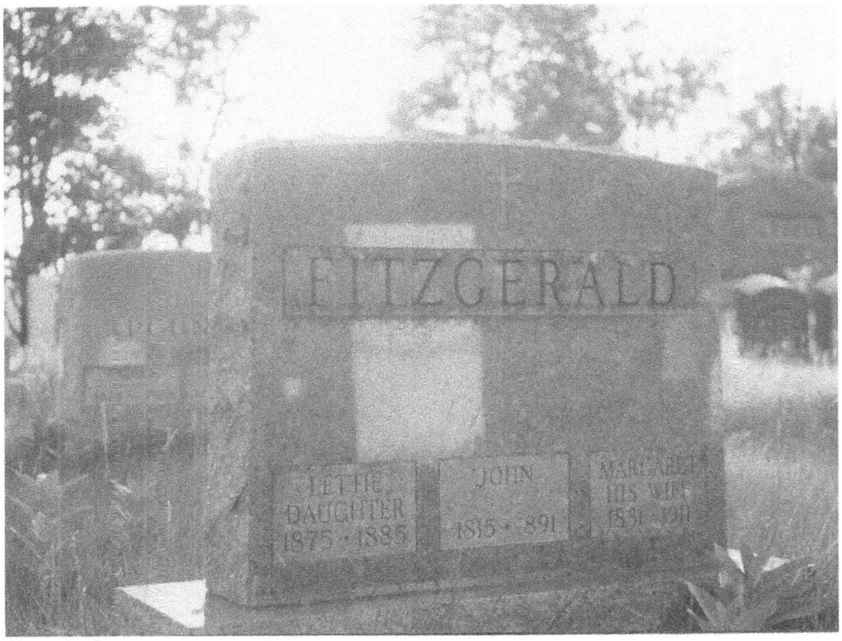

John and Margaret Fitzgerald tombstone; Rossie, New York

The Jack Fitzgerald problem was certainly not solved by locating this gravestone, but it presented positive and exciting new information which could (and did) lead to more important things. It was almost too late in the evening to take a photograph of the headstone, but I gave it a try, and fortunately it turned out fine. Because of the late hour, we drove back to the main highway and followed it north to Ogdensburg, then we drove east a few miles to Canton, the county seat, where we got a motel.

Early the following morning, Monday the 8th of July 1968, I was in the St. Lawrence County Court House copying records with renewed vigor and enthusiasm. I started with the probate court records (Surrogate Court in New York) and began copying Fitzgerald entries from the index. There were many Fitzgerald names listed, but only one John prior to 1900, just as officials had reported to us earlier.

After copying two pages of Fitzgerald entries from the index, I began pulling down the original files from special metal boxes housed high in the walls of room, hoping to find references to our people. This proved very time consuming, so I walked over to the clerk and asked him if I might use my own camera to take pictures of the documents in order to save time. I had recently purchased a new Cannon camera with a macro lens and could make good document copies without enlargements. His answer was very blunt and direct. He said: "Hell No! You can't use your own camera; if I let you do that, I wouldn't make any money!" Then he pulled out a large desk drawer and showed me dozens of document copy orders waiting to be filled; he was charging $1.00 per page for copies. After his answer and demonstrative display, I returned to my station and resumed copying the Fitzgerald documents by hand.

At the very moment the clerk had given me his blunt answer about not using my camera, a middle aged lady, whom I assumed to be an employee, walked by. She heard the clerk make

St. Lawrence County Court House; Canton, New York

PROBATE RECORD EXTRACTS
ST. LAWRENCE COUNTY, NEW YORK
SURROGATE COURT
(Testate Estates)

NAME	DEATHDATE	PROBATED
#6786 Dennis Fitzgerald Will Book 17:205	25 Sep 1879	21 Jul 1881
#7337 John Fitzgerald Will Book 19:477	23 Nov 1884	2 Feb 1885
#7487 Bernard Fitzgerald Will Book 21:227	26 Nov 1885	3 May 1886
#1477 Mary Fitzgerald Will Book 29:535	19 Jul 1896	2 Nov 1896
#3407 Michael Fitzgerald Will Book 38:16	19 Oct 1906	17 May 1906
#11375 Bessie Fitzgerald Will Book 45:417	4 Sep 1912	4 Nov 1912
#11624 John Fitzgerald Will Book 46:633	26 Mar 1913	13 May 1913
#7431 Richard Fitzgerald Will Book 53:109	4 Jan 1920	8 Mar 1920
#8611 John Fitzgerald Will Book 57:537	26 Mar 1922	18 Apr 1922
#9038 Mary G. Fitzgerald Will Book 59:157	7 Jan 1923	27 Mar 1923
#9107 Edward Fitzgerald Will Book 59:369	15 Apr 1923	4 Jan 1923
#9886 Sarah Fitzgerald Will Book 61:613	27 Dec 1922	6 Feb 1925
#14555 John Fitzgerald Will Book 76:226	17 May 1934	31 May 1934
#15715 Thomas Fitzgerald Will Book 80:370	12 Nov 1936	1 Dec 1936
#19260 Emmett Fitzgerald Will Book 87:192	4 Feb 1945	
#21739 Richard Fitzgerald Will Book 89:367	3 Aug 1950	

St. Lawrence County, New York probate extracts

his sharp remark as she passed, and I noticed that she took a backward glance at us. After I had returned to my copy work, she came over and said: "Why did you ask him that?" (about using my own camera) "He's not the boss here!" I thought "Oh, who is this?" And before I could reply, she said: "I'm the County Historian for St. Lawrence County; what is it you are doing?" I explained that I was trying to find genealogical information about Jack Fitzgerald, who was supposedly born in Rossie, New York in about 1857, and I showed her a copy of the Fitzgerald pedigree. She looked it over and remarked that she had done considerable genealogical research in county records, but the Jack Fitzgerald name didn't ring any bells with

St. Patrick's (Riverside) Cemetery; Rossie, New York

St. Patrick's Church; Rossie, New York - 7 July 1968

her. Then she gave me some suggestions about other sources which might be investigated; including naturalization/citizenship records and modern state censuses. After that, she said: "When you're finished here, you should come down to my office in the basement; I have some records which might help you." Her name was Mary H. Biondi, and meeting her was another positive step on the path leading to the solution of the Jack Fitzgerald problem.

PROBATE RECORD EXTRACTS
ST. LAWRENCE COUNTY, NEW YORK
SURROGATE COURT
(Intestate Estates)

NAME	DEATHDATE	ADMINISTR.
John Fitzgerald	1 Nov 1840	27 Jun 1842
Henry Fitzgerald	3 Jun 1884	19 Sep 1888
Lawrence Fitzgerald	2 Mar 1902	3 Apr 1902
Patrick E. Fitzgerald	(GRDN 5:260)	3 Apr 1902
James Fitzgerald	3 Mar 1908	16 Mar 1908
John Fitzgerald	(GRDN 5:766)	4 Jan 1913
Louise Fitzgerald	(as above)	
Elizabeth Fitzgerald	(as above)	
Thomas P. Fitzgerald	9 Sep 1914	21 Dec 1914
John Fitzgerald	13 Feb 1921	17 feb 1921
Kenneth Fitzgerald	(GRDN 6:548)	11 Sep 1924
Ellen Fitzgerald	(as above)	
Thomas E. Fitzgerald	19 Dec 1931	29 Dec 1931
Michael J. Fitzgerald	19 Mar 1932	11 Nov 1932
Frances Fitzgerald	7 Feb 1935	3 Dec 1936
Margaret Fitzgerald	(Adoption 72:465)	
John H. Fitzgerald	26 Oct 1945 (Min: 105:451)	

St. Lawrence County, New York probate extracts

There were excellent indexes for the probates; separate ones for testate and intestate estates, and I was able to copy all Fitzgerald names in a fairly short time, but it took much longer to look at the files and decide whether they were applicable or not. Extracts were made from each Fitzgerald file, but no apparent connections to Jack nor to John and Margaret were evident. At least three of the extracts would prove to be significant, but that would come much later after several other searches were completed. Extracts were also made from county land records (deeds, mortgages, and leases), but no connections to John and Margaret were found in them.

Several Fitzgerald names were located in the naturalization and citizenship records, but none were found for John nor Margaret. Copies were made of those listed, thinking they might later prove to be relatives. Copies of selected modern census records were also checked, and several Fitzgerald entries were noted, but John and Margaret couldn't be found. I did, however, find a Michael Fitzgerald in the 1905 census, who was listed as "Bartender" in Rossie, and he later proved to be a son of John and Margaret.

Most of the day was spent in the county clerk's records, but in the late afternoon I went down stairs to the County Historian's office where some really helpful information was found.

Mrs. Biondi was very kind and considerate in identifying record collections in her care; even making some searches for me herself. Her office had many early non-current records of the county; including birth, marriage, and death notices for 1847-1852; cemetery/sextons' records for a few burial grounds, some newspaper obituary notices, and other miscellaneous historical records.

BIRTHS, DEATHS, AND MARRIAGES
IN ST. LAWRENCE COUNTY, NEW YORK
1864-1902
as clipped from the Gouverneur Herald

MARRIED: Jackson-Fitzgerald; On the evening of the 14th, inst., (1883) by the Rev. Dr. Edwards, Mr. Samuel J. Jackson to Miss Margaret Fitzgerald, all of Gouvernour.

MARRIED: Fitzgerald-Nelson; At the residence of Dr. Frazier, Portland Drive May 29th 1890, Mr. James Fitzgerald of Gouverneur, N.Y. and Miss Cora M. Nelson of Potsdam, N. Y.

MARRIED: Fitzgerald-Hilts; In Brooklyn, N.Y. April 9, 1891 by Rev. T. De'Witt Talmage, Mr. John Fitzgerald of Butte City, Montana, and Miss Nellie Hilts of Gouverneur, N.Y.

MARRIED: Orford-Fitzgerald; In the Methodist Parsonage Aug 18, 1892 by Rev. C. A. Peck, William D. Orford and Mrs. Millie A. Fitzgerald, both of Gouverneur.

MARRIED: Clapp-Fitzgerald; In Gouverneur July 20, 1887 by Rev. E. C. Laramie, Homer Clapp and Mary Fitzgerald.

DIED: Fitzgerald; In this town, Oct. 17, 1885, Lottie Fitzgerald, dau. of John Fitzgerald, aged 10 years and 7 months.

DIED: Fitzgerald - In Gouverneur Oct 25, 1891 by being struck by railroad engine, John Fitzgerald aged 76 years and 1 month.

Births, Deaths, and Marriages from the Gouverneur Herald

The early vital records for 1847-1852 were on a town basis, and I searched them first, hoping to find the marriage of John and Margaret and perhaps some of their children, but nothing relevant was found. Then I began checking obituary collections, and one in particular proved very interesting. Someone had clipped birth, death, and marriage notices from the Gouverneur Herald, for the period 1864-1902, and had glued them on the pages of a history book in chronological order; Gouverneur was only a few miles east of Rossie and about 12 miles south of Canton. The first entry to catch my eye was one in 1885 which listed the death of Lottie Fitzgerald, daughter of John, who died aged 10 years and 7 months. This was one of the names on the Fitzgerald tombstone found in St. Patrick's cemetery at Rossie the night before. Only a few entries beyond that was one for a John Fitzgerald who died October 26, 1891 aged 76 years and 1 month after being struck by a railroad engine. This was undoubtedly the death notice for John Fitzgerald whom we presumed to be Jack's father, and my excitement increased. Unfortunately, entries in that collection didn't extend beyond 1902, so Margaret's death in 1911 wasn't included.

The marriage entries also proved interesting, and I copied all Fitzgerald names. A John Fitzgerald of Butte City, Montana married Miss Nellie Hilts of Gouverneur in Brooklyn, New

Gouverneur, New York - July, 1968

York on the 9th of April 1891, and at first I thought this might be our Jack from Park City, because he was a miner and Butte, Montana was a western mining town, but it dawned on me later that our man had married Martha Eleanor Lunceford in 1889 and they hadn't yet separated. A Homer Clapp and Mary Fitzgerald marriage in 1887, at Gouverneur, also looked interesting; it was contemporary with Jack's (1889) and Mary could have been his sister.

The town of Gouverneur began popping up more and more as Fitzgerald names were identified, and the next record checked gave it even more importance. Mrs. Biondi had a collection of Interment Records (burial records) for St. Lawrence County, and one document included several Fitzgerald names from St. Patrick's cemetery in Rossie. It listed the John, Margaret, and Lettie (or Lottie) with the same information I had found on the Fitzgerald tombstone, but it also listed three other Fitzgeralds buried there; including a Lawrence who died in 1880 aged 50 years, a Margaret (O'Rielly) Fitzgerald who died in 1922 aged 82 years, and a younger Lawrence Fitzgerald who died in 1902 aged 53 years. Written immediately under their names, was a special note indicating the latter three had been disinterred on June 15, 1932 and buried in the Riverside cemetery at Gouverneur. Why weren't all of the Fitzgeralds' disinterred and buried at Gouverneur; why just the latter three? That answer would come much later and would be logical, but now the Rossie/Gouverneur tie was definite. Another thing that puzzled me was the fact that both St. Patrick's cemetery and the one at Gouverneur were referred to as "Riverside" cemeteries; were they one and the same or were they different?

ST. PATRICK'S CEMETERY INTERMENT RECORD
County Historian's Office
Canton, New York
8 July 1968

JOHN H. FITZGERALD 1815-1891 (Oct 26) age 76 yrs
MARGARET W. FITZGERALD 1831-1911
LETTIE FITZGERALD; daughter, 1875-1885 (Oct 17)
LAWRENCE FITZGERALD; died Sept 1880 age 50 yrs
MARGARET O. FITZGERALD; died Mar 26, 1922 age 82 yrs
LAWRENCE FITZGERALD died Mar 2, 1902 age 53 yrs

NOTE: "3 Fitzgeralds disinterred and buried in Riverside Cemetery (Gouverneur) June 15, 1932"

Interment record from St. Patrick's Cemetery; Rossie, New York.

After completing searches in the Historian's Office, and just before the court house was ready to close, Mrs. Biondi suggested that I drive to the town of Gouverneur and make further investigations there. She said Gouverneur had a good library, which remained open until the late evening, and she knew there was a large cemetery near the center of town. While I was preparing to leave, she made a call to her close friend Ms Mitchell--the Librarian at Gouverneur--to determine the actual closing time; she also confirmed that the Library had microfilm copies of two local newspapers extending well beyond 1911.

A lesson was learned in St. Lawrence County about using a camera for copy work, but it wasn't fully realized until after the New York trip was completed and my film was developed. Having purchased my Cannon camera just before the New York trip, and being an amateur photographer, I had asked a professional which type of film would be best for document copy work. He had insisted that I use high contrast copy film, which was expensive and required special skills. I had taken photo's of many documents in the County Historian's Office and had used my last roll of film as the court house was closing, so I stopped at a local drug store to buy more film. They didn't carry the special film I was using and referred me to another store in town. That store didn't handle it either, but they referred me to a local professional who knew about such things. He said that I was a fool for using such expensive film for the type of work I was doing. He said I should use ordinary black and white plus x 125 speed film; It cost less that $1.00 for a 36 exposure roll, while the high contrast copy film sold for $5.00 a roll. Every exposure I took that day using the expensive film was indecipherable; either to dark, too light, or simply blank, while the copies I took using the cheaper film turned out great.

After the court house closed in Canton, we drove south about twelve miles to the town of Gouverneur where we found the Riverside cemetery without difficulty; there was no doubt about its name being "Riverside." It was a large metropolitan cemetery comprising about two city blocks, and a sexton's office stood at the entrance. Inquiry at that office failed to locate the sexton, so we drove slowly along the winding cemetery roads trying to spot Fitzgerald headstones. In the older section of the cemetery, we got out of the car and walked among the different headstones; many shaded by beautiful large deciduous trees and standing on small green rolling hills. Near the extreme southwest corner of the cemetery, I spotted a large Fitzgerald tombstone which proved to be that of the Lawrence and Margaret Fitzgerald family; three of whom had evidently been transferred from the Rossie cemetery. There was one large tombstone with "Fitzgerald" beautifully engraved on it, then smaller stones were in a single line identifying Lawrence Fitzgerald as father, Margaret as mother, Lawrence as brother, and Michael J. and Thomas E with no relationship given. Lawrence was old enough to be the brother of John from Rossie, but further research would have to be completed before that could be confirmed. I copied the names and dates listed on each stone, and we searched for other Fitzgerald names in the immediate area, but without success.

RIVERSIDE CEMETERY
Gouverneur, New York

"FITZGERALD"
Lawrence Fitzgerald 1830-1880, Father
Margaret Fitzgerald 1840-1922, Mother
Lawrence Fitzgerald 1869-1902, Brother
Michael J. Fitzgerald 1866-1932
Thomas E. Fitzgerald 1877-1931

Lawrence Fitzgerald family tombstones; Gouverneur, New York

After completing our search in the cemetery, we arranged for lodging and had a bite to eat, then we spent the rest of the evening at the Gouverneur Free Public Library. There were only two or three other people using the large facility when we arrived, and the Librarian (Ms Mitchell) was anything but friendly as we asked to use microfilm copies of early newspapers. The library had an old microfilm reading machine which had to be moved across the main isle before it could be plugged in, and the film had to be gotten from a special storage area which wasn't easily accessible. I had some difficulty moving the machine into place, and it took me some time to find the correct microfilms, but I finally got things working and began searching issues of the Gouverneur Free Press for Fitzgerald obituaries.

My prime objective was to find Margaret's obituary in 1911, but I began searching issues for earlier years first; finding the death notices again for Lettie (or Lottie) in 1885 and for John in 1891. I also found an entry for the younger Lawrence Fitzgerald, who died at the home of his mother on Somerville Road in 1902, but it didn't shed any further light on his relationship to our John and Margaret of Rossie. Ironically, on the day after John Fitzgerald was killed by a railroad engine in 1891, there was a font page article in the Free Press where an engineer explained how it felt to run over a man with a train. Even though no name was given, I'm sure the article had reference to old John Fitzgerald's death the day before.

Not knowing the exact date of Margaret's death in 1911, I began looking at the 1911 issues beginning with January, but that was very time consuming. It was a large newspaper, and death notices appeared in various sections of each issue. If the person who died was a political figure or an important socialite their death notice might make the front pages, but if they were

NEWSPAPER OBITUARY EXTRACTS
The Gouverneur Free Press
Gouverneur, New York

(Issue for Wednesday October 21, 1885 - Deaths)

"FITZGERALD - In this town, October 17, Lottie Fitzgerald, daughter of John Fitzgerald, age 10 years and 7 months."

(Issue for Friday March 78, 1902 - Deaths)

"Lawrence Fitzgerald died at the home of his mother on Sommerville Street Sunday morning at the age of 32 years. The funeral was conducted by Father Gallivan from the Catholic Church Wednesday morning and the remains taken to Rossie for interment."

Lottie (Lettie) and Lawrence Fitzgerald obituaries

of lesser importance, but still well known, their listing would typically be on the front page of the second or third section of the newspaper. Death notices and obituaries of ordinary people were scattered throughout the second and third sections of the paper; probably wherever extra space was available. It was not until much later in those newspapers that obituaries were listed together in a special section. At any rate, I had only gotten through July of 1911 when Ms Mitchell informed us the library would be closing; I hadn't yet found Margaret's death entry. It was only 9:30 p.m., but Ms Mitchell insisted the library was closing and we must go. She said we were welcome to return on the morrow, after 10:00 a.m., but for now we would have to give up our search.

By this time my wife and I and little Nathan were the only persons in the library, other than Ms Mitchell, and as we assisted in putting the reading machine back and helping return the microfilms, she became more friendly and inquired about our purpose in her library. She recognized that we were from the west, because of our accents, and when I told her I was a professor at Brigham Young University she almost fainted; I didn't look nor sound the part, wearing at the time a sport shirt, light slacks, and karochies (sandles) without stockings. Those were the "Hippy" years, and in her eyes I probably fit that mold. I explained that we were seeking information about Jack Fitzgerald who was born in Rossie, New York in about 1857 and died in Utah in 1901. I said we figured John and Margaret Fitzgerald of Rossie were his parents, and explained that I was trying to locate the obituary notice of Margaret who died in 1911. With that, Ms Mitchell said: " Why, I grew up with Tinnie Fitzgerald in Gouverneur (I would judge Ms Mitchell to have been sixty-five-ish at that time); she and I helped Father Gallivan raise funds for the new St. James Catholic church in town." Then she said: "You should visit St. James church, because they have good records! Would you like me to call Monsignor McCarthy and see if he will give you an audience? He's a personal friend of mine."

There was little hesitancy on my part to accept her offer, and both my wife and I expressed our heartfelt appreciation for her interest and help. We were standing beside her desk and the check-out counter at the time, and we listened as she made the call. Unfortunately, Monsignor McCarthy was on vacation at Plattsburg for two weeks, but Father Lewis was present; however, he couldn't see us that evening, but he would be happy to give us audience the following morning.

Early the next morning, after bed and breakfast, I was knocking on the parsonage door of St. James church in Gouverneur. A sweet "Sister" answered the door and escorted me into the foyer of a larger reception area where she invited me to wait. In a very short time a young priest appeared wearing a white "T" shirt and black trousers; he looked more like a football player than a priest, but this was Father Lewis who was filling in for the vacationing Monsignor McCarthy.

Father Lewis invited me to follow him into his office, and after we were both seated, he asked how he could help me. I had my Fitzgerald pedigree and yellow pad with me, and I explained the Jack Fitzgerald problem to him in some detail, asking him if St. James church might have records which would help identify the family. He said he was sure they had records, but he wasn't entirely sure where they were nor how to get at them, but he would certainly give it a try. With that, he left the office and I remained seated waiting for his return.

After what seemed to be an hour, but which was really only about twenty minutes, he returned carrying several large volumes of church books; "El Morto; El Nuptial; and El Baptiso" (not sure of the spelling). His first remark was: "I'm sorry it took so long; I couldn't unlock the safe!" He said it was a combination lock and he couldn't get it to opened at first, but finally it clicked and he was able to enter the vault and get the records. He was jovial about the whole affair, and he continued joking as he placed the large books on his hardwood desk.

My immediate interest was to find an exact death date for Margaret Fitzgerald who died in 1911, so I could return to the library and locate her obituary, but Father Lewis didn't attempt to look for that entry; he simply picked up the earliest volume and began thumbing through the pages. After some time, I became restless and stood up, saying: "Perhaps I could be looking at another volume while you're searching that one," but he snapped right back: "Do you read Latin?" I said: "No!" He said: "Sit down and relax!" Then he continued looking for Fitzgerald entries, turning the pages slowly, one at a time. After a few more minutes, he looked over at me and said: "I like this sort of work!" and flashed a big smile.

He found a christening entry dated February 19, 1874 for a James Charles Fitzgerald, son of Lawrence Fitzgerald and Margaret O"Rielly, which I jotted down on my yellow pad, and then after thumbing through nearly half of the book, he said: "Here's something which might be of interest," and he began reading: "The town of Rossie was serviced from Ogdensburg from 1841 until 1879 when St. Patrick's church was built." I thought to myself: "No wonder the Priest at St. Patrick's church couldn't find an entry for Jack; St. Patrick's didn't exist when Jack was born back in 1857." Continuing, Father Lewis said: "St. Mary's Cathedral Rectory in Ogdensburg is Diocesan headquarters; would you like me to call them and see if they have records?" You can imagine my eager and affirmative response. He didn't call at that moment; he just continued thumbing the pages looking for additional Fitzgerald entries, but he did call later. A death entry for Lawrence Fitzgerald was noted March 2, 1902; he was buried March 5, 1902 in St. Patrick's cemetery at Rossie, and a John Fitzgerald, son of Lawrence, married Mary Ellen Smith in 1918. While I was writing those down, he found the entry I really wanted. It said that Margaret Fitzgerald, widow of John Fitzgerald died December 16, 1911 age 78 and was buried December 19, 1911 in St. Patrick's cemetery at Rossie. He also noted that a Margaret Fitzgerald died March 26, 1922 age 82 and was buried March 29, 1922 at Rossie; this had to be Margaret (O'Rielly) Fitzgerald, wife of Lawrence, and I made note of it.

After making those searches, Father Lewis called St. Mary's Cathedral Rectory in Ogdensburg, asking if they had records covering the period 1841-1879, which they did; he also arranged for an afternoon appointment with them where I could visit and have the records searched. I was very appreciative of his help and offered him money for his time, but he wouldn't think of accepting it; he said: "If I can be of further help, just let me know." His help launched me on a new and even more successful journey, and I was soon back at the Gouverneur Free Public Library searching for the 1911 obituary.

My wife and young son had remained at our rented room while I visited St. James church, but they accompanied me to the Library where Margaret's obituary was found. Ms. Mitchell was much more friendly on our second visit and didn't object to our setting up the old microfilm reader in the isle. After obtaining the microfilm reels and placing the correct film on the reading machine, I began searching issues of the Free Press for December the 16th, Margaret's death date, but her obituary wasn't listed until Wednesday the 30th of December. There, on page four of the second section, was an obituary notice for "Mrs. John Fitzgerald" comprising three good sized paragraphs.

The obituary said she had gone to Yonkers to visit her daughter, Mrs. W. A. Smith, where she became ill and died. She was 78 years old and had been a resident of Gouverneur for the past 28 years. More importantly, her date of birth was given as December 19, 1833 (not 1831 as her tombstone indicated) and her place of birth was listed as Dublin, Ireland. Her maiden surname was Gillon, and she supposedly came to Rossie with her parents 60 years before her death. Her husband, John Fitzgerald, had preceded her in death, but she was survived by four daughters and two sons; namely Mrs. W. A. Smith of Yonkers, Mrs. Homer Clapp of Watertown, Mrs. William Pound of Silver City, New Mexico, Miss Tinnie Fitzgerald of Gouverneur, and Michael and James, both of Gouverneur; no Jack (or John) was mention.

ST. JAMES CHURCH RECORDS
FITZGERALD EXTRACTS
Copied by Father Lewis
July 9, 1968

19 Feb 1874, James Charles Fitzgerald christened the son of Lawrence Fitzgerald and Margaret O'Rielly.

2 Mar 1902, Lawrence Fitzgerald died age 32, buried 5 Mar 1902 in St. Patrick's cemetery at Rossie, New York.

16 Dec 1911, Margaret Fitzgerald, widow of John Fitzgerald died age 78; buried 19 December 1911
in St. Patrick's cemetery at Rossie.

1918, John Fitzgerald married Mary Ellen Smith.

26 Mar 1922, Margaret Fitzgerald died age

Fitzgerald entries from St. James Catholic Church at Gouverneur 9 July 1968

Excitement was there, and I wanted this to be Jack's family, but his name was not mentioned and my heart sank. Tinnie was there, whom Ms. Mitchell had known personally, and Mrs Homer Clapp (Mary Fitzgerald) was mentioned; whom I thought could be a sister of Jack; and Mrs William Pound was of Silver City, New Mexico, a western mining town like Park City, Utah, so there was still hope for a connection. After showing our find to Ms. Mitchell, she said it was a common practice to omit children from an obituary when they had preceded the parent in death, which made me feel better.

Shortly after noon, we finished our business in Gouverneur and drove back north through Canton, then proceeded west to Ogdensburg where we visited St. Mary's Cathedral Rectory and found further encouraging information. I had an hilarious experience there and was lucky to get away with any information. Ogdensburg is a rather large city, and we had a difficult time finding St. Mary's Cathedral, but after asking directions at three different service stations, we finally found it. I drove right in the main driveway, which led around the main edifice to the back of an adjoining office building, and parked the car. There was a large walkway leading from the parking lot to the back of the building, so I followed it and walk right into the main hallway. But as I entered through the large double doors, it was apparent it wasn't and office building; it was the bed chamber of several Priests, and just as I entered, one of them came out into the hall only half dressed. I don't know which one of us was the most embarrassed, but we both took evasive action. After covering himself with the robe he had in hand, the Priest said: "What are you doing in here?" I was too far along the hall to just turn around and exist, so after stammering and stuttering for a moment, I said: "Father Lewis sent me from St. James church to check some records. Are you the Priest who was going to search

NEWSPAPER OBITUARY EXTRACT
The Gouverneur Free Press
Gouverneur, New York
(Issue for Wednesday December 30, 1911 page 4)

"MRS. JOHN FITZGERALD: On Saturday morning at three o'clock at the home of her daughter in Yonkers, New York occurred the death of Mrs. John Fitzgerald a beloved and highly esteemed resident of this village. Death came suddenly aftera four days illness from pleurisy, age 78 years. Mrs. Fitzgerald went to Yonkerson the New York excursion and had planned on coming home last week in company with her daughter Mrs. W. A. Smith but was taken suddenly ill last Tuesday.

Mrs. Fitzgerald was born December 19, 1833 in Dublin, Ireland and came to this country 60 years ago, settling with her parents in Rossie where several years of her life were spent and where she was married to John Fitzgerald who died several years ago. Her maiden name was Margaret Gillon. She has resided in this village for the past 28 years.

She is survived by four daughters, Mrs. W. A. Smith of Yonkers, Mrs. Homer Clapp of Watertown, Mrs. William Pound of Silver City, New Mexico and Miss Tinnie Fitzgerald of this village, and two sons, Michael and James both of Gouverneur. The funeral was conducted by Father Gallivan and interment was in the Rossie cemetery."

Margaret (Gillon) Fitzgerald Obituary

them for me?" In a very disgusting voice, he said: "You're in the wrong place! Go around to the front of the building; you're in our private quarters."

Following his directions, I went back out the rear exit and walked around the building to the front entrance. A receptionist greeted me and asked how she might help. I explained the reason for my visit and reminded her that Father Lewis had called previously for an appointment to check their records. She knew nothing about that appointment but said she would get someone to help me. After waiting ten or fifteen minutes, who should appear but the Priest I had surprised in the rear bed chamber. He was very kind and considerate, however, and asked for details so he could make a search of their records. After explaining what I was looking for, the Priest made a few notes and left the reception area. I was not allowed to accompany him but was asked to remain seated in the reception area.

After another ten or fifteen minute wait, the Priest returned with a handwritten extract from their records. He had found a christening entry for a Michael Fitzgerald who was baptized February 27, 1854 in Canton, and one for a John Fitzgerald who was baptized August 17, 1856 (born July 24); also in Canton. I was really excited with this entry, because it fit our Jack, and even though the baptism took place in the town of Canton and not Rossie, I was delighted with the find and accepted it as Jack's. Of equal or perhaps more importance was a marriage entry the Priest had found for John Fitzgerald and Margaret Gillon who were married October 18, 1853 at Rossie; Thomas Clapom and Honora Maloney were listed as witnesses. By this time I was riding on cloud nine and was convinced the Priest had found the marriage of Jack's parents. The christening entry for Michael in February of 1854 presented a problem, however, because it was only four months after the marriage of John and Margaret in 1853. Was he their son and brother of Jack, or did he belong to another family? We wouldn't learn the answer to that question until much later.

Satisfied with the information we had located in St. Lawrence county, and realizing that we must soon be on our way to other locale's, we left Ogdensburg and drove south to Watertown, New York, where we made a rest stop for gasoline and goodies; it was then the late afternoon of July 9, 1968. Believe it or not, regular gasoline was selling for only twenty-five cents a gallon, and that was not self service.

While the attendant was filling our tank with gasoline, and recalling that Mrs Homer Clapp (Mary Fitzgerald) was listed of Watertown in the 1911 obituary, I casually glanced at the telephone book for Watertown and noted only two Clapp entries. I jotted down the numbers, and while the attendant was still servicing our car, I called the first one; it was the number of Katherine L. Clapp, and she answered the call. She seemed to be an older lady and I asked her if she might be related to Homer Clapp who had married Mary Fitzgerald in the 1880's. I explained that I was seeking information about a Jack Fitzgerald who was born in Rossie, New York and who died in Utah in 1901. Her answer astounded me and I couldn't believe what I was hearing. She said: "Why my son has his watch! (referring to Jack Fitzgerald of Utah) She continued by saying her father-in-law, Homer Clapp, went out to Utah when Jack Fitzgerald was "murdered" and brought back his personal belongings. What was this she was saying; "Jack murdered?" I knew nothing about that. This was shocking information and I couldn't respond for several seconds. Then I said: "Could I come to your home and speak with you further about this?" Her abrupt answer was, "No!" I'm leaving shortly for a meeting and won't be available." But she did give me additional helpful information before ending our telephone conversation.

ST MARY'S CATHEDRAL RECTORY
Box 538
Ogdensburg, New York 13669

Baptized in Canton:
Michael; Feb. 27, 1854
John; Aug. 17, 1856 (born July 24)

Married in Rossie:
John Fitzgerald to Margaret Gillon
on October 18, 1853

Witnesses:
Thomas Clapom
Honora Maloney

Fitzgerald extracts from St. Mary's Cathedral Rectory

Katherine was the wife of Thomas Clapp (known also as Roy) and they were the parents of three sons; Ross being the one who had Jack's watch and who lived in Atlanta, Georgia. Her husband Roy was deceased, but she remembered hearing stories about her father-in-law (Homer Clapp) and his brother-in-law (name not given) going to Utah when Jack Fitzgerald was murdered and bringing back his personal belongings. She (Katherine) also related a story she had heard from her husband, saying Homer and Mary (Fitzgerald) Clapp went to Ireland many years ago seeking family information, but returned very disappointed without learning much. Evidently their Irish relatives felt they had come to obtain family property and scorned them. I asked her if she knew where in Ireland they went, but she couldn't tell me. She did say she would be happy to receive correspondence from us, but for now she would have to say goodbye and our conversation ended. I jotted down her address (615 Academy) and made a mental note that the Lunceford family should get in touch with her right away.

As we left Watertown, my wife and I marveled at what had happened, not only in Watertown but in each of the places we had visited. We came into the area with very little information seeking an answer to a difficult problem, and now we were leaving with much important information. Each person we met and each place we visited added something to the puzzle, until the final piece fell into place at Watertown as we were leaving. We weren't really sure at first that the John and Margaret information from the Rossie cemetery was ancestral to Jack, but we believed it was and kept searching for additional facts to support our hopes and beliefs; finally, at Watertown, Katherine L. Clapp had voluntarily provided compelling proof of the connection. We both remarked that Providence had smiled on us, indeed.

EXCITING NEW FINDINGS BACK IN UTAH

Upon return from the 1968 trip to Rossie, New York, the newly found Fitzgerald information was summarized and sent to Clyde M. Lunceford along with a bill covering actual expenses. On the same day he received the report, President Lunceford came to my home in Pleasant Grove with a check which more than doubled the amount requested; this was a new experience for me, but it wouldn't be the last. He was excited with the information found and asked me to continue with the work, to which I happily agreed. One of his first remarks after receiving the report was: "I want to get a hold of Jack's watch!" (referring to Katherine Clapp's statement saying her son had it) When I brought up the point that Jack had been murdered, President Lunceford confirmed that his family had known that all along, but they didn't have any particulars about it, and he didn't think that fact was important in finding Jack's genealogy, so he hadn't mentioned it earlier; little did he know what would later be found because of it.

As research continued, one of the first steps taken was to evaluate the earlier census findings and correlate them with the new names found on the July trip. Correspondence was also initiated to obtain death records for Margaret (Gillon) Fitzgerald and Mary (Fitzgerald) Clapp from the State of New York.

There was little question about the 1880 census entry showing John Fitzgerald and Charles Ford living together in Park City, Utah; it had to be relevant even though there were some inconsistencies in it. The burial record for Jack said he had died in 1901 aged 44, which would make him born about 1857, and this census listed him as age 22 in 1880, which was pretty close. The fact his father's place of birth was listed as England rather than Ireland was a little disturbing, but again, census records are notoriously inaccurate, so little sleep was lost over that.

CENSUS EXTRACT
Summit County, Utah
1880

#94/110 - Park City		
FITZGERALD, John	WM 22 Single Miner	N.Y. Eng. Ire.
FORD, Charles	WM 21 Single Miner	Ill. N.H. N.H.

Jack (John) Fitzgerald in 1880

Previous searches in the 1850 and 1860 censuses for St. Lawrence County, New York failed to located a John and Margaret with a possible son of the right age to be Jack, and the John and Mary Fitzgerald family of Canton, which had been accepted earlier, proved to be non-ancestral after church and probate records were evaluated. A John and Margaret Fitzgerald family, which did include a younger John, appeared in the town of Rossie in 1870, but it hadn't been accepted previously because of birth place inconsistencies; however, after the new information was considered, that family looked very promising. The ages for John andrgaret were within acceptable parameters, though their places of birth were listed as Canada rather than Ireland, and the younger John was of the approximate age to be Jack. Also, there was a Michael as mentioned in Margaret's 1911 obituary, and there were ample females to have been Mrs. W. A. Smith, Mrs. Homer Clapp, and Mrs. William Pound; all mentioned in Margaret's obituary. Tinnie and James may not yet have been born when the 1870 census was enumerated.

When that same 1870 census was rechecked, and the new names from Margaret's obituary were considered, several additional interesting entries were found; a John and Mary

CENSUS EXTRACT
St. Lawrence County, New York
1870

#94/89 - Town of Rossie

FITZGERALD, John	50 M Works in Ore Bed	Canada
Margaret	40 F Keeping House	Canada
Anna	18 F	New York
John	**10 M**	**New York**
Maggie	9 F	New York
Catherine	8 F	New York
Amy	4 F	New York
Michael	2 M	New York

John and Margaret Fitzgerald family in 1870

Pound family was living right next door to John and Margaret Fitzgerald in Rossie, and there was a young William Pound in the household who could have married one of the Fitzgerald girls (Mrs. William Pound in the 1911 obituary). But to complicate matters, there was another Pound family living close by which also included a young William Pound who could be relevant. Through a series of later census searches and a marriage record, the family of Patrick and Teressa Pound proved to be germane; Margaret Fitzgerald (Maggie age 9 in the 1870 census) married William Pound (age 12 in the 1870 census) in 1881.

A Grace Gillin family was also noted in the town of Rossie, who could have been related, and another family of interest was that of Thos. C. Clapp living in Gouverneur. His family included a "Homer" who later proved to be the Homer Clapp who married Mary Fitzgerald on the 20th of July 1887 at Gouverneur (an obituary notice for Homer Clapp obtained later confirmed this). The Canada place of birth for Homer was also of interest, and it aroused more curiosity about John and Margaret's 1870 census listing. According to Jack's burial record, his parents were both born in Ireland, but the 1870 census listed them born in Canada; why? That question led to their whereabouts prior to 1870, and the credit for locating the family earlier must be given to Kip Sperry, then a genealogical major at Brigham Young University.

CENSUS EXTRACT
St. Lawrence County, New York
1870

#185/185 - Gouverneur

CLAPP, Thos. C.	35 M Cabinet Maker	Canada
Frances	33 F Keeps House	Canada
Fred	11 M	Canada
Allen	8 M	Canada
Homer	**6 M**	**Canada**
Aleda	3 F	New York

Homer Clapp in 1870

CENSUS EXTRACT		
St. Lawrence County, New York		
1870		
#95/90 - Rossie		
POUND, John	**45 M Day Laborer**	**Ireland**
Mary	**40 F Keeps House**	**Ireland**
John	**15 M WorksinOreBed**	**Ireland**
Ann	**13 F At Home**	**Ireland**
Patrick	**11 M**	**New York**
Julia	**9 F**	**New York**
William	**7 M**	**New York**
James	**5 M**	**New York**
Peter	**3 M**	**New York**
Edward	**1 M**	**New York**
#128/118 - Rossie		
POUND, Patrick	**43 M Farmer**	**Ireland**
Teressa	**32 F Keeps House**	**Switzerland**
Thomas	**15 M Works on Farm**	**New York**
Peter	**14 M**	**New York**
William	**12 M**	**New York**
Edward	**11 M**	**New York**
Mary A.	**9 F**	**New York**
Francis	**8 M**	**New York**
Teressa	**6 F**	**New York**
Julia	**4 F**	**New York**
Hannah	**3 F**	**New York**
Catherine	**1 F**	**New York**

John and Patrick Pound families in 1870

During the latter part of 1968, the university was in the process of establishing a research center to give "Gen. Tech."[1] majors practical experience in applied genealogical research. The LDS Genealogical Society in Salt Lake City was phasing out its research department and was encouraging private genealogists to fill the void, so BYU became involved. Under the direction of Ben E. Lewis of the Administration, Ray Beckham of University Development, and Ernest C. Jeppsen, Dean of the Technical Institute, the "BYU Genealogical Research Center" was organized and I became its first director. Selected accounts were transferred from the Genealogical Society in Salt Lake City, and the public was invited to participate in the program. Clyde M. Lunceford was one of the first patrons to establish an account (#3) by making a substantial deposit with the Center, and Gen. Tech. students began assisting with his research.

After Kip was assigned to work on the Lunceford account, and after the known facts had been evaluated, he did a little historical research on the town of Rossie and came up with some interesting information. He learned it had been first settled in 1813 by Scottish immigrants, from whom the town got its name, but by 1840, Irish immigrants were emigrating

[1] A degree program in "Genealogical Research Technology" was established at Brigham Young University in 1964 and continued until 1972.

by the hundreds to work in the iron and lead mining industry which was thriving along the St. Lawrence waterway. Many arrived at the port of New York and later found their way "upstate," while others landed at Quebec and migrated to "Upper Canada." They worked the "ore beds" on both sides of the river. Well, Kip put two and two together and began searching records on the Canadian side; Leeds and Grenville counties being immediately across the river from Rossie in Ontario.

After several hours of concentrated effort, Kip located what appeared to be the John and Margaret Fitzgerald family in the 1861 census of Wolford Township in Grenville County, Ontario. No wonder the family hadn't been located in earlier census searches; we were searching in the wrong country! The names, ages, and places of birth for each family member agreed with the facts shown in the 1870 census of St. Lawrence County, and the parameters still met the criteria of Margaret's 1911 obituary.

CENSUS EXTRACT
Grenville County, Ontario, Canada
1861

Page 49 - Wolford Township

John Fitzgerald	47-1861	Labr.	Ireland
Margaret	45-1861	Wife	Ireland
Ann	6-1861	Dau.	U.S.
John	3-1861	Son.	U.S.
Margret	1-1861	Dau.	U.S.

John and Margaret Fitzgerald family in the 1861 census of Canada

After completing the Canadian census searches, Kip checked the New York counties which surrounded St. Lawrence, and his efforts paid off again. He located the John and Margaret (this time Mary) Fitzgerald family in the 1880 census of Jefferson County, New York. They were living in the town of Antwerp, an iron ore refining town, and as a bonus, the Patrick and William Pound connection was reconfirmed. The Lawrence Fitzgerald family also came into focus while making this search.

Evidently, John and Margaret (or Mary) were operating a boarding house in Antwerp, and "Pat" and "Wm" Pound were boarders. There is little doubt but what this was the same Patrick Pound who was living next door to John and Margaret at Rossie in 1870; notice that the birthplace of William Pound's mother was listed as "Switzerland;" the same as Teressa Pound in 1870, wife of Patrick. Also notice that William Pound was aged 22 and Maggie Fitzgerald was aged 20. From other sources searched later, it was determined that William Pound, the son of Patrick and Teressa (also spelled Theresa), married Margaret Fitzgerald in 1881. William and "Maggie" were close neighbors at Rossie in 1870 and undoubtedly knew each other as young children; now, in 1880, they were young adults living in the same household and found an interest in each other which led to their marriage a year later.

Again, the names (except for Mary), ages, and places of birth fit the John and Margaret Fitzgerald family of 1861 and 1870. This time, James, Tina (Tinnie), and Letia (or Lottie) were included, which gave added strength to the assumption the families were the same. Notice also that Maggie was listed as born in "Ont." (Ontario, Canada) where the family was living in 1861; however, the 1861 Canadian census stated she was born in the "U.S." Later findings corroborate the Ontario place of birth which is probably correct. The Catherine Fitzgerald who was listed with the family in 1870 (age 8) was not listed in 1880; perhaps she was married by this time, or perhaps she had died young. The latter is probably true, because she cannot be accounted for in her mother's 1911 obituary nor in her mother's 1900 census listing where living and deceased children were numbered. The "Amy" in 1870 fits the description of "Mary" in 1880; she became the wife of Homer Clapp, which was documented later. The fact that John's wife was listed as "Mary" rather than Margaret in the 1880 census presented another problem, to which no easy answer existed; perhaps she used both names (Mary/Margaret), but more probably this latter entry was a transcription or an enumeration error. We will probably never know, but there is very strong evidence to show that John had but one wife (Margaret Gillon) from the time he was married in 1853 until his death in 1891.

CENSUS EXTRACT Jefferson County, New York 1880		
#176/201 - Antwerp		
FITZGERALD, John	WM 60 Miner	Ire. Ire. Ire.
Mary	WF 55 Wife	Ire. Ire. Ire.
Maggie	WF 20 Daughter	Ont. Ire. Ire.
Mary	WF 14 Daughter	N.Y. Ire. Ire.
Michael	WM 11 Son	N.Y. Ire. Ire.
James	WM 9 Son	N.Y. Ire. Ire.
Tina	WF 6 Daughter	N.Y. Ire. Ire.
Letia	WF 4 Daughter	N.Y. Ire. Ire.
KENNADY, Morgan	WM 22 Boarder	N.Y. Ire. Ire.
MCDONALD, Chas.	WM 22 Boarder	Can. Can. Can.
O'CONNEL, James	WM 40 Boarder	Ire. Ire. Ire.
MALLOY, John	WM 21 Boarder	Ire. Ire. Ire.
MCDONALD, George	WM 33 Boarder	Ire. Ire. Ire.
CONLY, John	WM 26 Boarder	Ire. Ire. Ire.
O'NIEL, Charles	WM 19 Boarder	Ire. Ire. Ire.
CARL, Walter	WM 40 Boarder	Ire. Ire. Ire.
LEE, William	WM 22 Boarder	N.Y. N.Y. Ont.
CIPHAS, Alexia(?)	WM 22 Boarder	N.Y. N.Y. N.Y.
POUND, Wm	WM 22 Boarder	N.Y. Ire. Switz.
POUND, Pat	WM 52 Boarder	Ire. Ire. Ire.
DAYTON(?), Wm	WM 20 Boarder	N.Y. N.Y. N.Y.

The John Fitzgerald family in 1880

CENSUS EXTRACT Jefferson County, New York 1880		
#172/189 - Antwerp		
FITZGERALD, Lawrence	WM 45 Miner	Ire. Ire. Ire.
Maggie	WF 35 Wife	Ont. Ire. Ire.
William	WM 18 Son	N.Y. Ire. Ont.
Edward	WM 16 Son	N.Y. Ire. Ont.
Michael	WM 14 Son	N.Y. Ire. Ont.
Lawrence	WM 12 Son	N.Y. Ire. Ont.
John	WM 9 Son	N.Y. Ire. Ont.
Charles	WM 6 Son	N.Y. Ire. Ont.
Thomas	WM 2 Son	N.Y. Ire. Ont.
Mary	WF 1 Daughter	N.Y. Ire. Ont.

The Lawrence Fitzgerald family in 1880

The Lawrence and Margaret Fitzgerald family, found living only a few doors from John and Margaret (Mary) in 1880, brought another interesting dimension to the search. It seemed that where ever John and Margaret were found, Lawrence and his family appeared also; they

clearly had to be related (a later interview with their daughter-in-law confirmed that Lawrence and John were brothers). You will recall that a Lawrence and Margaret (O'Rielly) Fitzgerald were buried next to John and Margaret (Gillon) Fitzgerald in the Rossie cemetery but were disinterred in 1935, along with the younger Lawrence, and were reburied in the Riverside cemetery at Gouverneur. Both families resided in Rossie for a time; undoubtedly in Canada for a few years; certainly in Antwerp of Jefferson County, New York; and then finally in Gouverneur.

During the July 1968 trip, Father Lewis found entries in St. James' church records relating to Lawrence and Margaret (O'Rielly) Fitzgerald as well as to John and Margaret. He located the baptism of James Charles in 1874, son of Lawrence and Margaret, the death and burial of their son Lawrence in 1902, and Margaret (O'Rielly) Fitzgerald's death and burial in 1922. No entry was found for the older Lawrence, who died in 1880 age 50, but he may have died in Jefferson County, where he was living that year. An obituary notice for the younger Lawrence was located, and his probate was also found, though its importance was not recognized until later. He died "intestate" and the total value of his estate was only $100. His wife Ellen was appointed guardian of their son Patrick E. Fitzgerald, who was probably their only child.

NEWSPAPER OBITUARY EXTRACT
The Northern Tribune
Gouverneur, New York
(issue for 7 Mar 1902)

"Lawrence Fitzgerald died at the home of his mother on Somerville street Sunday morning at the age of 32 years. The funeral was conducted by Father Gallivan from the Catholic church Wednesday morning and the remains taken to Rossie for interment."

Obituary of Lawrence Fitzgerald

The parents of Margaret (Gillon) Fitzgerald could not be identified in any of these earlier searches, even though, according to her 1911 obituary, she *"...came to this country 60 years ago, settling with her parents in Rossie where several years of her life were spent and where she was married to John Fitzgerald..."* **I located a Michael Gillen living in the town of Brasher in 1850, who could have been a brother, and a Grace Gillin was living in Rossie in 1870, who could have been a sister-in-law, but possible parents could not identified at that time; perhaps they had died early or removed to another location.**

The Right Reverend Monseigneur Joseph G. Bailey, of St. Mary's Cathedral Rectory in Ogdensburg, New York, responded to a September 1970 request, sending me a baptism record for Ann Fitzgerald dated October 12, 1854. She was listed as the daughter of John and Margaret Fitzgerald of Rossie and was their first child. I learned later that Ann (Anna) was Mrs William A. Smith of Yonkers, whom Margaret had been visiting in 1911. Monseigneur Bailey also determined that the baptism for John Fitzgerald, son of John and Mary, which took place on the 27th of July 1856 at Canton, and which I thought pertained to our Jack, actually applied to a John Fitzgerald who was long a resident of Canton and who couldn't possibly have been our man; that was a little disappointing, but his finding Anna's baptism was very encouraging.

On the 16th of January, 1970, I received a copy of Mary Clapp's death record from the New York State Department of Health, and it was equally interesting; confirming some facts but shading others. According to the record, she was married to "Homer B. Clapp" and died the 10th of June 1924 in Watertown, Jefferson County, New York. The record indicated she was born in "Rossie, N.Y. on Mar 16, 1867," but it said her father was "Garrit" rather than John. It listed her mother as Margaret "Fitzgerald" and not Margaret Gillon. The informant for her record was Thomas R. Clapp of 615 Academy St., Watertown; a nephew of Mary and son of Katherine L. Clapp whom we had contacted earlier.

Death Certificate of Mary (Fitzgerald) Clapp

1 PLACE OF DEATH (Dist. No. ______ To be inserted by Registrar) New York State Department of Health
DIVISION OF VITAL STATISTICS

STANDARD CERTIFICATE OF DEATH 31250
STATE OF NEW YORK

County Jefferson
Town ______ or Village ______ or City Watertown
Registered No. 205
(No. St. Joachim Hospital St.; ______ Ward)
(If death occurred in a hospital or institution, give its NAME instead of street and number)

2 FULL NAME Mary Clapp
(Ia) Residence No. 671 ______ St., ______ Ward.
(Usual place of abode) (If nonresident, give city or town and State)
Length of residence in city or town where death occurred 26 yrs. ______ mos. ______ ds. How long in U. S., if of foreign birth? ______ yrs. ______ mos. ______ ds.

PERSONAL AND STATISTICAL PARTICULARS

3 SEX Female
4 COLOR OR RACE white
5 SINGLE, MARRIED, WIDOWED OR DIVORCED (write the word) married
5a IF MARRIED, WIDOWED OR DIVORCED HUSBAND OF (or) WIFE OF Thomas Clapp
6 DATE OF BIRTH Mar. 16 1867 (Month) (Day) (Year)
7 AGE 57 Years 2 Months 25 Days. If LESS than 1 day, how many hrs. or min.?
8 OCCUPATION
(a) Trade, profession, or particular kind of work house wife
(b) General nature of industry, business, or establishment in which employed (or employer)
(c) Name of employer
9 BIRTHPLACE (City or Town) (State or Country) [illegible] N.Y.

PARENTS
10 NAME OF FATHER Garret Fitzgerald
11 BIRTHPLACE OF FATHER (City or Town) (State or Country) Ireland
12 MAIDEN NAME OF MOTHER Margaret Fitzgerald
13 BIRTHPLACE OF MOTHER (City or Town) (State or Country) Ireland

14 THE ABOVE IS TRUE TO THE BEST OF MY KNOWLEDGE
(Informant) Thomas Clapp
(Address) [illegible] Academy St. Watertown N.Y.

15 Filed 6/11 1924 M. E. [illegible] Registrar

MEDICAL CERTIFICATE OF DEATH

16 DATE OF DEATH June 10 1924 (Month) (Day) (Year)

17 I HEREBY CERTIFY, That I attended deceased from [illegible] 1922 to June 10 1924, that I last saw h[er] alive on June 10 1924, and that death occurred on the date stated above, at [illegible]
The CAUSE OF DEATH* was as follows:
Myocarditis

RECEIVED JAN 16 1970

(Duration) 4 yrs. ______ mos. ______ ds.
CONTRIBUTORY Diabetes & Bright's Disease (Duration) 4 yrs. ______ mos. ______ ds.
18 Where was disease contracted, if not at place of death?
Did an operation precede death? No Date of
Was there an autopsy? No
What test confirmed diagnosis?
(Signed) [illegible] M. D.
June 11, 1924 (Address) Watertown N.Y.

*State the Disease Causing Death, or in deaths from Violent Causes, state (1) Means and Nature of Injury, and (2) whether Accidental, Suicidal, or Homicidal.

19 PLACE OF BURIAL, CREMATION OR REMOVAL No. Watertown Cemetery
DATE OF BURIAL June 13 1924
20 UNDERTAKER E. A. Howland
ADDRESS 533 State St.

Burial or Removal Permit issued by M. E. [illegible] Date of Issue June 11 1924
See Instructions on Other Side

Death Certificate of Margaret (Gillon) Fitzgerald

BURIAL OR TRANSIT PERMIT No. 1756

New York State Department of Health

BUREAU OF VITAL STATISTICS

1 PLACE OF DEATH

County of Westchester

City of Yonkers

(No. 15 Riverdale Avenue 1 Ward)

STANDARD CERTIFICATE OF DEATH 245

STATE OF NEW YORK

Registered No. 26933

[If death occurred in a hospital or institution, give its NAME instead of street and number]

2 FULL NAME Margaret Fitzgerald

PERSONAL AND STATISTICAL PARTICULARS

3 SEX: Female

4 COLOR OR RACE: White

5 SINGLE, MARRIED, WIDOWED, OR DIVORCED (Write the word): Widowed

6 DATE OF BIRTH: December 18, 1833 (Month) (Day) (Year)

7 AGE: 77 yrs. 11 mos. 29 ds. If LESS than 1 day, ... hours or ...... min.?

8 OCCUPATION
(a) Trade, profession or particular kind of work: At home
(b) General nature of industry, business, or establishment which employed (or employer):

9 BIRTHPLACE (State or country): Ireland

PARENTS

10 NAME OF FATHER: John Fitzgerald

11 BIRTHPLACE OF FATHER (State or country): Ireland

12 MAIDEN NAME OF MOTHER: Mary Gillan

13 BIRTHPLACE OF MOTHER (State or country): Ireland

14 THE ABOVE IS TRUE TO THE BEST OF MY KNOWLEDGE

(Informant) John Smith

(Address) 15 Riverdale Ave

15 Filed Dec 16 191[1] Wm J Hanrahan

Marion J Edsall Asst Reg. REGISTRAR

MEDICAL CERTIFICATE OF DEATH

16 DATE OF DEATH: Dec 16, 1911 (Month) (Day) (Year)

17 I HEREBY CERTIFY, That I attended deceased from Dec 15, 1911, to Dec 16, 1911, that I saw her alive on Dec 16, 1911, and that death occurred, on the date stated above, at 3:30 a m.

The CAUSE OF DEATH* was as follows:

Myocarditis

(Duration) ...... yrs. ...... mos. 1 ds.

Contributory (SECONDARY) Arterio sclerosis and Senility (Duration) 10 yrs. ...... mos. ...... ds.

(Signed) O J McCormick, M.D.

Dec 16, 1911 (Address) 360 So Bway

*State the DISEASE CAUSING DEATH, or, in deaths from VIOLENT CAUSES, state (1) MEANS OF INJURY; and (2) whether ACCIDENTAL, SUICIDAL, or HOMICIDAL.

18 LENGTH OF RESIDENCE (FOR HOSPITALS, INSTITUTIONS, TRANSIENTS, OR RECENT RESIDENTS).

At place of death ...... yrs. ...... mos. ...... ds. In the State ...... yrs. ...... mos. ...... ds.

Where was disease contracted, if not at place of death?

Former or usual residence

19 PLACE OF BURIAL OR REMOVAL: Gouverneur, St Lawrence County N.Y.

21 DATE OF BURIAL: Dec 18, 1911

20 UNDERTAKER: Peter H. Hay & Sons

ADDRESS: Yonkers NY

It was a little more difficult to obtain a copy of Margaret (Gillon) Fitzgerald's death record, but when it was received it confused the issue more than it clarified things. The New York State Bureau of Vital Statistics couldn't locate a record for her, because she died before 1914 in a city (Yonkers) which recorded its own vital statistics; it was only after 1914 that copies were mandatorily filed at the State office in Albany. After I learned that, and wrote to Yonkers, a copy of her record was finally received. According to it, she was born "December 18, 1833 in Ireland" and died "Dec. 16, 1911 at No. 15 Riverdale Avenue, City of Yonkers, County of Westchester." Her father was listed as "John Fitzgerald" (her husband's name), and her mother was listed as "Mary Gillan" (probably her mothers married name). The informant for her record was her grandson John Smith, son of Anna. Learning the address of the informant, and the exact place of death, made it possible to locate the William Smith family later in the 1900 census and confirm other important information.

Productive research continued on the Lunceford account through 1970 and the early part of 1971. Kip Sperry continued his good work searching census, land, court, military, and immigration records for the New York and Canadian areas; and I continued searching vital, church, cemetery, and compiled sources, as time would permit (I was then teaching as well a directing the Center). Wilma Adkins, a former student who had become a professional genealogist, also contributed significantly to the work. Mrs Mary Biondi, the St. Lawrence County Historian who had been so helpful on the 1968 trip, responded to my written requests and provided additional information during 1969 and 1970. Letters were also sent to county and state officials requesting copies of selected birth, death, and marriage records; and I wrote to each of the Catholic churches, which had been contacted previously, and received additional information. I also sent letters to various libraries and publishers for newspaper obituary information, and I corresponded with Katherine Clapp of Watertown.

FAMILY HISTORY SERVICES TAKES OVER

During the Spring of 1971 the genealogical program at BYU began to change, and that had an effect on the Lunceford account. Jerry Wells, a British research specialist at the LDS Genealogical Society in Salt Lake City, was employed as Director of the Genealogical Research Center, and I returned to full-time teaching. Under the Center's new management, research accounts and assignments were systematized, and the Center was utilized as a laboratory for genealogical research courses. Qualified analysts were employed to direct the students in applied research, and the Lunceford account remained with them. Because of a sabbatical leave and the subsequent illness of my wife, which later resulted in her untimely death, my involvement with the Center and the Lunceford account ended for nearly five years.

During 1972 and ensuing years, the genealogical program at BYU went through even more decisive changes, with a new University President (Dallon H. Oaks) and academic reorganization. The "Gen. Tech." degree program was canceled, and genealogical course offerings were reduced to a minimum while two of its three full-time instructors were given leave to obtain doctoral degrees, in an effort to upgrade the program. As a result of these and subsequent changes, the genealogical program was transferred to the History Department under Family and Local History, and the Genealogical Research Center was reorganized to become Family History Services with only minimal student involvement. From 1972 until December of 1976, Family History Services worked on the Jack Fitzgerald problem for President Lunceford with little or no success, then, for personal reasons, he closed his account with them.

"NEW" RETURNS

In the Fall of 1976, President Lunceford approached me again and asked me to continue his research; to which I readily agreed. He gave me a generous retainer, and after obtaining the Lunceford files from Family History Services, I began building the Jack Fitzgerald pedigree again.

After reviewing the work done by Family History Services, research was continued; ship passenger lists for New York were checked, and a lot of my time was spent trying to extend the Gillon line. Searches were also made in selected Irish records on microfilm at the library in Salt Lake City, but no startling information was found.

CENSUS EXTRACT
Rensselaer County, New York
1850

#302/486 - TROY		
John Reardon	40 M Grover	Ireland
Joanna M. Rearson	23 F	New York
Michael Reardon	4/12 M	New York
JOHN FITZGERALD	**25 M Clerk**	**Ireland**
Joanna Brason	20 F	Ireland
Bridget Mermain(?)	70 F	Ireland
John Flaherty	27 M Labour	Ireland
Mary H. Flaherty	27 F	Ireland
Michael Flaherty	1 M	New York
#828/1356 - TROY		
Barney Murphy	29 M Grocer	Ireland
Maria Murphy	38 F	Ireland
James Murphy	2 M	New York
LAWRENCE FITZGERALD	**16 M Clerk**	**Ireland**

John and Lawrence Fitzgerald in 1850

I located a John and a Lawrence Fitzgerald in the 1850 census of Rensselaer County, who looked like good candidates to be ours, but that couldn't be proven from the records. I reasoned they had entered the United States through the Port of New York, had found their way up the Hudson to the town of Troy where they had worked for a season, then had proceeded west along the Mohawk to Rome or perhaps Utica; finally moving north to Rossie where employment was found in the iron and lead mining industry. That scenario was plausible, but they could also have entered Canada at Quebec and moved south and west along the St. Lawrence river to the same location.

An index to ship passenger lists for the Port of New York was located, covering the period 1820-1846, and a check of it showed more than two dozen John Fitzgeralds of the correct age to be our man, but no Lawrence Fitzgeralds were listed who met the needed criteria. Unfortunately, ship passenger lists for Canada were non-existent until about 1865, which was much too late for our purposes, so that approach ended for the time being.

After consulting with Irish specialists at the Library in Salt Lake City, a check was made of Irish Applotment Books (1824-1860), A Register of Labour Patients at the Rotunda Hospital in Dublin (1831-1836), and various Rateable Property Valuations for 1852. Fitzgerald and Gillon names were located and copied, but no direct connections to our people could be made. It soon became evident that a more definitive place than Dublin was necessary to find connecting information in Irish records, so I turned my efforts back to the American scene.

County records for New York were checked first, but this time I concentrated on the Gillon surname. Land and court records for St. Lawrence County were rechecked, and all Gillon information previously found was re-evaluated. Mrs Mary H. Biondi, the St. Lawrence

ROTUNDA HOSPITAL; DUBLIN, IRELAND
LABOUR PATIENTS 1831-1833
(Fitzgerald/Gillon births)

Bridget Fitzgerald, age 28; William (husband), Servant, Protestant; of St. Thomas Parish; admitted 13 May 1831; delivered 14 May 1831 (Girl). (page 19)

Anne Fitzgerald, age 33; James (husband), Painter, Roman Catholic; of St. Michael's Parish; admitted 4 Aug 1831; delivered 4 Aug 1831 (Boy). (page 33)

Catherine Fitzgerald, age 25; Garrett (husband), Soldier, Roman Catholic; of St. James Parish; admitted 5 Nov 1831; delivered 5 Nov 1831 (Boy). (page 46)

Mary Fitzgerald, age 30; William (husband), Servant, Protestatnt; of St. Annes Parish; admitted 31 Jan 1832; delivered 31 Jan 1832 (Girl). (page 57)

Margaret Fitzgerald, age 38; James (husband), Laborer, Protestant; of St. Michael's Parish; admitted 17 Feb 1832; delivered 18 Feb 1832 (Girl). (page 61)

Anne Fitzgerald, age 30; Charles (husband), Laborer, Roman Catholic; of Phippsoboro Parish; admitted 23 Feb 1832; delivered 23 Feb 1832 (Girl). (page 62)

Mary Fitzgerald, age 30; Robert (husband) Servant, Roman Catholic; of St. Michael's Parish; admitted 15 Apr 1832; delivered 16 Apr 1832 (Girl). (page 70)

Margaret Fitzgerald, age 30; Harry (husband), Laborer, Protestant; of St. Michael's Parish; admitted 9 July 1832; delivered 9 July 1832 (Girl). Child died 10 July 1832 (p. 83)

Bridget Fitzgerald, age 30; William (husband), Servant, Roman Catholic; of Clantaif Parish; admitted 341 Aug 1832; delivered 31 Aug 1832 (Girl). (page 91)

Catherine Fitzgerald, age 30; Henry (husband), Servant, Roman Catholic; of St. Mark's Parish; admitted 27 Dec 1832; delivered 27 Dec 1832 (Girl). (page 110)

Mary Fitzgerald, age 31; John (husband), Gardner, Roman Catholic; of St. Nicholas Parish; admitted 17 Mar 1833; delivered 17 Mar 1833 (Boy). (page 122)

Eliza or Eleanor Fitzgerald, age 26; a widow; Protestant; of the country; admitted 30 Mar 1833; delivered 30 Mar 1833 (Boy). Bapt 7 Apr 1833; named Henry. (page 125)

Eleanor Gillin, age 21; John (husband), Servant, Roman Catholic; of St. Andres's Parish; admitted 14 April 1833; delivered 15 April 1833 (Girl). Stilborn. (page 127)

Anne Fitzgerald, age 35; Charles (husband), Laborer, Roman Catholic; of Phippsboro Parish; admitted 8 May 1833; delivered 8 May 1833 (Boy). (page 132)

Mary A. Fitzgerald, age 22; Nicholas (husband), Laborer; of St. Mark's Parish; admitted 23 May 1833; delivered 23 May 1833 (Girl). (page 134)

Teresa Fitzgerald, age 28; Thomas (husband), Laborer, Roman Catholic, of St. Thomas Parish; admitted 16 July 1833; delivered 16 July 1833 (Girl). (Page 142)

Margaret Fitzgerald, age 26; John (husband), Laborer, Roman Catholic; of St. Michael's Parish; admitted 22 Sept 1833; delivered 22 Sept 1833 (Girl). (page 152)

CENSUS EXTRACTS
St. Lawrence County, New York
1870 and 1880

1870 census; Town of Rossie		
#17/17		
Gillin, Grace	36 F	Ireland
Rosannah	10 F	New York
Daniel	6 M	New York
William	3 M	New York
1880 census; Town of Rossie		
#163/172		
Gillin, Grace	46 F Widow	Ire. Ire. Ire.
Rosanna	20 F Daughter	N.Y. Ire. Ire.
Daniel	16 M Son	N.Y. Ire. Ire.

Grace Gillen family in 1870 and 1880

CENSUS EXTRACT
St. Lawrence County, New York
1850

#203/212 - Brasher		
Michael Gillen	34 M Farm Hand	Ireland
Lucy	34 F	Ireland
Thomas	12 M	New York
Betsy	9 F	New York
Michael Jr.	8 M	New York
John	5 M	New York
James	5 M	New York
George	4 M	New York
Lucy Ann	1 F	New York
Mary	1 F	New York
Catherine	2/12 F	New York

Michael and Lucy Gillen family in 1850

County Historian who had been so helpful on the 1968 New York trip, assisted by checking land and probate records for me. She determined that Grace Gillin, who appeared in the 1870 census of Rossie, was the wife of a Daniel Gillon who died intestate on the 1st of April 1870 in St. Lawrence County. At his death, Daniel left three children; Rosannah, Daniel, and William. They were listed in the household of their mother in 1870; ages 10, 6, and 3 respectively. According to Mrs Biondi, Grace was the daughter of Michael McMullin and Mary Cary and died the 15th of December 1902, age 69. Before his death, the father Daniel owned and operated a liquor store in Rossie, which he had purchased from George Parish. After Daniel's death, his daughter Rosannah ran it as a grocery store and later became postmistress at Rossie. Daniel was about the same age as our Margaret and could have been her brother, but that couldn't be proven.

I had located a Michael Gillen in the 1850 census of St. Lawrence County, living in the town of Brasher which was about fifty miles north of Rossie, and I first thought he might have been the father of Margaret; however, the ages of his wife and children made that idea implausible. If they were related, Michael would more than likely have been an older brother or an uncle. Also, a John Gillon was listed in the 1860 census of Rossie, and he could have been Margaret's brother, but that couldn't be proven either; he was listed with a Margaret and younger Michael Gillon.

CENSUS EXTRACT Franklin County, New York 1850		
#1297/1327 - Fort Covington		
James Gillon	40 M Farmer	Ireland
Mary	40 F	Ireland
Michael	16 M Laborer	Ireland
Patrick	14 M	Ireland
Catherine	13 F	Ireland
James	11 M	New York
Sarah	4 F	New York

John and Mary Gillon family in 1850

While rechecking some of the earlier census findings, I noticed a James and Mary Gillon family, who had previously been overlooked, but now they stood out like a beacon signal. The family was enumerated in Franklin County in 1850 (the county immediately north of St. Lawrence); and the names, ages, and places of birth were remarkable when compared with the family of John and Margaret Fitzgerald. James and Mary Gillon were old enough to be the parents of Margaret; both age 40 in 1850, and the names of their children had an incredible similarity to those of John and Margaret. They had a Michael, Patrick, Catherine, James, and Sarah. John and Margaret Fitzgerald named a son Michael, a son James, a daughter Mary and another daughter Catherine. Of course those name similarities were not proof of kinship, because nearly every Irish family in that time and place had a Michael and Mary, but the probability of kinship between the two families was high. Also, after reviewing the extracts taken from St. Lawrence County land records, I noticed that a James Gillon was living in Brasher in 1856; the town where Michael and Lucy were resident. In my thinking, the three families simply had to be related.

CANCER CAUSES A DELAY

After making those searches, reports were sent to President Lunceford in January of 1977 and again in March, informing him of my findings and giving suggestions for continued research. He was positive in his responses, but because of the continued illness of my wife Carolyn and her unexpected death from cancer on April 20, 1977, little work was done on the Fitzgerald line until the Spring of 1978; exactly twenty years after Thelda Moss Lunceford had first asked the Genealogical Society for help in identifying Jack Fitzgerald.

President Lunceford was very understanding and considerate during the interval of my anxiety and stress, and he refused to take back the retainer given earlier; in fact, he wanted to give me additional money. At the time of my wife's death, our second son was serving an LDS mission in Lima, Peru, and our third son was preparing to enter the Missionary Training Center in Provo, Utah for a mission to Argentina. Our other six children, ranging in age from 22 to 9, were at home. I spent most of the spring and early summer of 1977 with them; camping in the mountains, and traveling across the country visiting relatives trying to ease the terrible heartache caused by my wife's death.

I was having very little success relieving that anguish until Daniele Yvonne Michele Piquee came into my life during mid-summer; we were married on the 30th of September 1977. She lifted my heartache completely and brought a new happiness into my life which could not be explained. She also became involved in the Jack Fitzgerald quest and was a critical part of its final solution. She entered my life in an unusual way, and I can't help but feel unseen forces had been directing our paths.

A SECOND TRIP TO NEW YORK

During the early part of 1978, Daniele and I made several personal visits to the Lunceford home, where plans were laid for a second visit to Rossie and Gouverneur, New York;

Daniele and Norm Wright - September 1977

this time in company with President Lunceford himself. We mixed a little business with the pleasure of genealogical research, and a strong and lasting bond of fellowship developed between us. During the first week in May, Daniele and I drove to Horseheads, New York, in our little red Volkswagen Beetle, where we participated in one of Brigham Young University's Education Week Programs. At the same time, President Lunceford flew to Michigan, where he carried out some cherry-orchard business. After that, we made a rendezvous at the Syracuse, New York Airport and then drove to Watertown, where we had new and exciting genealogical experiences.

The drive from Syracuse to Watertown took us about three hours--arriving at our destination near sunset. Daniele and I had called ahead to reserved a motel, and during the long drive we laid careful plans for our itinerary. We wanted to visit Katherine Clapp in Watertown, but it was getting late, so we had to decide whether to visit her first or check into our motel. We reached a compromise, deciding to stop at the motel to see if our reservation was in force, without carrying in our bags and formally checking in, then driving to the Clapp home. Our reservations at the Holiday Inn were in order, and after a very short drive, we were at the Clapp residence; interestingly, the Inn and the Clapp home were both on Academy Street in Watertown.

It was still quite light when we arrived at the residence (615 Academy), but there was a light on in the front room, and a car was parked in the driveway with two persons sitting in it. President Lunceford asked me to go knock at the door, which I did, and a middle aged gentleman answered. His first words were: "How did you know I was here?" I was a little puzzled with his question and simply answered: "I didn't know you were here; I just knocked and found you here." Again, in a more stern voice, he said: "But how did you know I was here?" With that, I told him my real purpose was to talk with Katherine Clapp. His curt response was: "She died six months ago; in February!" By this time, President Lunceford and Daniele had gotten out of the car and walked up to the porch where we were talking. I explained that we were seeking genealogical information about Jack Fitzgerald, the brother of Mary (Fitzgerald) Clapp; and with that, his attitude mellowed considerably and he became very friendly. Warm greetings were exchanged between him and President Lunceford, and they proved to be second cousins. We were speaking with Emerson Clapp, the son of Ross and Katherine Clapp, and grandson of Mary (Fitzgerald) and Homer Clapp. President Lunceford was the son of Joseph Alvin Lunceford (Fitzgerald), who was the son of Jack Fitzgerald; brother of Mary (Fitzgerald) Clapp.

Emerson said he had been taking care of some business in another part of the county and had stopped at his mother's house, which had been unoccupied for the past three months, to make a quick phone call; his home was in Ogdensburg which was several miles to the north. He had been trying to sell his mother's house and had stopped to make a local call to confirm some facts about the proposed sale. He hadn't been there more than five minutes when we drove up; in fact, his wife and son were waiting in the car and had honked the horn once or twice already, wonder what his delay was about. If we had been ten minutes earlier or ten minutes later, we would have missed him and missed a very important genealogical connection. He seemed to be in no hurray to end our conversation, even though his wife, who remained in the car, continued to honk the horn trying to get his attention. I quickly ran to our car and got my camera, then I took a picture of Emerson and Clyde standing together on the porch. After the photo, he invited us into the house where we talked for a few minutes longer. He took the time to show us an old photograph of Mary (Fitzgerald) Clapp, sister of Jack, and I also took a picture of it. Emerson's wife and son remained in the car all this time and never did come into the house. After a short but pleasant conversation, we made arrangements to meet Emerson at his home in Ogdensburg the following morning where we could discuss family history in more detail, then he went to his car and headed north while we returned to the Inn where we enjoyed a fine stake dinner and later retired to comfortable beds.

Emerson Clapp and Clyde M. Lunceford; 2nd Cousins

Photo of Mary (Fitzgerald) Clapp

Bright and early the following morning, we drove north to Ogdensburg where we met with Emerson and his wife. We learned that she had been very upset with our intrusion the night before at Watertown, but her disposition had changed dramatically and she showed us unusual hospitality. For the next hour or so, we talked about the Fitzgerald family over a scrumptious breakfast of eggs and bacon, orange juice and toast, followed by milk and donuts.

Emerson had first hand knowledge about several of the Fitzgerald children, and he related events and circumstances in their lives with great detail. He said Tina (Tinnie) lived a spinster's life in Gouverneur and died in the 1960's. James had been a fireman in Gouverneur for many years, and he too never married. Michael married Margaret Leonard, in Gouverneur, and they were the parents of three sons; Stanley, Clarence, and Leslie. Stanley married Jessie Link, and they had a daughter and five sons. Jessie was then living in a rest home (St. Joseph's Health Related Facilities) in Yonkers, New York. Stanley had been a pharmacist in Brooklyn, New York; he had been "mugged" in Brooklyn and died there several years ago. Anna was the oldest sister, and she had married a William Smith who died in Brazil on a business trip after World War II; they had a son John who lived in Yonkers.

Emerson said that Lawrence Fitzgerald, who married Margaret O'Rielly, was a brother of John and had a large family. He said their four oldest sons all went west; William, Edward, Lawrence and Michael. Edward died in a California hospital before 1922. A son Ted was killed in an auto accident, but Emerson couldn't remember where or when. A son John married Mary Smith and died in Gouverneur sometime in the 1940's. He said Lawrence senior was killed in Gouverneur in 1880. Emerson related all of these facts from memory, without referring to any documents or written records, which seemed quite amazing to us. I had my pen and yellow pad with me and jotted down each of the facts as he gave them.

After an enjoyable visit with Emerson and his wife, we left Ogdensburg and resumed our quest for Fitzgerald and Gillon information along the St. Lawrence. Our plan had been to drive north from Ogdensburg and visit each of the main towns looking for Gillon information, but President Lunceford wanted to visit the town of Rossie, so we drove there first. We took photographs of St. Patrick's church and then visited the cemetery, taking several pictures of the John and Margaret Fitzgerald tombstone. President Lunceford was really excited about visiting this historic family location, and he spent a lot of time walking about the cemetery and contemplating what might have happened had his lot been different. As we were gathered around the Fitzgerald tombstone chatting, Daniele happened to noticed the name "Pound" carved in large letters on a tombstone directly behind that of John and Margaret; neither President Lunceford nor I had noticed it before. As we looked more closely, it proved to be a combined tombstone for the Patrick Pound family. Theresa (Teressa in the census) Flick was listed as his wife, and Alice and Mary were listed as daughters. It was their son William who married Maggie, the daughter of John and Margaret Fitzgerald. To me, this was very interesting; because in life these two families had lived and associated together, and in death their remains had been buried next to each other. In 1968, when the John and Margaret Fitzgerald tombstone was first located, I had no idea about a "Pound" connection, but it does show that a person should take special interest in those buried next to relatives.

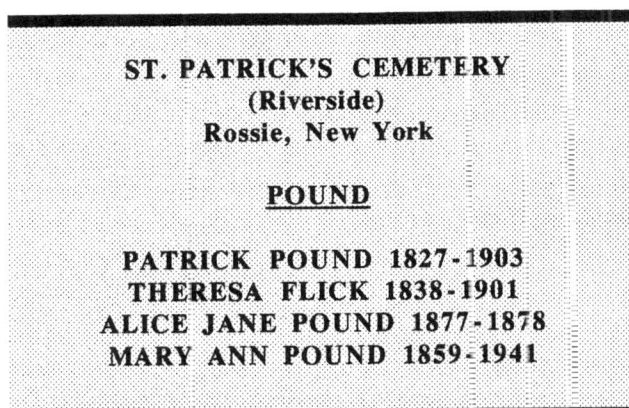

ST. PATRICK'S CEMETERY
(Riverside)
Rossie, New York

POUND

PATRICK POUND 1827-1903
THERESA FLICK 1838-1901
ALICE JANE POUND 1877-1878
MARY ANN POUND 1859-1941

The Patrick and Theresa (Flick) Pound Tombstone

That principle was confirmed again when Daniele identified the tombstone of James Mahoney and Hanora his wife, which

Clyde M. Lunceford at St. Patrick's Cemetery; Rossie, New York

The John and Margaret Fitzgerald Tombstone; Rossie, New York

ST PATRICK'S CEMETERY
(Riverside)
Rossie, New York

JAMES MAHONEY died Jan 2 1878 aged 64 years
HANORA his wife died Dec 21, 1893 aged 75 years
JAMES MAHONEY JR died April 2 1878 aged 24 years

James and Hanora Mahoney Tombstone Inscriptions

was situated just to the north of the Fitzgerald stone. According to St. Mary's church records, also searched in 1968, "Honora Maloney" (the Hanora Mahoney spelling is correct) was a witness to John and Margaret's marriage in 1853; again, family and friends were found together in life as well as death. We were careful to copy inscriptions from other tombstones surrounding those of John and Margaret.

After finishing our morning visit to Rossie, we headed north along the St. Lawrence, visiting every major town between Ogdensburg and the Canadian border. We talked with local residents and visited cemeteries, hoping to find Gillon relatives, but the trip turned out to be nothing more than a wild goose chase. Oh, we found a lead or two, but each person contacted could relate nothing about earlier Gillon residents, and each of them chose not to talk about themselves. We did enjoy the scenery, and we were fascinated with the rural culture of Upstate New York, but our genealogical findings turned out to be zero. The weather had been beautiful during the morning and early afternoon, but as we headed south toward the town of Gouverneur, dark clouds began to gather and light rain began to fall; our spirits matching the dark clouds.

It was after 4:00 o'clock in the evening when we arrived at Gouvernour, and President Lunceford suggested we visit the Riverside cemetery before returning to our motel. He thought we should try to locate the tombstones of Tinnie, Michael, and James, who should have been buried there. Daniele and I weren't too excited about the idea, because that's what we had been doing most of the day; however, we yielded to his request and drove to the cemetery without comment. The rain had subsided, but there was still a slight drizzle as we began our search.

We couldn't arouse anyone at the sexton's office (a small house at the entrance to the cemetery), so we began a systematic search of the entire place, walking along each row looking for Fitzgerald headstones. We found the Lawrence Fitzgerald plot, which I had located in 1868, and we spotted one or two other Fitzgerald stones which we couldn't identify, but we couldn't locate those for Tinnie, Michael, and James. After searching for more than an hour, and after reaching the outer perimeter of the cemetery, Daniele walked over a large knoll and disappeared from our view. President Lunceford and I continued searching within sight of each other, but Daniele didn't reappear for quite a long time. Finally, she came trudging back over the knoll, telling us she had met the sexton who had been sitting in his car drinking beer. His car had been out of sight on a small road, near the cemetery's northern boundary, when Daniele approached and apparently surprised him. They carried on a short conversation, and when he said he was the sexton, Daniele asked him if he would go check his records for the Fitzgerald names we were seeking. He was harsh in his refusal to help her, so she left him immediately and walked back over the hill to us; at the same time saying a short prayer that his heart would be softened.

After finishing our search for Fitzgerald headstones, we headed back to our car, which was parked at the southwest entrance to the cemetery. As we reached the car, who should drive up but the sexton Daniele had talked with a few minutes earlier; her silent prayer had apparently been answered. He had gone to his office and checked the records for the

Clyde M. Lunceford and the Fitzgerald Headstones; Riverside Cemetery; Gouverneur, New York

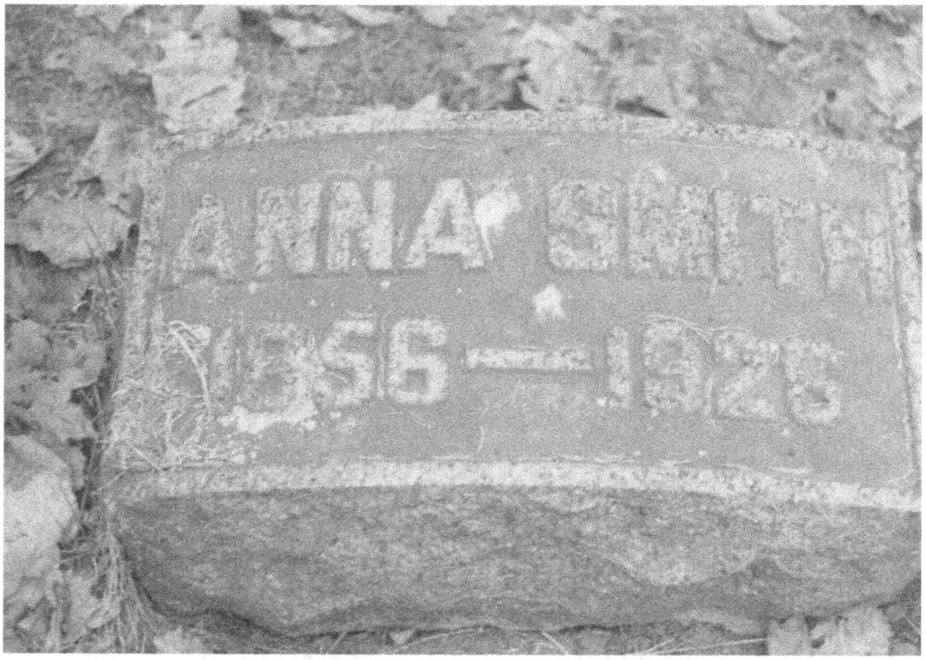

Anna (Fitzgerald) Smith Headstone; Riverside Cemetery

Michael Fitzgerald Headstone; Riverside Cemetery;
Gouverneur, New York

James Fitzgerald Headstone; Riverside Cemetery
Gouverneur, New York

Tinnie Fitzgerald Headstone; Riverside Cemetery; Gouverneur, New York

Fitzgerald names, but unfortunately, he couldn't find any of them. However, he told us there was an older Catholic cemetery about a mile south of Riverside which we should check, and he gave us directions how to get there. We were disappointed that he hadn't found our people in his records, but we were happy with this new lead.

We found the older Catholic cemetery without difficulty and began searching for Fitzgerald headstones. Daniele located one for a William Fitzgerald right off the bat, but his epitaph said he was from Massachusetts, and the dates were much too early for our family. We couldn't find any other markers with the Fitzgerald or Gillon names in the entire cemetery, so we headed back to our car with natural disappointment. Interestingly, however, as we were getting into our car, the Riverside sexton drove up behind us and sounded his horn. He got out of his car and hurried toward us, waving a paper and shouting: "I found them! I found them!--They were listed under the name Smith, not Fitzgerald." After leaving us at the Riverside cemetery, he had gone back to his office and rechecked his records; finding entries for Anna Smith, Tinnie, Michael, and James Fitzgerald. Evidently the names had been indexed under Anna Smith (the older sister), and that was apparently why he couldn't find them earlier. It was then clear to us that Daniele's silent prayer had been answered; yes, by a half inebriated sexton. He seemed to sense our excitement and led us back to the other cemetery, where he pointed out the burial plot and witnessed our intense joy.

Section D, lot 165, at the Riverside cemetery had been purchased by Anna Smith, and she along with her sister Tinnie and her brothers Michael and James were buried there. The individual headstones were similar in size, each being horizontal in style and rising about ten or twelve inches above the ground. Anna's headstone was the oldest and was convex, but the others were flat; all beautifully carved. Daniele began writing down the names and dates from the headstones while President Lunceford and I took photos of them. Ironically, each one of us; President Lunceford, Daniele, and I had walked right by these headstones earlier without recognizing them. As President Lunceford looked at Tinnie's headstone, he remarked: "You know, if I had gotten on a plane and flown to Rossie when we first began research on Jack (in 1957), I could have talked with his sister, Tinnie!" Yes, and I have since thought: "If I had only checked copies of the Deseret News and Salt Lake Tribune for August 26, 1901 (the day after Jack's murder), I would have learned that his mother Margaret and his brothers, Michael and James, were living in Gouverneur."

TOMBSTONE INSCRIPTIONS
Riverside Cemetery
Gouverneur, New York

ANNA SMITH 1856-1956
MICHAEL FITZGERALD 1870-1939
JAMES FITZGERALD 1872-1942
TINNIE FITZGERALD 1875-1961

Brothers and Sister of Jack Fitzgerald

President Lunceford later remarked that we must not dwell on our mistakes, even in genealogical research; but rather, we should learn from them and move forward with new determination and resolve. He said each mistake provides us with a new experience which can be used to move ahead, whether it be in genealogy or in any other of life's pursuits.

We were happy with our findings at Riverside, but Daniele and I were eager to get back to the motel and relax, because it had been a very long and busy day; little did we realize our rest was still several hours away. As we left the cemetery, supposedly heading for our motel, President Lunceford suggested that we try to find the stonecypher who created the Fitzgerald headstones and see if he might have additional information. I had never done that sort of thing before and discounted it, but Daniele thought it was a good idea, so we made inquiry at a convenience store and were directed to the Sprague Funeral Home, which was only a few blocks distant. President Lunceford followed his usual pattern and asked me to knock at the door and inquire, which I did, and the owner, Mr Sprague, answered the door himself. He invited me in and graciously listened to my request for information. He not only operated the only funeral home in town, but his organization was an outlet for the sale of monuments, headstones, tombstones, and the like. He was kind enough to check his records for the Fitzgerald names I provided him, but he couldn't locate an entry for any of them in his files. When I explained the headstone style for Anna Smith, which was convex with raised letters, he said: "Oh, if we had done that stone I would have remembered it; those are difficult to make and are very expensive!" We talked for a few minutes longer, and as I was preparing to leave, he said: "You should go talk to Bill Fitzgerald; he lives just down the street from here; he might be able to help you." That seemed like a good idea, so I thanked him for his assistance and returned to the car.

I explained my experience with Mr Sprague to Daniele and President Lunceford, and they both agreed that we should visit Bill Fitzgerald immediately; it was then about 6:30 p.m. When we arrived at the house, a young boy about ten or eleven years old was riding a skate board on the front sidewalk. We inquired of him if this was the Bill Fitzgerald residence, and he said yes, but as we got out of the car, he said: "My dad is not here, he's at the school coaching pony league." We asked him for directions to the school, but he had a difficult time trying to explain it, so he said: "I'll show you how to get there," and he climbed into our car. We should never have allowed that, because his father was very upset with us when we arrived at the school. The father threatened me as the driver and was ready to report me to the local police for abducting his young son. After we explained our purpose, he calmed down a bit, but he was still very upset with us.

We asked him about his family and explained that we were seeking information about the John and Margaret Fitzgerald family, which had resided in Gouverneur for several years. He said he was not related to them but descended from a William Fitzgerald who came to New York from Massachusetts in the 1790's. He said his ancestry was English and not Irish; I reasoned the William Fitzgerald tombstone we had found earlier in the old Catholic cemetery belonged to his ancestor. As we were preparing to leave, he said: "You might contact Mary Fitzgerald who lives on Main Street; she's a very old lady and might know something about your family." He began to explain how to get to her home when his young son, who had shown us how to get to the school, blurted out: "I know where she lives, I'll show you how to get there!" But the father said: "Oh no you won't!" and pushed him back. It was then well after 7:00 o'clock p.m. and was getting dark.

After receiving instructions from Mr Fitzgerald, we drove back to town and began looking for "160 West Main," the address he had given us. It was too dark to read some of the house numbers, so I got out of the car and was crossing the street toward the home which I thought was number 160. At that very moment, someone behind me honked his horn and hollered out the window: "Wrong house! Wrong house! It's on the other side of the street!" Bill Fitzgerald had followed us from the school in his car; perhaps to see if we were really looking for the Fitzgeralds or up to some other kind of mischief, but he was now giving us directions.

After finding the correct house, I knocked on the door and an elderly lady answered. She was nearly deaf, however, and I had to shout to make her hear me. I told her I was seeking information on a John and Margaret Fitzgerald family and wondered if she could help me. With that, she said: "Won't you please come in." Before entering, I beckoned to Daniele and President Lunceford to come in also, and we had a rewarding conversation with another relative. We had experienced some genealogical highs and lows during the past two days, but this visit proved to be the highest one yet. This sweet lady proved to be the wife of John Fitzgerald who was the son of Lawrence and Margaret (O'Rielly) Fitzgerald; she was a first cousin (in-law) to our Jack Fitzgerald.

Even though we were strangers, Mrs Fitzgerald showed us unusual hospitality by inviting us into her home and seating us comfortably in her front room; she even offered us refreshment. Our conversation was somewhat unusual, because we had to shout with our questions, but we were successful in learning important facts about the Fitzgerald family. She was over ninety years old, and though somewhat hard of hearing, she was mentally bright and able to carry on an intelligent conversation with us. In this instance, I didn't have my trusty yellow pad with me, but I did have a family group record of the John and Margaret in my shirt pocket, so I took it out and wrote down the genealogical facts she gave us.

It was the evening of the 8th of May 1978, and the place was number 160 West Main Street in Gouverneur, New York. Mrs John Fitzgerald said her maiden name was Mary Smith; that she was born on the 16th of September 1888 in Potsdam, Jefferson County, New York the daughter of Frederick and Margaret (Donahue) Smith. She had a sister and four brothers; two of the brothers being school teachers in New Jersey. She said she married John Fitzgerald, the son of Lawrence and Margaret Fitzgerald, in Potsdam, New York (I failed to record the date but learned later it was in 1918). Her husband John was born on the 14th of August 1871, also in Potsdam, and died the 26th of October 1945 in Gouverneur. She said he experienced a tragic and unusual death while attending the County Fair. He had been standing beside a horse drawn wagon and happened to rest his foot on one of the wooden wheel spokes while chatting with the driver. Something frightened the horses and they bolted forward, dragging John to his death. Mary was able to relate this tragic event without showing much emotion.

On a happier note, she had been in regular contact with Jessie Link Fitzgerald, the wife of Stanley Fitzgerald who had been mugged in Brooklyn some years earlier; in fact, a letter from Jessie to Mary was sitting on the piano at that very moment, and we were permitted to read it. She said Stanley and Jessie had at least one daughter, but she couldn't recall their names. She said Stanley and his two brothers, Clarence and Leslie, (sons of Michael) who lived with their Aunt Tinnie Fitzgerald when they were young, were later placed in an orphanage. Stanley had died in Brooklyn several years earlier; Clarence had died in Utica; and Leslie was also deceased, but Mary couldn't recall when or where he died. She said her husband, and several others of the family, were all buried in Gouverneur.

Mary showed us a copy of the obituary notice for Katherine L. Clapp, which she had clipped from the Gouverneur Free Press, and she allowed me to keep it. She was able to recall several other important facts about the family; including the following:

MRS. CLAPP DIES IN OGDENSBURG

Ogdensburg - Mrs Katherine L. Clapp, 89 formerly of 615 Academy St., Watertown, widow of Thomas R. Clapp, died Tuesday at 7:10 p.m. in St. Joseph's Nursing Home where she had been admitted Feb. 6.

She had previously been a patient at the Cedars Nursing Home.

The funeral will be Friday at 10:30 a.m. at the Cummings Funeral Home, Watertown and 11 a.m. at Holy Family Church, Watertown. Spring burial will be in Glenwood Cemetery, Watertown.

Calling hours are 2 to 4 and 7 to 9 p.m. today at the funeral home.

She is survived by two sons, Carroll J., Atlanta, Ga., and Emerson, Ogdensburg; a daughter, Mrs. James H. (Dorothy) Cody Kostyk, 151 Park Ave.; six grandchildren; five great grandchildren, nieces and nephews. Two brothers, Carroll Loughlin and Edmund Loughlin, died before her.

Obituary of Katherine L. Clapp

When Margaret O'Rielly Fitzgerald died in 1922, her husband's body (also that of their son Lawrence) was moved from the Rossie cemetery to the Riverside cemetery in Gouverneur (Interment records said this happened in 1935 not 1922). She had heard of the Pound family but couldn't give us any details about them. She knew nothing about Catherine or Letia, children of John and Margaret, and she knew nothing about our Jack, but She did recall that James was a policeman in Gouverneur for several years and lived with his sister Tinnie in a house at the corner of Clinton and Hospital Road. Anna Smith, the sister of Tinnie, had a son John who lived in Yonkers. He was tall and good looking, with red hair, but he never did marry; he was a salesman in Yonkers. She knew that Homer and Mary (Fitzgerald) Clapp had gone to Ireland and contacted family members there, but when I asked her "Where in Ireland?" she said: "If you hadn't asked me I could have told you, but now I can't remember;" and she was not able to recall that information during the remainder of our visit.

After providing us with some light refreshment, Mary related more facts about the Lawrence and Margaret (O'Rielly) Fitzgerald family, confirming several things we already knew but adding more. She corroborated Emerson Clapp's assertion the older boys went west, but she said he was wrong in saying Lawrence was one of them; he died in 1902 at the home of his mother "on Somerville Road" in Gouverneur, which we had also confirmed. Lawrence senior and his sons worked in the Iron mines near Antwerp, New York. but they belonged to St. James Parish in Gouverneur. "Tom" (Thomas) and "Mae" (Mary), the two youngest children, never married and lived in Gouverneur. We had located the tombstones of Michael J. (1866-1932), Lawrence (1869-1902), and Thomas E. (1877-1931) in the Riverside cemetery earlier, but we hadn't found those for John, Charles, and Mary.

The evening had been well spent, and it was after 9:00 o'clock p.m., so we expressed our thanks to Mary Smith Fitzgerald for the helpful information we had receive, and for her kind hospitality, then we returned to our motel for dinner and a good nights rest. President Lunceford insisted that we celebrate the day's success by have a "New York steak" dinner with all the trimmings, and he picked up the tab.

The following morning as we drove back to the Syracuse Airport where President Lunceford would catch his flight home, we reviewed our findings and outlined the research steps which might be taken when we got back to Utah. We had obtained a wealth of information in less than two days, and the list of things we could yet do was astounding; other living relatives could be contacted, modern death records and obituaries could be obtained, and a variety of new sources might be investigated. We all agreed that providence had smiled on us again, and we expressed our thanks for the unseen help.

THE IRISH ORIGIN

President Lunceford arrived home from the 1978 New York trip in less than three hours by plane, but it took Daniele and me more than three days to get there in our little red volkswagen. We did some research on my Haines and Doty ancestry in Ohio and Indiana as we traveled west, but our success was nothing like that we had experienced on the Fitzgerald line in New York. We were excited about the new information which had been located, and we were anxious to begin investigating the new leads which had been uncovered.

A few days after we had returned, Daniele and I visited President Lunceford at his home in Orem, and after reminiscing about our recent New York experiences, we began formalizing plans to continue building the Jack Fitzgerald pedigree. There were a hundred things we could do; including writing for modern death records and newspaper obituaries, contacting living relatives in New York and the west, checking modern census records for the children of John and his brother Lawrence, and reevaluating the material which had been located previously; correlating it with our new findings. Ironically, the Genealogical Society had just begun microfilming county records for New York, some of which we had already searched, and many more which we were interested in, so there were abundant records available to investigate right in Salt Lake City. Most of the summer of 1978 was spent with my family; Daniele's parents had arrived from France for an extended visit, so little work was done until fall when school began, but by September and October, interesting things were happening, and exciting new facts were being found concerning Jack Fitzgerald.

One of the first things I did was request copies of death records from the State of New York for Michael, James, Tinnie, and Anna (Smith) Fitzgerald; each of whom had died in a modern period; Anna in 1926, Michael in 1939, James in 1942, and Tinnie in 1961. Because of a heavy backlog of orders, however, the New York State Department of Health told me to expect a six-month delay before receiving them. In the mean time, modern census records were searched, newspaper obituaries were obtained, living family members were contacted, and

(HUSBAND): Richard A. STUMPF
(born): 3 Aug 1933 in Yonkers, Westchester, New York
(married): 1 Sep 1956 in St. Denis Church; Yonkers, New York

(WIFE): Ann Patricia FITZGERALD
(born): 8 Mar 1937 in Yonkers, Westchester, New York

(CHILDREN):

1-John Stanley STUMPF
(born): 23 Jun 1957 in Yonkers, Westcherst, New York
2-Kim Ann STUMPF
(born): 27 Sep 1958 in Yonkers, Westchester, New York
3-Keith William STUMPF
(born): 12 Feb 1960 in Nyack, Westchester, New York
4-Stephen Andrew STUMPF
(born): 26 May 1962 in Nyack,Westchester, New York
5-Richard Andrew STUMPF
(born): 14 Jan 1966 in Nyack, Westchester, New York

(Family Address): 295 Eisenhower Drive; Orwigsburg, Pennsylvania 17961

interesting new family connections were discovered. Of equal importance, was the detailed information learned about Jack Fitzgerald's murder in Park City, Utah in 1901. Original court records revealed a fascinating tale about him and about early Utah history. We were also able to determine who had Jack's watch, which President Lunceford was so interested in getting.

I had written to Jessie (Link) Fitzgerald, the wife of Stanley (nephew of Jack), in September of 1978, asking her for family information, but she did not reply, so on the 29th of November 1978, I placed a long distance telephone call to St. Joseph's Health Related Facilities in Yonkers, New York and was able to talk with her personally for an extended period of time. She was 72 years old and responded smartly and intelligently to my questions. She said she had received my September letter but was embarrassed that an answer had not yet been sent. Her sister had recently passed away, which had caused her concern, but she assured me she still planned to send me her family genealogy. She had known Jack's brothers and sisters personally and was particularly well acquainted with Anna, the oldest sister. She said Anna's husband, William Smith, had died several years earlier while in Brazil on a business trip, and she said their only son John had died in Yonkers, New York in about 1927.

As our conversation continued, Jessie said her husband Stanley had been a graduate of Albany College in New York and later became a pharmacist in Yonkers. She and Stanley had lived on Clinton Street in Gouverneur when they were first married, right close to Tinnie and James Fitzgerald. She said Stanley had died about eight years earlier in Yonkers (Emerson Clapp had said that Stanley was "mugged" in Brooklyn). Jessie said she was born on the 8th of March 1906 at Gouverneur "or one of those little towns near by" the daughter of Webster Link and Anna Ferry. She said that she and Stanley were married on the 8th of July 1929 at St. James Church in Gouverneur and were the parents of one child; a daughter Ann who had five children; the first a son, the second a daughter, and the other three sons.

As our conversation ended, Jessie reminded me that she would be sending me more details about her family; she seemed very excited about my call and was happy to learn of our interest in the Fitzgerald family and her relationship to Clyde M. Lunceford. A short time later, on the 25th of June 1979, she sent me a five page letter summarizing her life's history with Stanley and included a document from her daughter which provided genealogical facts on her son-in-law and five grandchildren. Her daughter Ann was a grandniece of Jack and a second cousin to President Lunceford. Who would have imagined that we would be finding great grandnieces and nephews of Jack Fitzgerald in 1979 living in Orwigsburg, Pennsylvania? (see copy which follows)

On the 4th of December 1978, in response to an earlier request, I received copies of two certificates of marriage from St. James Church in Gouverneur, New York; one for Michael Fitzgerald and Margaret A. Leonard (Stanley's parents), dated 26 September 1893; and one for Stanley A. Fitzgerald and Jessie M. Link, dated 9 July 1929 (Jessie said she was married on the 8th of July rather than the 9th). These two documents confirmed information I had found earlier, and they added new facts about the family which was helpful. The names of the parents were listed on the back of each document, and the clerk had included the baptism dates and places for Stanley and Jessie on the back of their record. (see copies which follow)

Shortly after my telephone conversation with Jessie, I placed another long distance call, this time to Atlanta, Georgia, in an effort to speak with Carroll J. Clapp the brother of Emerson whom we assumed had Jack Fitzgerald's watch. But on this call, the results were not nearly as productive as they were with Jessie. Carroll's wife answered the telephone and was very guarded in her responses. After I had explained my connection and interest in the Fitzgerald family, she said Carroll had just gone through heart surgery and couldn't receive any calls. I told her we were interested in identifying the descendants of John and Margaret Fitzgerald of Rossie, New York, but she declined to give me genealogical facts about her family. She did say that she and Carroll had two daughters and a son, but she wouldn't disclose their names nor give me their places of residence. She said that if I would give her my name and address, which I did, she would get in touch with me later, but I haven't heard from her since.

Marriage Certificate of Michael Fitzgerald and Margaret E. Leonard

Certificate of Marriage

Church of

St. James

Gouverneur, N.Y.

This is to Certify

That Michael Fitzgerald

and Margaret E. Leonard

were lawfully Married

on the 26 day of September ~~19~~ 1893

According to the Rite of the Roman Catholic Church

and in conformity with the laws of

the State of New York

Rev. E. C. Laramee officiating,

in the presence of Alexander Renard

and Philomena Laurens Witnesses,

as appears from the Marriage Register of this Church.

Dated 12-4-78

Joseph A. Lagamer

Pastor

No. 312 F. J. REMEY CO., Inc. MINEOLA, N. Y.

Michael's Parents
John Fitzgerald
&
Margaret Gillen

Margaret (non catholic)
Peter Leonard
Maria Scott

Marriage Certificate of Stanley A. Fitzgerald and Jessie M. Link

Certificate of Marriage

Church of
St. James
Gouverneur, N.Y.

This is to Certify

That Stanley A. Fitzgerald
and Jessie M Link
were lawfully Married
on the 9 day of July 1929
According to the Rite of the Roman Catholic Church
and in conformity with the laws of
the State of New York
Rev. M F. Gallivan officiating,
in the presence of Walter Mason
and Edith Kennedy Witnesses,
as appears from the Marriage Register of this Church.
Dated 12-3-76

(Cmy) [signature]
Pastor

No 312 F J REMEY CO. Inc MINEOLA, N.Y.

Parents of Stanley — Michael Fitzgerald, Margaret Leonard

Jessie — Webster Link, Anna Ferry

he baptized May 21, 1898 St. James Gouverneur

She June 26 1910 St. Mary's Canton, N.Y.

CENSUS EXTRACT
Grant County, New Mexico
1900

#39/39 - Town of Pinos Altos, Precinct #2			
POUND, William;	Gold Miner;	Oct 1857; 42 M-19;	N.Y. Ire. Switz.
Maggie	Wife;	Apr 1862; 38 M-19;	Can. Ire. Ire.
Fred	Son;	May 1886; 14 S;	New Mex. N.Y. Can.
Marie	Dau;	Feb 1888; 12 S;	New Mex. N.Y. Can.
Roy	Son;	Sep 1892; 7 S;	New Mex. N.Y. Can.
Charles A.	Son;	Nov 1899; 6/12 S;	New Mex. N.Y. Can.
#20/20 - Town of Pinos Altos, Precinct #2			
ROBINSON, Lewis;	Doctor;	Sep 1858; 41 M-9;	Penn. Penn. Penn.
Katie	Wife;	Jan 1869; 31 M-9;	N.Y. Ire. Switz.
Shelburn	Son;	May 1894; 6 S;	New Mex. Penn. N.Y.
Edgar J.	Son;	Dec 1895; 4 S;	New Mex. Penn. N.Y.
Lewis S.	Son;	Mar 1898; 2 S;	New Mex. Penn. N.Y.
Mary E.	Dau;	Apr 1900; 1/12 S;	New Mex. Penn. N.Y.
POUND, Hannah	S-i-law;	Jan 1867; 33 S;	N.Y. Ire. Switz.

William Pound and Lewis Robinson families in 1900

On the 27th of November 1978, while visiting the Family History Library in Salt Lake City, I made an important find in the 1900 Federal U.S. census of New Mexico which helped me better identify Jack's older sister Margaret (Maggie). Remembering that Jack's mother, was survived by a "Mrs. William Pound of Silver City, New Mexico" in 1911, I searched the 1900 census for Grant County, New Mexico, where Silver City was located, and found the William Pound family living in the town of "Pinos Altos," which was only a few miles north of Silver City. As a bonus, William's brother-in-law, Lewis Robinson, and two of his sisters, Hannah and Catherine (Kate), were found living only a few houses away. Hannah and Catherine had been listed as ages "3" and "1" respectively in the household of Patrick and Teressa (Theresa) Pound in the 1870 census for Rossie, New York; and here in the 1900 census of Grant County, New Mexico, they were listed as ages "33' and "31." The places of birth for their parents were listed as "Ireland" for their father and "Switzerland" for their mother, which supported my belief that they were the children of Patrick and Theresa Pound.

Back in December of 1969, after my first New York trip, I had written to the New Mexico State Department of Health, asking them to search their files for possible death records of William and Margaret Pound who may have died in their state after 1911. They were kind enough to make a general search for me and found a death record on file for a William but none for a Margaret. The document they did find was for a "William Adelbert Pound" who had died in San Juan, New Mexico in May of 1922. The record indicated he had been born September 3, 1852 near Buffalo, New York; that his wife was Mary A. Pound; that his father was Geo. Pound; and that a Kate Pound of Denver, Colorado had been the informant. This William Pound did not fit the criteria to be our man, but I did follow through and obtained a newspaper obituary for him, and after carefully evaluating both records, it was evident that William Adelbert Pound was not the person we were seeking. He was living in the northwestern corner of the state, while our William Pound was living in the southwestern corner (see copies).

DEATH CERTIFICATE OF WILLIAM ADELBERT POUND - 1922

STATE OF NEW MEXICO, DEPARTMENT OF HEALTH

CERTIFICATE OF DEATH

1 PLACE OF DEATH County of San Juan Registered No. 19

School District of .... or Village of ....

or City of Near Aztec No. .... St., ... Ward

(If death occurred in hospital or institution, give its NAME instead of street and number)

2 FULL NAME William Adelbert Pound

(a) Residence. No. .... St., ... Ward.

(Usual place of abode) (IF NONRESIDENT give city or town and State)

LENGTH OF RESIDENCE in city or town where death occurred 9 yrs 1 mos 20 days. How long in U. S., if of foreign birth? yrs. mos. ds.

PERSONAL AND STATISTICAL PARTICULARS

3 SEX	4 COLOR OR RACE	5 Single, Married, Widowed, or Divorced (write the word.)
male	white	married

5a If married, ~~widowed, or divorced~~ HUSBAND OF ~~(or) WIFE of~~ Mary A. Pound

6 DATE OF BIRTH Sept month 3 day 1852 year

7 AGE 69 Years 8 Months 16 Days. If LESS than 1 day .... hrs. or .... min.

8 OCCUPATION OF DECEASED (a) Trade, profession, or particular kind of work Farmer

(b) General nature of industry, business, or establishment in which employed (or employer)

(c) Name of employer Self

9 BIRTHPLACE (city or town) (State or county) Near Buffalo New York

PARENTS

10 NAME OF FATHER Geo. Pound

11 BIRTHPLACE OF FATHER (City or town) (State or county) ✓

12 MAIDEN NAME OF MOTHER ✓

13 BIRTHPLACE OF MOTHER (City or town) (State or county) ✓

14 Informant Kate Pound

(Address) Denver Colo.

15 Filed June 15 1922 Mrs. E. B. Deacon Sub. REGISTRAR

MEDICAL CERTIFICATE OF DEATH

16 DATE OF DEATH May (MONTH) 19 (DAY), 1922 (YEAR)

17 I HEREBY CERTIFY, That I attended deceased from May 12, 1922 to May 19, 1922 that I last saw h........ alive on May 19, 1922 and that death occurred, on the date stated above, at 3 A. m.

The CAUSE OF DEATH* was as follows:

Angina Pectoris

(duration) 89 yrs. 3 mos. ds.

CONTRIBUTORY (SECONDARY) .... (duration) .... yrs. .... mos. .... ds.

18 Where was disease contracted if not at place of death? ✓

Did an operation precede death? no Date of ....

Was there an autopsy? no

What test confirmed diagnosis? clinical

(Signed) M. D. Taylor M. D.

Date ...., 19 .... (Address) Aztec, N. Mex.

*State the Primary Disease causing death. See reverse for instructions as to statement of cause of death.

19 PLACE OF BURIAL, CREMATION OR REMOVAL	DATE OF BURIAL
Aztec, N. Mex.	May 20, 1922

20 UNDERTAKER	ADDRESS
J. W. Dial	Aztec, N.M.

NEWSPAPER OBITUARY
The Aztec Independent Review
May 26, 1922

William Adelbert Pound was born in New York, September 1852 and died at his home near Aztec, New Mexico on Friday morning, May 19 at three a.m. From New York, he moved to Iowa, then to South Dakota, where he was married to Mary A. Grimwood. Five Children were born to this union, three died while small, and Miss Kate and John survive. They moved to Aztec nine years ago. besides the two children, his wife and many friends mourn his sudden passing.

(from same paper, same date)

W. A. Pound passed away very suddenly last Friday morning. He had been ill but a short time and his illness was not thought dangerous until the last few days. Miss Kate Pound who was in Denver and John Pound, professor at Pueblo, Colo., were notified. miss Pound arrived Thursday night in time to see her father before the end, but John did not arrive until Friday night. Funeral services were conducted by Rev. John Cox at the Methodist Church, Saturday afternoon.

CENSUS EXTRACT St. Lawrence County, New York 1870		
#128/118 - Rossie		
POUND, Patrick	48 M Farmer	Ireland
Teressa	32 F Keeps House	Switzerland
Thomas	15 M Works on Farm	New York
Peter	14 M	New York
William	12 M	New York
Edward	11 M	New York
Mary A.	9 F	New York
Francis	8 M	New York
Teressa	6 F	New York
Julia	4 F	New York
Hannah	3 F	New York

Patrick Pound family in 1870

After finding our William Pound in the 1900 census, I wondered what the odds might have been for two William Pounds' to have been living in New Mexico in the 1900's; both born in state of New York, and both born at the same approximate time--they would certainly have to have been high. interestingly enough, I had faced a "two-William-Pound-problem" earlier in the Rossie, New York 1870 census, and now I was facing it again in the 1900 schedules for New Mexico. The two William Pounds' in Rossie were very probably first cousins, but was there a relationship between these two in New Mexico? That answer would have to come later.

More helpful information about Margaret was learned from Michael Fitzgerald's obituary, which was obtained much later. It said he was survived by a "Mrs. Margaret Pound" who was residing in "San Pedro, California" in 1939, so I wrote to the California State Department of Health Services in Sacramento and was able to get a copy of her death record. It said she died on the 26th of November 1940 in St. Mary's Hospital at Long Beach, California, and it stated that she had been a resident of California for "36 years." Evidently she, and perhaps other members of her family, had left New Mexico and had settled in California by 1904. The record indicated that she was the "Widow" of William Pound, and it confirmed her Canadian birth as well as her parentage. A Mrs. Marie Meagher (her daughter) was the informant and was listed as a resident of Long Beach, California when Margaret died.

From James Fitzgerald's 1942 obituary (another brother), which was also obtained later, I learned that he (James) was survived by "a niece, Mrs. Meager (Marie Pound) of Long Beach, Calif" and also by "Roy Pound and Charles Pound of El Paso, Texas." An attempt was made later to locate Roy and Charles Pound in El Paso, Texas; and I also tried to find Fred Pound in New Mexico and California, but to date both of those efforts have failed. Nevertheless, four more nephews of Jack Fitzgerald were identified in these searches; Fred, Marie (Meagher), Roy, and Charles Pound, and more valuable information was learned about Jack's sister Margaret. The following census extract shows Margaret (Maggie) in her parent's household in 1870:

A few days before I had located the William Pound family in the 1900 census of New Mexico, I had written to the California Department of Health, asking them to try and locate a death record for an Edward Fitzgerald who had died in a California hospital before 1922. Emerson Clapp had provided us with that information in our July 1978 interview at Ogdensburg, New York. At that time, I had no idea that Margaret (Fitzgerald) Pound had also

DEATH CERTIFICATE OF MARGARET (FITZGERALD) POUND - 1940

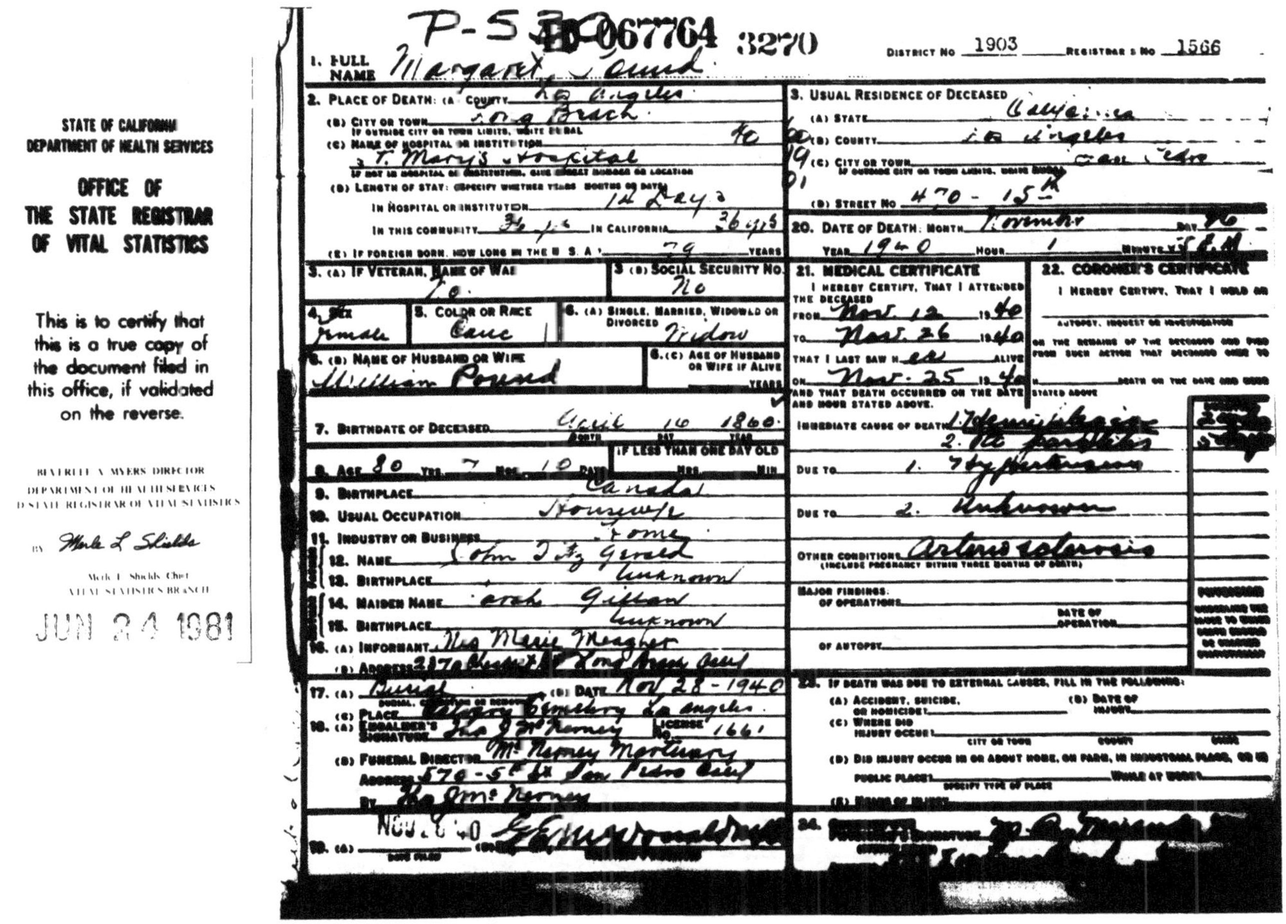
STATE OF CALIFORNIA
DEPARTMENT OF HEALTH SERVICES

OFFICE OF
THE STATE REGISTRAR
OF VITAL STATISTICS

This is to certify that this is a true copy of the document filed in this office, if validated on the reverse.

BEVERLEE A. MYERS DIRECTOR
DEPARTMENT OF HEALTH SERVICES
& STATE REGISTRAR OF VITAL STATISTICS

BY Merle L. Shields
Merle L. Shields Chief
VITAL STATISTICS BRANCH

JUN 24 1981

P-53 40-067764 3270

DISTRICT NO. 1903 REGISTRAR'S NO. 1566

1. FULL NAME Margaret Pound

2. PLACE OF DEATH: (A) COUNTY Los Angeles
(B) CITY OR TOWN Long Beach
(C) NAME OF HOSPITAL OR INSTITUTION St. Mary's Hospital
(D) LENGTH OF STAY: IN HOSPITAL OR INSTITUTION 14 Days
IN THIS COMMUNITY 36 yrs IN CALIFORNIA 36 yrs
(E) IF FOREIGN BORN, HOW LONG IN THE U.S.A. 79 YEARS

3. USUAL RESIDENCE OF DECEASED
(A) STATE California
(B) COUNTY Los Angeles
(C) CITY OR TOWN San Pedro
(D) STREET NO. 470 - 15th

3. (A) IF VETERAN, NAME OF WAR No
3. (B) SOCIAL SECURITY NO. No
4. SEX Female
5. COLOR OR RACE Cauc
6. (A) SINGLE, MARRIED, WIDOWED OR DIVORCED Widow
6. (B) NAME OF HUSBAND OR WIFE William Pound
6. (C) AGE OF HUSBAND OR WIFE IF ALIVE YEARS
7. BIRTHDATE OF DECEASED April 16 1860
8. AGE 80 YRS. 7 MOS. 10 DAYS
9. BIRTHPLACE Canada
10. USUAL OCCUPATION Housewife
11. INDUSTRY OR BUSINESS Home
12. NAME John FitzGerald
13. BIRTHPLACE Unknown
14. MAIDEN NAME Norah Gillan
15. BIRTHPLACE Unknown
16. (A) INFORMANT Mrs Marie Meagher
(B) ADDRESS Long Beach Calif

17. (A) Burial (B) DATE Nov 28 - 1940
(C) PLACE Calvary Cemetery Los Angeles
18. (A) EMBALMER'S SIGNATURE LICENSE NO. 1661
(B) FUNERAL DIRECTOR McNerney Mortuary
ADDRESS 570 - 5th St. San Pedro Calif

19. (A) NOV 26 1940 DATE FILED

20. DATE OF DEATH: MONTH November DAY 26 YEAR 1940 HOUR 1 MINUTE 5 A.M.

21. MEDICAL CERTIFICATE
I HEREBY CERTIFY, THAT I ATTENDED THE DECEASED FROM Nov. 12 1940 TO Nov. 26 1940 THAT I LAST SAW H alive ON Nov. 25 1940 AND THAT DEATH OCCURRED ON THE DATE AND HOUR STATED ABOVE.
IMMEDIATE CAUSE OF DEATH
DUE TO 1. Hypertension
DUE TO 2. Unknown
OTHER CONDITIONS Arteriosclerosis
MAJOR FINDINGS: OF OPERATIONS
OF AUTOPSY
DATE OF OPERATION

22. CORONER'S CERTIFICATE
I HEREBY CERTIFY, THAT I HELD AN AUTOPSY, INQUEST OR INVESTIGATION ON THE REMAINS OF THE DECEASED AND FIND FROM SUCH ACTION THAT DECEASED CAME TO DEATH ON THE DATE AND HOUR STATED ABOVE

23. IF DEATH WAS DUE TO EXTERNAL CAUSES, FILL IN THE FOLLOWING:
(A) ACCIDENT, SUICIDE, OR HOMICIDE
(B) DATE OF INJURY
(C) WHERE DID INJURY OCCUR
CITY OR TOWN COUNTY STATE
(D) DID INJURY OCCUR IN OR ABOUT HOME, ON FARM, IN INDUSTRIAL PLACE, OR IN PUBLIC PLACE? WHILE AT WORK
(E) MEANS OF INJURY

24. PHYSICIAN'S SIGNATURE

DEATH CERTIFICATE OF EDWARD FITZGERALD - 1920

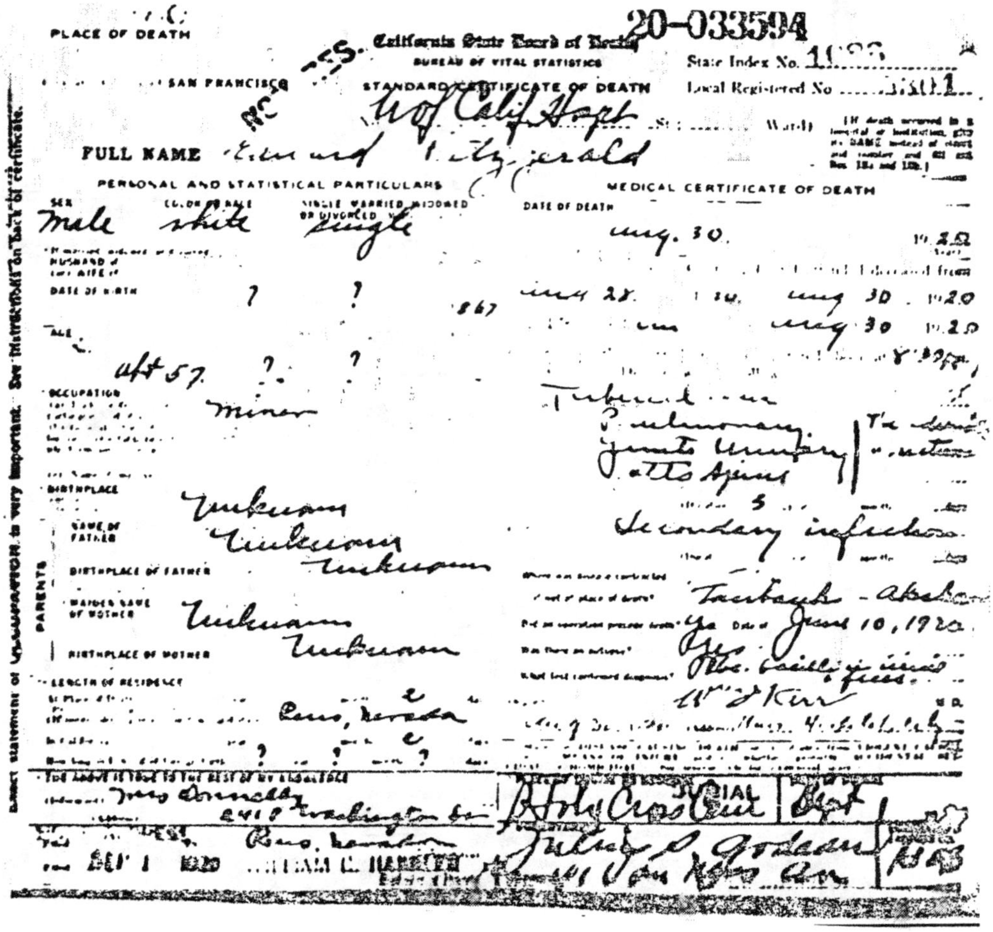

20-033594

PLACE OF DEATH

SAN FRANCISCO

California State Board of Health

BUREAU OF VITAL STATISTICS

STANDARD CERTIFICATE OF DEATH

State Index No.

Local Registered No.

U of Calif Hosp

FULL NAME Edward Fitzgerald

PERSONAL AND STATISTICAL PARTICULARS

MEDICAL CERTIFICATE OF DEATH

SEX Male

COLOR OR RACE white

SINGLE, MARRIED, WIDOWED OR DIVORCED single

DATE OF DEATH Aug. 30, 1920

DATE OF BIRTH ? ? 1867

AGE abt 57 ? ?

OCCUPATION miner

Tuberculosis Pulmonary

Secondary infection

BIRTHPLACE Unknown

NAME OF FATHER Unknown

BIRTHPLACE OF FATHER Unknown

MAIDEN NAME OF MOTHER Unknown

BIRTHPLACE OF MOTHER Unknown

June 10, 1920

Reno, Nevada

Holy Cross Cem

SEP 1 1920

died in California. On the 19th of January 1979, the California Registrar of Vital Statistics sent me copies of two death records for Edward Fitzgeralds' who had died before 1922.

CENSUS EXTRACT
Jefferson County, New York
1880

#172-189 - Town of Antwerp		
FITZGERALD, Lawrence	WM 45 Miner	Ire. Ire. Ire.
Maggie	WF 35 Wife	Ont. Ire. Ire.
William	WM 18 Son	N.Y. Ire. Ont.
Edward	WM 16 Son	N.Y. Ire. Ont.
Michael	WM 14 Son	N.Y. Ire. Ont.
Lawrence	WM 12 Son	N.Y. Ire. Ont.
John	WM 9 Son	N.Y. Ire. Ont.
Charles	WM 6 Son	N.Y. Ire. Ont.
Thomas	WM 2 Son	N.Y. Ire. Ont.
Mary	WF 1 Dau.	N.Y. Ire. Ont.

Edward Fitzgerald, son of Lawrence

The first record was for a "Major Edward H. Fitzgerald, U.S.A. Retired," and it was apparent that he was not the person I was seeking. The other was for Edward Fitzgerald, a "Miner," who had died in a San Francisco hospital on the 30th of August 1920, and he fit the picture nicely to be Jack's cousin. He was listed as a single white male, aged "abt. 57." but his place of birth and parentage were unknown. A Mrs Donnelly was the informant on his record and was probably his landlady. Because of the incomplete nature of this record, I had given it only casual attention at first, but now I'm convinced it is the death record of Edward Fitzgerald, son of Lawrence and Margaret (O'Rielly) Fitzgerald of Gouverneur, New York. Edward was listed with his parents in the 1880 census of Jefferson County, New York as "16" years old, and this 1920 listing with his age "abt. 57" is within a year of that, so there is a good possibility they are one and the same person. I have included a copy of the 1880 census for comparison.

In September of 1978, after I had requested copies of the death records for Anna, Michael, James, and Tinnie, and after I had written a follow-up letter to see what was taking so long for a response, the New York State Department of Health answered my letter and stated the following:

> "...In reply to your inquiry regarding your genealogy request, dated September, we are now searching requests received in April. Please be assured that you will hear from us just as soon as possible..."

They did keep their word, however, and on the 12th of March 1979, I received certified copies of each record I had requested. Each document provided excellent confirming information, but more importantly, two of them; those for Michael and James, listed the Irish places of birth for their parents, John and Margaret (Gillon) Fitzgerald). The father John was listed as born in "Knockskmoling, Ireland," and the mother Margaret was listed as born in "New Town, Ireland." This was, without a doubt, the most exciting information I had yet received, but unfortunately, I couldn't identify either locality in available reference materials at BYU.

DEATH CERTIFICATE OF ANNA (FITZGERALD) SMITH - 1926

1 PLACE OF DEATH (Dist. No. 5907) To be inserted by Registrar — New York State Department of Health — Division of Vital Statistics — 69661

County Westchester

STANDARD CERTIFICATE OF DEATH

STATE OF NEW YORK

Town or Village or City Yonkers (No. 55½ Hudson Street St.; 1 Ward) Registered No. 11

(If death occurred in a hospital or institution, give its NAME instead of street and number)

2 FULL NAME Anna Smith

(Usual place of abode) Residence No. 55½ Hudson St St. 1 Ward. (If nonresident, give city or town and State)

Length of residence in city or town where death occurred 30 yrs. mos. ds. How long in U. S., if of foreign birth? yrs. mos. ds.

PERSONAL AND STATISTICAL PARTICULARS

3 SEX Female — 4 COLOR OR RACE White — 5 SINGLE, MARRIED, WIDOWED, OR DIVORCED (Write the word) Widow

5a IF MARRIED, WIDOWED OR DIVORCED HUSBAND OF (or) WIFE OF William Smith

6 DATE OF BIRTH Oct. (Month) 12 (Day) 1857 (Year)

7 AGE Years 69 Months Days 29 If LESS than 1 day, how many hrs. or min.?

8 OCCUPATION (a) Trade, profession, or particular kind of work At home

(b) General nature of industry, business, or establishment in which employed (or employer)

(c) Name of employer

9 BIRTHPLACE (City or Town) (State or Country) Rossie N.Y.

PARENTS

10 NAME OF FATHER John Fitzgerald

11 BIRTHPLACE OF FATHER (City or Town) (State or Country) W. Stafford Ireland

12 MAIDEN NAME OF MOTHER Margaret Dillon

13 BIRTHPLACE OF MOTHER (City or Town) (State or Country) Unknown Ireland

14 THE ABOVE IS TRUE TO THE BEST OF MY KNOWLEDGE

(Informant) Fennie Fitzgerald

(Address) 55½ Buena Vista Ave.

15 Filed Nov 11, 1926 Francis M. Zeile Registrar

MEDICAL CERTIFICATE OF DEATH

16 DATE OF DEATH Nov (Month) 10 (Day) 1926 (Year)

17 I HEREBY CERTIFY, That I attended deceased from Aug 1 [illegible], 1926, to Nov 10, 1926 that I last saw her alive on Nov 10, 1926 and that death occurred on the date stated above, at [illegible]

The CAUSE OF DEATH* was as follows:

[illegible]

(Duration) yrs. 2 mos. 1 ds.

CONTRIBUTORY [illegible] (Secondary) (Duration) yrs. 3 ds.

18 Where was disease contracted, or injury sustained if not at place of death?

Did an operation precede death? Yes Date of [illegible]

Was there an autopsy? No

What test confirmed diagnosis? [illegible]

(Signed) Phillip [illegible], M. D.

11/11, 1926 (Address) Yonkers

*State the Disease Causing Death, or, in deaths from Violent Causes, state (1) Means and Nature of Injury, and (2) whether Accidental, Suicidal, or Homicidal.

19 PLACE OF BURIAL, CREMATION OR REMOVAL Riverside Cem. Gouverneur, N.Y. — DATE OF BURIAL Nov 13, 1926

20 UNDERTAKER (License No.) 4463 Foley & Flynn Inc. — ADDRESS Yonkers N.Y.

Burial or Transit Permit issued by Francis M. Zeile Date of issue Nov 11 1926

See Instructions on Other Side

NEWSPAPER OBITUARY
The Gouverneur Free Press
Wednesday 17 June 1926

MRS ANNA SMITH DIES IN YONKERS, BURIAL IS HERE

The body of Mrs. Anna Smith, age 70, a former resident of this village, who died at her home in Yonkers Wednesday night, was brought to this village Thursday where funeral services were held Saturday morning at 10 from St. James Catholic Church, of which she was a member for many years.

Mrs. Smith had been in failing health for many months. Sometime ago she underwent an operation and never fully recovered. Her condition grew steadily worse, until her death Wednesday.

She was born in this village and spent her life here until about 20 years ago when she removed with her husband, William Smith, to Yonkers. He was engaged in the horse trading business and it was while in Brazil on a trip in connection with his business that he died. Mrs. Smith continued her residence in Yonkers with her one son, John Smith, who died during the influenza epidemic of 1918.

Mrs. Smith leaves two sisters, Miss Tinnie Fitzgerald of this village and Miss Kate Fitzgerald who resides in the west, and two brothers Michael and James Fitzgerald of this village.

Interment was made in Riverside cemetery.

DEATH CERTIFICATE OF MICHAEL FITZGERALD - 1939

1 PLACE OF DEATH [District No. 4423]

STATE OF NEW YORK

County St Lawrence

Town Gouverneur

Village Gouverneur

City

(No. St. Ward) (If death occurred in a hospital or institution, give its NAME instead of street and number)

New York State Department of Health

DIVISION OF VITAL STATISTICS

CERTIFICATE OF DEATH 39414

Registered No. 6

2 FULL NAME Michael Fitzgerald

3 Residence (Usual place of abode) No. 117 Clinton St. City or Ward, Village Gouverneur State N.Y.

County St Lawrence Town Gouverneur Is residence within limits of city or incorporated village? Yes

4 Length of residence in district where death occurred: Years 53+ Months Days

5 How long in U. S., if of foreign birth? Years Months Days

PERSONAL AND STATISTICAL PARTICULARS

6 SEX: Male

7 COLOR OR RACE: White

8 Single, Married, Widowed, or Divorced (Write the word): Widowed

8a If MARRIED, WIDOWED OR DIVORCED Husband of (or) Wife of: Margaret Leonard

9 DATE OF BIRTH (month, day and year): July 20 1870

10 AGE: Years 69 Months 0 Days 14 If LESS than 1 day, ...hrs. or ...min.

OCCUPATION

11 Trade, profession, or particular kind of work done, as spinner, sawyer, bookkeeper, etc.: Mechanic

12 Industry or business in which work was done, as silk mill, sawmill, bank, etc.: Marble Quarry

13 Date deceased last worked at this occupation (month and year)

14 Total time (years) spent in this occupation

15 BIRTHPLACE (City or Town) (State or Country): Rossie New York

FATHER

16 NAME: John Fitzgerald

17 BIRTHPLACE (City or Town) (State or Country): Kilkenny [?] Ireland

MOTHER

18 MAIDEN NAME: Margaret Ditton [?]

19 BIRTHPLACE (City or Town) (State or Country): Newtown Ireland

20 THE ABOVE IS TRUE TO THE BEST OF MY KNOWLEDGE (Signature of Informant): Lynn A. Spragu[e]

(Address) Gouverneur N.Y.

21 PLACE OF BURIAL, CREMATION OR REMOVAL: Riverside [cemetery] Gouverneur — DATE OF BURIAL: Aug. 7 1939

22 UNDERTAKER: Lynn A. Sprague — (Registration) 1375 — (Address) Gouverneur N.Y.

23 Filed Aug 7 1939 [illegible] Registrar

MEDICAL CERTIFICATE OF DEATH

24 DATE OF DEATH (month, day and year): August 4 1939

25 I HEREBY CERTIFY, That I attended deceased from Feby 1939, to Aug 4, 1939

I last saw h[im] alive on Aug 3, 1939

To the best of my knowledge, death occurred on the date stated above, at 12:40 P.m.

CAUSE OF DEATH*: Carcinoma of Rectum — DURATION OF CONDITION: Yrs. Mos. 6 Dys.

CONTRIBUTORY CAUSES

(a)

(b)

(c) 46.7

(d)

26 Where was disease contracted, or injury sustained?

27 Name of operation, if any ... Date

Condition for which performed.

Organ or part affected

28 What laboratory test assisted diagnosis? Biopsy

29 Was there an autopsy?

(Signed) Harry L. Mills M.D.

Aug 7 1939 (Address) Gouverneur N.Y.

*See reverse side for instructions

Burial or Removal Permit issued by E. M. McCarran [?] Dep. Date of issue Aug 7 1939

THIS CERTIFICATE MUST BE FILED WITH THE LOCAL REGISTRAR WITHIN 72 HOURS AFTER DEATH

NEWSPAPER OBITUARY
The Gouverneur Tribune Press
Wednesday 9 August 1939

FUNERAL SERVICES HELD FOR MICHAEL FITZGERALD

A solemn high mass of requiem was celebrated Monday morning for Michael Fitzgerald, 69, former marble quarry worker, who died Friday afternoon at the home of his sister, Miss Tinnie Fitzgerald, Clinton Street, where he had resided the past four years. Celebrants of the mass in St. James Church were Rt. Rev. Cornelius J. Crowley and Rev. William E. Capron. Burial was in Riverside Cemetery.

Mr. Fitzgerald was born in Rossie on July 20, 1870, the son of John and Margaret Dillon Fitzgerald. His father was employed in the Rossie lead mines. When Michael Fitzgerald was a small boy the family moved to Gouverneur and he resided in this village all his life. His father and an older brother were employed as miners in the Caledonia Iron Ore Mines at Kein's. He himself started work in marble quarries here as a young man and was employed in the quarries until they shut down several years ago.

He married in 1893 Miss Margaret Leonard of Gouverneur who survives. He was a member of the Gouverneur fire dept. for many years in the days when the firemen wore red flannel shirts and large fire helmets. He was a member of the exempt firemen's association of Gouverneur. he was a member of St. James Roman Catholic Church.

Surviving besides the widow and sister are another sister, Mrs. Margaret Pound of San Pedro, Calif., 3 sons, Leslie of Utica, Clarence of Syracuse and Stanley of Yonkers; one brother James Fitzgerald of Gouverneur, and one granddaughter.

DEATH CERTIFICATE OF JAMES FITZGERALD - 1942

New York State Department of Health
DIVISION OF VITAL STATISTICS
CERTIFICATE OF DEATH

53261

Dist. No. (To be inserted by registrar)

Registered No. 62

1 PLACE OF DEATH: STATE OF NEW YORK
County St. Lawrence
Town Gouverneur
Village Gouverneur
City
No. 117 Clinton St. Ward
(If a hospital or institution give its NAME instead of street and number)
Length of stay: -
In hospital or institution ...... yrs. ...... mos. ...... days
In town, village or city 60 yrs. ...... mos. ...... days

2 USUAL RESIDENCE OF DECEASED: (If an institution, give place of residence prior to admission)
State New York
County St. Lawrence
Town Gouverneur
Village or City Gouverneur
No. Clinton St.
Is residence within limits of city or incorporated village? Yes
2a Citizen of foreign country (alien)? No (Yes or no)
If yes, name country —

3 Full Name James Fitzgerald
4 (a) Social Security No. —
4 (b) If Veteran, Name War —
5 Sex male
6 Color or Race white
7 Single, Married, Widowed, or Divorced (Write the word) single
8 If Married, Widowed or Divorced, Name of Husband (or) Wife — Age if alive ...... years
9 Date of Birth (month, day, year) Jan. 6. 1872
10 Age Years 70 Months 8 Days 19 If Less than 1 day ...... hrs. or ...... min.
11 Usual occupation Laborer
12 Industry or business State Highway
13 Birthplace (State or Country) [illegible]
14 Name John Fitzgerald
15 Birthplace (City or Town) (State or Country) [illegible]
16 Maiden Name Margaret [illegible]
17 Birthplace (City or Town) (State or Country) [illegible]
18 The above is true to the best of my knowledge
Informant's own signature Thomas A. Fitzgerald
Address Gouverneur N.Y.
19 [illegible] Gouverneur Sept 27 1942
20 Funeral Director [illegible]
Address Gouverneur N.Y.
Registration No. 1373
21 Date received Sept 27 1942 E. M. [illegible] Registrar
Burial or Removal Permit issued by [illegible] Deputy Date of issue Sept 27/1942

MEDICAL CERTIFICATION
22 DATE OF DEATH (Month, Day and Year) Sept. 25th. 1942
23 I HEREBY CERTIFY, That I attended deceased from Sept 22, 1942, to Sept 25, 1942
I last saw him alive on Sept 25, 1942
To the best of my knowledge, death occurred on the date stated above, at 8 P. m.
Immediate cause of death Cerebral Hemorrhage — Duration 4
Due to Hypertension — 2
and Myocarditis
Due to
Other conditions (Include pregnancy within 3 months of death)
Major findings: Of operations
937 Date
Of autopsy
What laboratory test was made?
24 If death was due to external causes, fill in the following:
(a) Accident, suicide, or homicide (specify)
(b) Date of occurrence
(c) Where did injury occur? 83 (City or town) (County) (State)
(d) Did injury occur in or about home, on farm, in industrial place, in public place? (Specify type of place) While at work?
(e) Means of injury
25 Signature [illegible] M. D.
Address Gouverneur Date 9-26-42

NEWSPAPER OBITUARY
The Gouverneur Tribune Press
Wednesday 30 September 1942

JAMES FITZGERALD, 70, DIES AFTER LONG ILLNESS

James Fitzgerald, 70, lifelong resident of the Gouverneur area, passed to his reward Friday night about 9:00 PM at his home, 117 Clinton Street, after an illness of several years. He suffered a stroke the previous Tuesday.

He was born at Rossie Jan. 6, 1872, the son of John and Margaret Dillon Fitzgerald, and during his early childhood his family lived at Spraqueville for a few years.

After obtaining his education in Spragueville and Gouverneur, he worked at the Gouverneur marble quarries in the early days when the industry flourished here. Later he became night patrolman and served on the village police force for 16 years.

retiring from police work, he was employed for some time at the milk plant now operated by the Pioneer Ice Cream Division of the Borden Co. he was later employed at the Capital International Co. Mill and on state road patrol work. Mr. Fitzgerald had lived with his sister at 117 Clinton Street for about 16 years. He was a member of St. James Catholic Church and the Sacred Heart League of that Church

Surviving are one sister, Miss Tinnie Fitzgerald; a brother-in-law, Homer Clapp of Watertown; a niece, Mrs. Meager of Long Beach, Calif. and eight nephews; Ross Clapp and Roy Clapp of Watertown, Stanley Fitzgerald of Yonkers, Leslie Fitzgerald of Utica, Clarence Fitzgerald of Syracuse, Roy Pound and Charles Pound of El Paso, Texas.

Funeral Services were held at St. James Catholic Church at 10:00 AM yesterday, Rt. Rev. Mesgr. C. J. Crowley, Pastor, officiating, assisted by Rev. Fredrick Pshue. Burial was in Riverside Cemetery.

DEATH CERTIFICATE OF TINNEY (TINNIE) FITZGERALD - 1961

New York State Department of Health
OFFICE OF VITAL RECORDS

44263

Dist. No. 4483
To be inserted by registrar

CERTIFICATE OF DEATH

Registered No. 46

1. PLACE OF DEATH, STATE OF NEW YORK
a. COUNTY St. Lawerence
b. TOWN Gouverneur
e. LENGTH OF STAY IN TOWN, CITY OR VILLAGE 85 Yr.
c. CITY OR VILLAGE Gouverneur
d. NAME OF HOSPITAL OR INSTITUTION (If not in hospital or institution, give street address or location) Edw. John Noble Hosp.

2. USUAL RESIDENCE (Where deceased lived. If institution: residence before admission).
a. STATE New York
b. COUNTY St. Lawerence
c. TOWN Gouverneur
d. CITY OR VILLAGE Gouverneur
Is residence within its corporate limits? YES [X] NO [ ]
e. STREET ADDRESS 117 Clinton
f. IS RESIDENCE ON FARM? YES [ ] NO [X]

3. NAME OF DECEASED (Type or Print) Tinnie Fitzgerald
4. DATE OF DEATH (Month) June (Day) 12 (Year) 1961
5. SEX F
6. COLOR OR RACE W
7. SINGLE, MARRIED, WIDOWED, DIVORCED (Specify) Single
8. IF MARRIED, WIDOWED OR DIVORCED, Name of Husband (or) Wife Single
9. DATE OF BIRTH Dec. 19, 1875
10. AGE (In years last birthday) 85
IF UNDER 1 YEAR Months Days
IF UNDER 24 HRS. Hours Min.
11. BIRTHPLACE (State or foreign country) Gouverneur, N.Y.
12. CITIZEN OF WHAT COUNTRY? U.S.
13a. USUAL OCCUPATION (Give kind of work done during most of working life, even if retired) Cateress
13b. KIND OF BUSINESS OR INDUSTRY Serving Food
14. FATHER'S NAME John Fitzgerald
15. MOTHER'S MAIDEN NAME Margaret Dillon
16. WAS DECEASED EVER IN U.S. ARMED FORCES? (Yes, no, or unknown) (If yes, give war or dates of service) No
17. SOCIAL SECURITY NO. None
18. INFORMANT'S NAME Mae Fitzgerald ADDRESS Gouverneur, N.Y.

MEDICAL CERTIFICATION

19. CAUSE OF DEATH (Enter only one cause on a line)
PART I. DEATH WAS CAUSED BY:
IMMEDIATE CAUSE (a) Auricular fibrillation + cardiac decompensation
INTERVAL BETWEEN ONSET AND DEATH: 1 wk.
Conditions, if any, which gave rise to above immediate cause (a), stating the underlying cause last.
DUE TO (b) Myocarditis — 4-5 yrs.
DUE TO (c) Arterio Sclerosis + Chronic Nephritis
PART II. OTHER SIGNIFICANT CONDITIONS CONTRIBUTING TO DEATH BUT NOT RELATED TO THE TERMINAL CONDITION GIVEN IN PART I(a)
Chronic Arthritis
4331
20. WAS AUTOPSY PERFORMED? YES [ ] NO [X]

21a. ACCIDENT, SUICIDE, HOMICIDE (Specify)
21b. DESCRIBE HOW INJURY OCCURRED. (Enter nature of injury in Part I or Part II of item 19.)
STATE DEPT. OF HEALTH RECEIVED
21c. TIME OF INJURY Hour Month, Day, Year a. m. p. m.
21d. INJURY OCCURRED While at Work [ ] Not While at Work [ ]
21e. PLACE OF INJURY (e.g., in or about home, farm, factory, street, office bldg., etc.)
21f. WHERE DID INJURY OCCUR? City or town County State

22. I hereby certify that I attended the deceased from June 5, 1961, to June 12, 1961, that I last saw the deceased alive on June 12, 1961, and that death occurred at 1:15 a.m., from the causes and on the date stated above.
Signature: Francis L. Mills M.D.
Address: Gouverneur, N.Y.
22c. DATE SIGNED June 13 1961

Burial, Cremation, Removal: Riverside Cem. Gouverneur, N.Y.
Date: 6/14 61
Signature of Undertaker: James A. Spencer Jr.
Address of Undertaker: Gouverneur, N.Y.
License No.: 104725
Signature of Registrar: Mildred Ryan

Issued by: [signature] Deputy Registrar
Date of Issue: June 13 1961

NEWSPAPER OBITUARY
The Gouverneur Tribune Press
Wednesday 14 June 1961

MISS TINNIE FITZGERALD GOUVERNEUR NATIVE DIES

Miss Tinnie Fitzgerald, 85, 117 Clinton Street, died 11:10 A.M. Monday in the E. J. Noble Hospital, Gouverneur where she had been a patient since May 30. She had been in ill health with arthritis and a heart condition for a number of years.

Funeral services will be at the St. James Church at 10 A.M. today, (Wednesday) with Very Rev. Msgr. R. J. McCarthy officiating. A rosary was recited at the Sprague funeral home Tuesday evening. Burial will be in Riverside cemetery. Several nieces and nephews survive her.

Miss Fitzgerald was born Dec. 19, 1875 in Gouverneur, the daughter of John & Margaret D. Fitzgerald. She attended Gouverneur schools. She worked as a cateress most of her life retiring because of ill health. She was a member of the St. James Church.

The Harold B. Lee Library at Brigham Young University had an excellent map collection, and it had several good gazetteers and atlases for Ireland, but I couldn't locate Knockskmoling in any of them. I did find a "Newtown" as a suburb of Dublin, which made sense for Margaret's place of birth, but the reference for John was more elusive. I consulted with reference personnel at the Library and also talked with Irish specialists in the History Department, but none of them could help me solve the problem. I even made a special trip to the Family History Library in Salt Lake City and consulted with Irish Specialists there, but they too were unable to locate Knockskmoling in their reference books.

Here again, I had one of those unusual experiences where help from an unexpected quarter provided the solution to a difficult problem. At the time I was trying to identify the town of "Knockskmoling" in Ireland, my son Jerry was serving an LDS mission in that country, and of course we were corresponding with one another. He was then billeted at #4 Hanover Place, Coleraine, Derry, North Ireland, and in one of my letters to him, I mentioned that I had been trying to identify an Irish town but was having little success. I didn't ask him to conduct any genealogical research for me, knowing that he was busily engaged in his own work, but I did ask him to keep his eyes open, and if the opportunity arose, "he might try and locate the town of Knockskmoling for his Dear Old Dad." Well, some time later (August 31, 1979) I received a large brown envelope from him with several xerox pages listing Irish place names, a detailed map of Wexford County in Ireland, and a letter from the Public Record Office of Ireland saying:

> "Knockskemolin, in County Wexford, is situated near Gorey, in the parish of Kilmannagh."

Also included in the package, was a list giving the name and address of the incumbent minister at Kilmannagh. What more could a person ask for? Jerry confided to me later that he had simply picked up the telephone and called the Public Record Office in Dublin, asking them for help in identifying an Irish place name. They had solved the problem in a very short time and had sent him the supporting materials without charge. He then forwarded the information to me, and we both benefitted from the experience. (see copies of Public Record Office letter and map which follow)

On September 7, 1979, I wrote to the incumbent priest at Kilmannagh, asking him to search his records for possible entries of John and Lawrence Fitzgerald, but I received no reply. However, more than a year later (July 1981) I received a letter from "Seamas S. de Val," parish priest at Kilmannagh who explained what had happened to my earlier correspondence. (see copy of letter which follows)

Evidently, after the English took control of Ireland, and after Protestants were strongly established in the North, the Catholic Irish were forbidden to keep church records. Many of the records which had been kept were destroyed by the English, and unfortunately, many of those which remained were destroyed later by the forces of nature. The Catholic priests were evidently not permitted to continue their record keeping until well after 1800, which was too late for our Fitzgerald problem, so my efforts had to return to the family's American roots. Hopefully, the family's early Irish roots are recorded elsewhere and will come to light sometime in the future.

LETTER DATED 28 AUGUST 1979 FROM AIDAN O'ROURKE

AN OIFIG TAIFEAD POIBLÍ
PUBLIC RECORD OFFICE OF IRELAND

Na Ceithre Chúirt Baile Átha Cliath 7
Four Courts, Dublin 7.

Do thagairt Your reference	Do scéala dar dáta Your communication of	Ár dtagairt Our reference	Teil. Tel. 01—[redacted]	Dáta Date
		1657/12	725275	28 August 1979

J

Mr. Jerry Wright,
4 Hanover Place,
Coleraine,
Derry,
N. Ireland.

Dear Mr. Wright,

Thank you for your telephone enquiry of 27 August.

Knockskemolin, in County Wexford, is situated near Gorey, in the parish of Kilmannagh. The district can be found on sheet 21 of the Wexford 6" Ordnance Survey Maps.

LETTER DATED 16 JULY 1981 FROM SEAMAS S. DE VAL

Oulart, Gorey,
Co. Wexford, Ireland
16 July 1981

NORMAN E. WRIGHT
520 East 200 North
Pleasant Grove, Utah 84062

Dear Mr. Wright,

I received your letter dated 12 June 1981 in which you seek information concerning John Fitzgerald, born 26 September 1815 at Knockskemolin. I regret that I can give you no information about this person as the register of this parish begins only in 1824. The earliest occurrence of the name Fitzgerald is in a marriage entry dated 9 November 1826, the marriage of James Fitzgerald and Margaret Monihan. No address is given. The name Fitzgerald is met with only rarely in the register for that period so that it is not unlikely that James was a relative of John.

You mention in your letter that you wrote last year and did not receive a reply. I am sorry to say that your previous letter, which I received, was addressed to "Parish Priest, Kilmannah Parish" (--recte Kilnamanah). Now, the name of this, the Roman Catholic parish, is Qulart, while the name of the corresponding Church of Ireland (Protestant) parish is Kilnamanah. It would appear that your first letter was delivered by the mailman to the clergyman of Kilnamanah parish, that is, the rector, Reverend Robert Stuart, who, I regret to say, has since died. He had been ill for some time during last year and probably never got round to answering your letter.

Although I have been unable to assist you on this occasion, I would be most willing to help in any way I can, and if you think I can give you any further information do not hesitate to write to me.

In view of the fact that I have not unearthed any information for you, I shall not cash your check!

I am Yours sincerely,
Seamas S. de Val
(parish priest)

P.S. Just when I had finished typing this letter, I discovered another entry which may be of interest to you:

Baptism of WALTER FITZGERALD of Noscomolin(sic),
child of WILLIAM FITZGERALD and
ANNE DEMPSY on 18 August 1826

MAP OF IRELAND SHOWING TOWN OF GOREY IN WEXFORD COUNTY

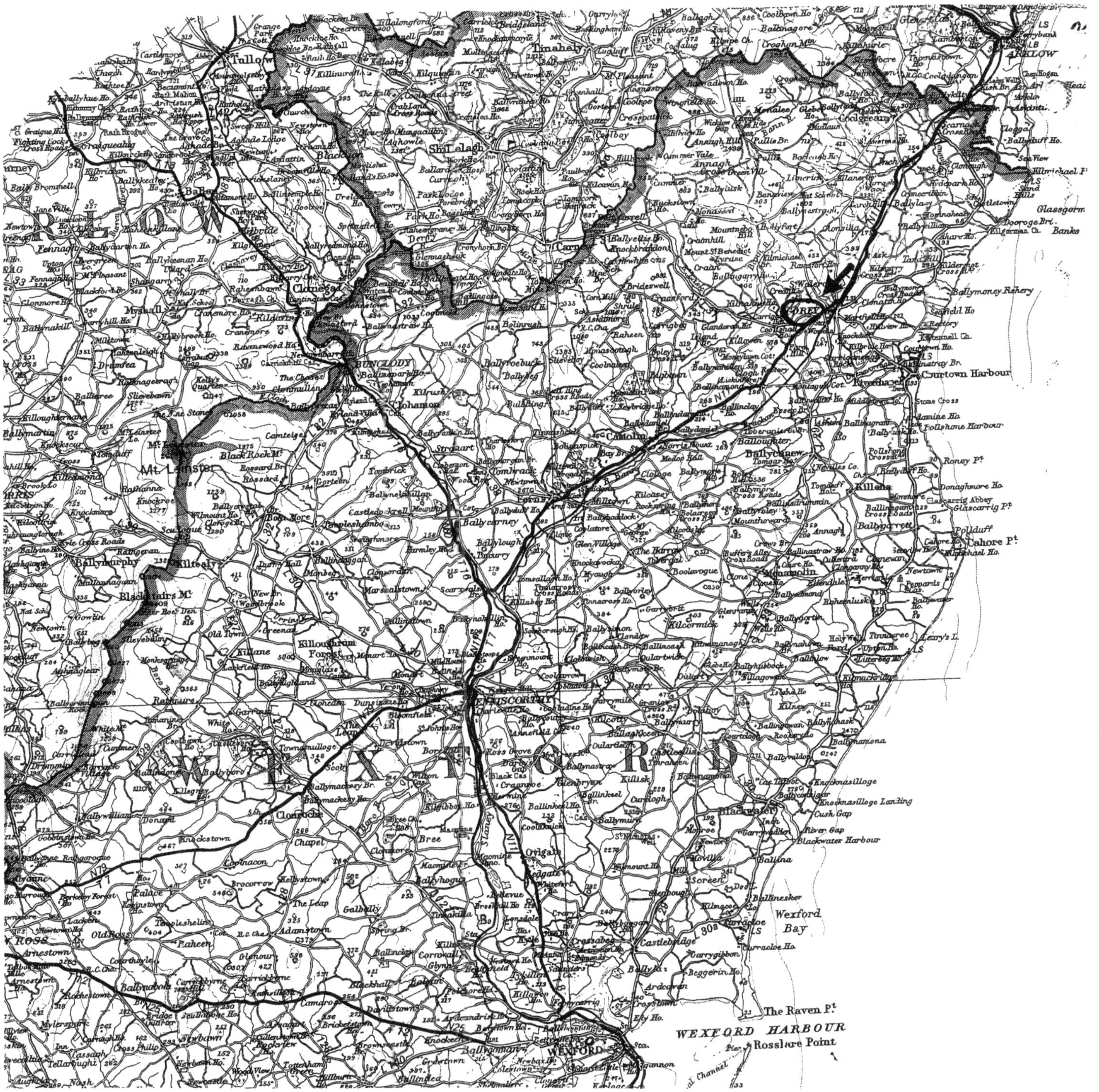

MODERN CENSUS RECORDS REVEAL MUCH

Shortly after receiving the informative death records for Anna, Michael, James, and Tinnie Fitzgerald, I began checking New York State census records, which had recently been microfilmed and were on file in Salt Lake City. New York took decennial censuses between the Federal enumerations, and those 1855 through 1925 were nominal. Unfortunately, the 1855 and 1875 records for St. Lawrence County were missing, and our John Fitzgerald family was residing in Canada when the 1865 census was enumerated, so I was unable to locate them in the earlier state records, but I was able to locate certain members of the family in the 1905 and 1925 schedules.

NEW YORK STATE CENSUS EXTRACTS
St. Lawrence County
1905

Town of Gouverneur; 2nd District, Page 28
FITZGERALD, Margaret (Head) 72 FW Housework Ireland (65 years in country)
James (Son)33 MW Night WatchmanU.S.

Town of Rossie; 2nd District, Page 10			
WHITNEY, Vivian	(Head)	28 FW Hotel Keeper	Canada
Dewit B.	(Husband)	39 MW Day Laborer	U.S.
FITZGERALD, Michael	(Servant)	35 MW Bartender	U.S.
Town of Gouverneur; 1st District, Page 3			
IRWIN, Andrew	(Head)	55 MW	Canada
Nina F.	(Wife)	50 FW Housework	U.S.
Fredrick	(Son)	22 MW At School	U.S.
FITZGERALD, Tinney	(Servant)	29 FW Servant	U.S.

Margaret, Michael, and Tinney in the 1905 New York State Census

A Michael Fitzgerald was found listed as "Bartender" in the household of one Vivian Whitney (Hotel Keeper) in the 1905 state census for Rossie, New York; I had found that listing in the original books at the court house in Canton on my 1968 trip, but I had failed to record the particulars. I also located a "Tinney" Fitzgerald listed as "Servant" in the household of Andrew Irwin at Gouverneur. A Margaret and James Fitzgerald were listed at #10 Wall Street in Gouverneur and were undoubtedly family. Interestingly, Margaret was identified as having been "65 years in (the) country," and if that fact was correct, she would have entered the U.S. in 1840 rather than in 1850 as her 1911 obituary indicated.

In the 1925 schedules, a James, Tinnie, and Stanley Fitzgerald were all listed together, living on Wall Street in Gouverneur. James was shown as the "head" of household with Tinnie listed as "sister" and Stanley shown as a "brother." Stanley was actually a nephew of James, rather than a brother, but that's the way it was shown. I also located three of Lawrence Fitzgerald's children in the 1925 enumeration for Gouverneur; all living in "Hailesboro." Charles Fitzgerald was shown as the head of household with Thomas E. listed as "brother" and Mae A. as "sister." According to earlier interviews with Emerson Clapp and Mary Smith

NEW YORK STATE CENSUS EXTRACTS
St. Lawrence County
1925

Town of Gouverneur; 35 1/2 Wall Street

FITZGERALD, James	(Head)	WM	52	Repairman	United States
Tinnie	(sister)	WF	50	Housekeeper	United States
Stanley	(brother)	WM	26	Pharmacy	United States

#9 Hailesboro

FITZGERALD, Charles	(Head)	WM	50	Mechanic	United States
Thomas E.	(brother)	WM	43	Mechanic	United States
Mae A.	(sister)	WF	46	Housekeeper	United States

James and Tinnie, their nephew Stanley, and their cousins Charles, Thomas, and Mae in 1925

Fitzgerald, the other children of Lawrence and Margaret (O'Rielly) Fitzgerald had gone west; and their son John, who had married Mary Smith in 1918, was supposedly living in Gouverneur, but I didn't locate him in the State schedules.

After these state census searches were made, and after having received the modern death records for Michael, James, Tinnie, and Anna (Smith) Fitzgerald, I initiated searches to locate newspaper obituary notices for each of them. My first attempts were only partly productive, primarily because copies of the appropriate newspapers were not available to me, but later efforts really paid off when Cory Meyerink came to my rescue. Cory had been a student of mine at BYU and had heard the Jack Fitzgerald story several times over. After graduation, he moved to Michigan and was doing some private genealogical research, and I hadn't heard from him until the 7th of August 1979 when he gave me a call. He said he was going to visit his sister in Westboro, Massachusetts and would be happy to do some research for me in New York on his way, if there was a need. His call had come at just the right time, and I authorized him to spend two or three days working on the Fitzgerald problem in St. Lawrence County, New York. The newspaper obituaries he found, and the additional information which he provided, opened new Fitzgerald horizons and added a wealth of information to the Jack Fitzgerald saga. He found obituary notices for Michael, James, Tinnie, and Anna (Smith) Fitzgerald, and as an additional bonus, he located a New York newspaper account of Jack (John) Fitzgerald's murder in 1901. (see obituary notices next to their respective death certificates above)

From the detail provided in Anna's obituary, it would seem that her husband William Smith was an electrical engineer rather than a horse trader, as one obituary states, but he probably did die in Brazil. It is also interesting to note that one notice said Anna's son John died in the flu epidemic of 1917 while the other said 1918; either one could have been correct, because that epidemic occurred in both of those years. This also corrected Jessie Link Fitzgerald's statement that Anna's son John died in "1927."

The statement that Anna was survived by "Mrs. Jacob Pounds, formerly Miss Kate Fitzgerald, who resides in the west" was interesting but somewhat puzzling. Anna's sister "Margaret" was then residing in the west, but she was "Mrs. William Pound." Was there another daughter in the family named "Kate" (Catherine) who married a "Jacob Pound" or did this reference pertain to Margaret who married William Pound? The 1870 census of Rossie, New

CENSUS EXTRACT			
St. Lawrence County, New York			
1870			
#94/89 - Town of Rossie			
FITZGERALD, John	**50 M**	**Work in Ore Bed**	**Canada**
Margaret	**40 F**	**Keeps House**	**Canada**
Anna	**18 F**	**At Home**	**New York**
John	**10 M**		**New York**
Maggie	**9 F**		**New York**
Catherine	**8 F**		**New York**
Amy	**4 F**		**New York**
Michael	**2 M**		**New York**

John and Margaret Fitzgerald family in 1870

York did list a Catherine (see above) in the John Fitzgerald family, so there was a Catherine (Kate), and she may well have married a Jacob Pound and moved west. There is a problem with that, however, because her mother's 1911 obituary only mentions one Pound as a survivor ("Mrs. William Pound" whom we know to be Margaret). A Catherine did exist, but other than the 1870 census and the Anna Smith obituary reference, I have been unable to identify her further. Perhaps additional information about her will come to light in the future.

Each of the newspaper obituary notices located provided a wealth of information, particularly when it came to identifying family members, and in spite of the fact they did contained some errors, they were invaluable in helping us reconstruct the Fitzgerald family.

A TELEPHONE INTERVIEW WITH EMERSON

On the 2nd day of January, 1979, while visiting with President Lunceford at his Orem home, we placed a long distance telephone call to Ogdensburg, New York and spoke with Emerson Clapp, a nephew of Jack with whom we had consulted in 1978. He provided us with additional information about his own family, and he disclosed that he, in fact, had the watch which had originally belonged to Jack Fitzgerald of Park City, Utah. This came as a real shock to us, because we had spoken to him about the watch previously without results. The facts from his interview follow:

He (Emerson Clapp) was born 11 February 1917 in Watertown, New York and married Faye Kingsley on the 10th of May 1940. He and Faye had a daughter, Nancy, born 26 September 1947 in Watertown, who married Henry Edward Parker II; Nancy and Henry were living in Glenns Falls, New York.

> **Emerson and Faye also had a son, David, born 19 January 1957 in Ogdensburg. David was not married at the time and was living with his parents in Ogdensburg.**
>
> **Carroll Joseph Clapp was Emerson's older brother and was born 18 September 1913 in Watertown, New York. He married Marilyn Reader and they had three children; a son Carroll who lived in California; a daughter Mary Lynn who married Gary Conner and lived at Union Springs, New York; and a daughter**

Susan Clapp who was working in Albany, New York and was a college graduate. Susan was not married at the time of the interview.

Emerson said his brother Carroll had open heart surgery about two months ago (November 1978) and was living in Atlanta, Georgia. He said Carroll handles real estate business for what used to be the Kentucky Fried Chicken Organization in Atlanta.

Emerson said he also had a sister, Dorothy, who first married a Mr. Cody, who died, then she married James Kostyk, but they were separated. Dorothy was living in Watertown, New York at the time of the interview.

Emerson's father, Thomas Roy Clapp, had a brother, Ross Clapp, who married Mabel Fletcher. Ross died about ten years ago (1968). Emerson said Mabel wasn't quite right when she was old and sold the family home for a very small sum of money. This was evidently the home of Homer Clapp and Mary (Fitzgerald) Clapp, Emerson's grandparents. Emerson said he got nothing from his grandfather's estate, but a nephew of Mabel, Robert Shaw (a retired Air Force man who lived in San Francisco), got the proceeds and family items from the estate of Ross as well as the family items belonging to Homer and Mary.

Emerson said that he had a watch which was given to him 30 or 40 years earlier by his father, Thomas Roy Clapp, and it could well have been the watch which belonged to Jack Fitzgerald of Park City, Utah. He said it was a plain gold watch, with no cover, but is was highly prized by him.

Emerson said his mother, Katherine Loughlin Clapp, died 21 February 1978 at Ogdensburg, New York and was buried in the Glenwood Cemetery at Watertown, New York. He said his mother's maiden name was Carroll and that's why the oldest son carried that name.

As the interview concluded, Emerson expressed his appreciation for the work we were doing in attempting to gather the genealogy of the Fitzgerald family, and he said he would be happy to assist in any other way that he could. He had been unusually kind to us when we consulted with him at Watertown, New York on our 1978 trip, and he remained a gentlemen through this later interview.

It had been our understanding that Ross Clapp, an uncle of Emerson, had possession of Jack Fitzgerald's watch, and President Lunceford was a little chagrined to learn that Emerson actually had it. One of President Lunceford's remaining goals, however, was to gain possession of that watch, because it did belong to his grandfather Jack, and he believed he should have first right to it. Notwithstanding the frustration he felt in not being able to gain immediate possession of it, President Lunceford was thrilled with the family information Emerson provided, and a deep feeling of kinship continued between the two men.

After our interview with Emerson, we began to summarize the Fitzgerald family information which had been gathered since work first began on Jack's genealogy in 1958, and we were astonished with the results. It had been twenty years since Thelda Moss Lunceford first established the account with the Genealogical Society, and very little information had been located during the first ten years, but since our trip to New York in 1968, a wealth of family information had been gathered, and it continued to come forth in abundance.

When research on the line first began, we knew little more than Jack (John) Fitzgerald's date and place of death. We knew that he had married Martha Eleanor Lunceford in Park City, Utah in 1889, that they had a child, Joseph, in 1890, and that Martha and Jack divorced in 1895, but we knew little else about him. Now, we had excellent genealogical facts on his parents and his brothers and sisters; on several aunts and uncles, and on several nieces and nephews. We had learned the Fitzgerald and Gillon family's Irish places of origin, and a vast amount of historical information had been gathered which pertained directly to the family.

As our research efforts were concluding in 1978, the details about Jack's untimely death and murder came to light and served as a fitting conclusion to the Jack Fitzgerald narrative.

JACK'S MURDER

I have purposefully left the details and circumstances surrounding Jack Fitzgerald's 1901 murder for the conclusion of the book. They were most unusual, and in many ways unjust and unfair, but they were part of one family's heritage and should be considered as such. Jack was murdered in cold blood, of that there is little doubt, but there were also extenuating circumstances indicating he was the aggressor in a dispute. His assailant certainly didn't have to resort to the drastic action taken, but he did, and Jack suffered the physical consequences. It can be truthfully said that Jack paid the ultimate price for his aggressive actions, but according to one newspaper account, "...before he died Fitzgerald exonerated James from all blame and requested that he be freed..." Another said: "...After languishing several hours it was seen that he (Fitzgerald) could not live and was told that his end was near. He received the fatal news calmly and asked that James be set free as he himself was the aggressor in the quarrel..." In my mind, through this last act, Jack asked his assailant for forgiveness; the best thing he could possibly do before dying. We can only hope that his assailant finally expressed a similar contrition.

In 1968, after Katherine L. Clapp told me that Jack Fitzgerald had been murdered, I wrote to Ms. Mitchell at the Gouverneur Public Library and asked her to try and locate a newspaper account of that event. I reasoned that family members in New York would have learned of it soon after it happened, and perhaps a local paper would have carried an account of it. Ms. Mitchell reported to me later that she did make a search for the account, but she was unable to find a reference to it; perhaps she didn't extent her search far enough, because it was surely there.

One of the interesting finds which Cory Meyerink made on his 1979 New York research trip, was a notice of Jack's murder carried in the Gouverneur Free Press on 11 September 1901 (Vol. 20, No. 27, Page 3). Cory located it at the Gouverneur Public Library, the very place Ms. Mitchell had made her searches, and he included it in his report to me dated the 9th of September 1979. It was succinct and to the point, as follows:

> **"John Fitzgerald, a brother of James Fitzgerald, of this village, was murdered in Park City Utah, Aug. 25th. Fitzgerald had trouble with a livery man by the name of James who shot him twice. James has been held for murder."**

My reasoning was all right when it came to thinking an account of Jack's murder might have been carried in New York newspapers, but it was certainly deficient earlier when it came to searching Utah newspapers. True, I had attempted to find a notice of Jack's death in the "Park Record" back in 1958 when research was first begun; and true, I had no idea that he had been murdered, but it is evident that I should have searched newspapers of surrounding towns, such as Coalville and Salt Lake City--my lack of historical research technique in 1958 was only exceeded by my naivety and amateurism. Nevertheless, "what goes around comes around," and Jack's murder finally unfolded before me in a most interesting way, and with an abundant amount of detail as well as excellent documentation.

On the 15th of November 1978, after fall semester had begun at BYU, and after the New York trip with President Lunceford, I was teaching at a genealogical seminar in the Harold B. Lee Library on the BYU campus and was using the Jack Fitzgerald problem as a case study. After I had presented the preliminary facts about his pedigree, a middle aged woman named Robinson (I've forgotten her first name) raised her hand and asked to make a comment. She said she was a historian and had done a lot of research concerning the Park City, Utah area. She remembered an account in a Salt Lake City newspaper of a shooting in Park City in the

time period I was talking about, and to the best of her recollection, it did concern a man named Fitzgerald. She couldn't recall the details, but she was sure of the account, and she was sure it had been reported in the Salt Lake Tribune or the Deseret News. I was excited about her comment, to say the least, and immediately after class, I went directly to the third floor of the Library and located accounts of Jack Fitzgerald's murder in both the Salt Lake Tribune and the Deseret News. A similar article was located in the Coalville Times the following day. Why hadn't I checked any of those newspapers back in 1958 when the Lunceford account was first opened? (see newspaper accounts which follow)

Those newspaper accounts of Jack's murder were astonishing to me, and I was in somewhat of a trance as I read them. Park City, Utah had been well known to me from my youth; I had known many of her people, traveled her streets, eaten in her restaurants; why I had lodged sheep herders at the very hotel where Jack died. My father, my uncles, and my grandfather before them were sheepmen and owned grazing lands east of Park City; over 32 Sections extending north and east to Peoa, Oakley, and the Kamas Valley. Three of my uncles were also important land owners in Coalville, Utah during the early 1900's, running their sheep on the Chalk Creek Range in Summit County.

Park City was a center of activity for all of them, particularly during the springtime when it was lambing season, and when the sheep were being trailed to the summer range, but it was also important in the fall when the sheep were being shipped to the winter range. Prior to World War II, the railroad was critical to the sheep business, and Park City was a center for shipping as well as a supply base for many sheep and cattle men. The Union Pacific Railroad's main line, of course, traversed Ogden through Weber Canyon, and "Echo Junction" was important to Park City traffic through "Silver Creek Junction." But in my youth, there was also a railroad line from Salt Lake City, east through Parley's Canyon to Kimball's Junction and points south as well as east.

Highway 40, America's "National Highway" followed that same route east from Salt Lake City through Parley's Canyon to Kimball's Junction. There, it continued east while many local travelers turned south and found their way past Mecham's Ranch (now Park West) to Park City and Heber City. During my childhood in the 1930's, going to the "sheepherd" during the spring or summer was the most exciting experience I could have. It was a three hour drive in our old two-ton Chevy truck loaded with supplies. We would travel north to 27th South from Mill Creek, then east to Sugar House where 21st South was followed east past the old red State Prison to the mouth of Parley's Canyon. Then we followed a two-lane asphalt highway which traversed the canyon floor several miles, switching back and forth across the railroad tracks, and gradually reaching Mountain Dell Reservoir, which had been constructed in the 1930's and was always a scare for us young children. We could imagine the brakes failing and our truck running over the edge into the water where we would all be drowned; or we would think of a car coming down the canyon out of control, crashing into us and sending us into the deep waters. A road at the top of the Reservoir led north to "East Canyon" and we understood that a person would come out "Emigration Canyon" if he followed it north and west. It wasn't far from Mountain Dell reservoir to an old Texaco service station situated on the south side of the road near a railroad crossing, then it was on to Lambs Canyon, where our family also summered sheep. The climb from Lambs Canyon to Parley's Summit was steep, and it wasn't unusual to see cars stalled along the way with overheated radiators. The railroad crossed the summit through a tunnel, which was south of the main highway, then it took a longer roundabout way to the bottoms on the east side of Parley's summit, passing Jeremy's Ranch and then heading east to Kimball's Junction. The main highway passed directly over Parley's summit, then it followed a steeper route down the east side of the mountain, crossing the railroad tracks a couple of times, then passing Roach's store and heading toward Kimball's Junction where the road branched; one leading east past Bitner's Ranch toward Wanship and Coalville, and the other turning south following the foot of the mountains, passing Mecham's Ranch and finally reaching Park City.

Most everyone stopped at "Coffee John's" for a bite to eat or just to chat; his restaurant was on the main road as one entered Park City or proceeded east and south to Hailstone and Heber City. Coffie John knew all the local people on a first-name basis, and many others as well, and it was exciting to hear them in conversation. A traveler could turn east at Hailstone and pass through Francis, then turn south to Kamas, or he could continue east to Woodland and travel over Wolf Creek summit to Tabiona and Duchesne country. He could also continue south from Hailstone to Heber City and follow the canyon back south and west past Deer Creek Reservoir to Provo.

Sheep and cattle herders on the trail, or those being hired or seeking recreation, spent lots of time walking the streets of Park City, and many of them frequented her establishments. I've heard many an interesting story from the lips of "old timers" who have walked her "boardwalks" after midnight and frequented her "sporting houses." After I told the Jack Fitzgerald story to my father, who was born in 1893 and died in 1990, he said: "Why I've dealt with the McPolin livery stables on many occasions; once when I was a kid, I slept in their hay-loft." He also said he had slept in the Park City Hotel on more than one occasion, the hotel where Jack Fitzgerald died. Yes, Park City held great fascination for me, and now it had become even more important because of the Jack Fitzgerald experience.

PARK CITY MAN SHOT.

Jack Fitzgerald Killed Saturday by Frank James.

Jack Fitzgerald, a prominent man of Park City, was shot last Saturday night by Frank James, also prominent in the Park, and died Sunday night about 7:00 o'clock.

Fitzgerald visited the livery stable of McPolin & James about 2:00 o'clock Sunday morning and asked for a horse to ride up to the Silver King mine. He had at one time been employed by Mcpolin & James, but had been discharged by the latter and bad blood existed between them. He did not get the animal, the reason being that there were none at hand. Fitzgerald did not believe this was the case and a dispute followed in which Fitzgerald struck James in the mouth with his fist. James then drew a revolver and fired, the bullet striking Fitzgerald in the neck, whirling him half around, when another shot was fired striking him in the back and passing clear through the body. A third shot failed to stike the object aimed at.

The wounded man was then taken to the hotel and his injuries attended to, but they were so serious that no hopes were entertained for his recovery and he died at the time stated above.

James was brought to Coalville Tuesday morning by Sherriff Mair and lodged in the county jail. He will be taken back to the Park tomorrow, when a preliminary hearing will be held. James has a family in the Park. He realizes very strongly the seriousness of his crime. His wife came down from the Park with him, but returned the same day.

(Coalville Times; Summit County, Utah; Issue for August 30, 1901; vol. VII No. 34, page 1, column 4; BYU C63; copied 11/17/1978)

FATAL SHOOTING AT PARK CITY

Jack Fitzgerald Shot by Frank James in latter's Livery Stable

----

HE DIED LAST EVENING

Tragedy the Outcome of a Quarrel in Which Fitzgerald Was Said to be the Aggressor.

[Special to the "News"]

Park City, Aug. 26.--At 2 o'clock yesterday morning Frank James shot Jack Fitzgerald during an altercation in the former's livery stable, and the latter died at 7:10 last night. After firing two bullets into Fitzgerald's body James walked directly to the police headquarters and gave himself up. But before he died Fitzgerald exonerated James from all blame and requested that he be freed.

The trouble grew out of James' refusing to let Fitzgerald have a saddle horse. The latter had formerly been employed at the McPolin & James stables and was discharged by James. The consequence was there grew up a mutual enmity between them and when Fitzgerald applied for a horse James told him there was no saddle horse in. Presently another man came in and secured a horse and Fitzgerald was much angered by the slight and stepping up to James dealt him a blow over his mouth with his fist. James quickly drew his gun and fired. The bullet entering Fitzgerald's neck and turned him partially around. James fired again and the bullet passed through the wounded man's body. A third shot was fired but the bullet went wide of the mark.

A large crowd was soon attracted to the scene of the shooting, and while James was accompanied to the jail to give himself up, Fitzgerald was carried to the hotel where he received surgical aid. After languishing several hours it was seen that he could not live and was told that his end was near. He received the fatal news calmly and asked that James be set free as he himself was the aggressor in the quarrel.

Frank James is an old resident of Park City and has a family. Fitzgerald has also resided here a long time, but was unmarried.

(Salt Lake City Deseret News; Issue for Monday, August 26, 1901, page 8, column 3; BYU D45d; copied 11/15/1978)

PARK CITY MAN SHOT

Jack Fitzgerald Is Fatally Wounded by Frank James

TWO BULLETS STRIKE HIM

One Passes Through His Neck, the Other Through His Body--He Succumbed to the Wounds at 7:10 O'clock Last Evening--Tragedy the Outcome of a Quarrel, in Which Fitzgerald Appears to Have Benn the Aggressor--Shooting Occurs at 2 O'clock Sunday Morning.

[TRIBUNE SPECIAL]

Park City, Utah. Aug. 25.--Jack Fitzgerald lies dead at the hotel here. Frank James is in prison charged with killing the first named. Both men are well known in this city.

At 2 o'clock this morning Fitzgerald visited the livery stable of McPolin & James and asked for a horse for the purpose of riding to the Silver King mine. He had formerly been employed by the firm and had been discharged by James, and as a result ill-feeling is said to have existed between the men.

His request for an animal was refused, the reason assigned being that no saddle horses were in. Mr. James was in charge of the barn at the time. His reason for refusing the request was questioned by Fitzgerald, and a dispute followed.

CAUSE OF TRAGEDY

In this dispute Fitzgerald struck James in the mouth with his fist. James then drew a revolver and fired, the bullet striking Fitzgerald in the neck, whirling him half around. Another shot followed, this one striking Fitzgerald in the back and passed clear through his body, tearing his liver on its course. A third shot failed to strike the object aimed at.

WOUNDED MAN DIES

People attracted by the shooting rushed to the stable and Fitzgerald was taken to the hotel. James surrendered to officers and was placed in jail. Surgeons were summoned and the injuries of Fitzgerald attended to, but it was seen that he was fatally hurt, and at 7:10 o'clock tonight he died.

STATEMENT FROM VICTIM

This afternoon County Attorney Callis came up from Coalville to investigate the affair. He secured an antemortem statement from Fitzgerald, which accords with the above statement.

During the day Fitzgerald declined to talk or make any statement regarding the shooting, merely saying, "Oh, turn him loose, I don't want him held." but when told that he could not live late this afternoon made the statment mentioned to the County Attorney.

JAMES HAS A FAMILY

James has a family and is a well known citizen, as is also the victim of the shooting. Tonight the Sheriff was advised to place additional guards around the jail, but this was considered unnecessary.

(Salt Lake Tribune; Issue for Monday, August 26, 1901, page 1, column 1; BYU SA37; copied 11/15/1978)

THE PARK CITY HOMICIDE

Inquest to Be Held Today--James's Examination Saturday.

Park City, Aug. 26.-- The body of John Fitzgerald, who was killed by Frank James yesterday, was taken to Undertaker Richardson's, where it was viewed by the Coroner's jury composed of Arthur Williams, Peter McPherson and Thomas Paull. Owing to the absence of Dr. Donohue, who first attended Fitzgerald, the Inquest will not be held until tomorrow at 4 p.m.

James will be taken to Coalville tomorrow morning and lodged in the county jail, pending his preliminary examination on the charge of murder in the first degree, which will be held in Park City on next Saturday at 11 a.m.

Mr. James has secured Judge Powers as attorney for the defense, and was in consultation with him today, the Judge coming up on the morning train and returning this evening.

Fitzgerald's people have been comunicated with at Gouverneur, N.Y., *where his mother and two brothers reside*, and directions received to bury the body here. The funeral will take place some time tomorrow.

(Salt Lake Tribune; Issue for Tuesday, August 27, 1901; page 1, column 2; BYU SA37; copied 11/15 1978)

THE FITZGERALD INQUEST

Death Caused by James's Shooting
With Felonious Intent.

[TRIBUNE SPECIAL]

Park City, Aug. 27.--The inquest held here today on the body of John Fitzgerald, who was killed on Monday, resulted in the jury returning a verdict that Fitzgerald came to his death from a bullet wound shot from a gun in the hands of Frank James, and that James fired the shot with felonious intent.

The Funeral of Fitzgerald will take place this afternoon at 4:30 o'clock from the Catholic church.

(Salt Lake Tribune; Issue for Wednesday, August 28, 1901, page 1, column 5; BYU SA37; copied 11/15/1978)

On the 17th of November 1978, two days after finding those newspaper accounts of Jack's murder, Daniele and I took the day off and drove to the County Court House in Coalville, Utah, where we located and copied over one hundred and twenty documents relating to Jack's murder and the subsequent trial of his assailant Frank James.

We had no difficulty locating an entry in the docket book showing the State of Utah vs Frank James in 1901, but we couldn't find the corresponding criminal court files at first. We determined the correct case file numbers from the index, but when we looked in the corresponding boxes (in this case cans), the documents we were seeking were not included. The deputy clerk assisted us, but she couldn't find them either. Finally, Mrs. Elizabeth Laird, the County Clerk (a sweet gracious lady and a sister of Robert Young the movie star) came to our rescue. She rechecked the docket book to make sure we had the correct file number, then she went to the corresponding file box and removed the papers from it. They had nothing to do with the Frank James case, which was a criminal case--they pertained to a civil court case which carried the same number. Mrs. Laird concluded that someone had misfiled the records, and after checking the appropriate civil court files, she located the Frank James papers and gave us access to them. They were unusual in their content and provided remarkable detail from the time Jack was shot, on the 25th of August 1901, until Frank James was acquitted of murder, on the 26th of March 1902. Unfortunately, the trial proceedings had not been transcribed from the court reporter's records, so I was not able to get copies of the actual trial proceedings.

Before we began copying the Frank James documents, our conversation with Mrs. Laird turned to Park City and its local newspaper the "Park Record." In our conversation, I had suggested to her that copies of the paper were not available for the early 1900's, but she strongly disagreed with me, saying that she new for a fact the University of Utah Library had a complete set of the paper dating from the 1890's. "What is that?" I said, "Do you mean to tell me that copies of that newspaper were right in Salt Lake City while I was trying, unsuccessfully, to find copies of it in Colorado and New Mexico?" With a chuckle, Mrs. Laird responded: "I'm afraid so!" And she left us to our copy work.

On our return to Salt Lake City that same afternoon, we visited the University of Utah Library and were able to find a detailed account of Jack Fitzgerald's murder in the Park Record (see copy which follows). When compared to the court documents we found, its account was much more accurate and detailed than those located in the Salt Lake Tribune or Deseret News, and the reporter seemed to be much more sensitive to Jack's predicament than the others had been.

SHOT TO DEATH

Frank James Kills John Fitzgerald.

TROUBLE OVER A HORSE.

Victim Shot in the Neck and the Back--Died in a Few Hours--Slayer Held to the District Court for Murder in the First Degree.

A terrible tragedy was enacted in Park City about 1:30 o'clock Sunday morning which ended in the death of John Fitzgerald. The scene of the tragedy was McPolin and James' livery stable on upper Main street, and the man who inflicted the wounds which resulted in the death of his victim was Frank James one of the proprietors of the stable.

THE SHOOTING.

The trouble, it seems grew out of the refusal of James to hire a horse to Fitzgerald, the latter wanting the animal to ride to the King mine. Fitzgerald was somewhat under the influence of liquor, and when James refused to let him have the horse, and but a few minutes afterwards let another applicant have one it angered Fitzgerald, who, it is alleged stepped up to James, and with the remark that he, James, would let anyone but himself, Fitzgerald, have a horse, struck James a blow in the face with his open hand. James immediately whipped out a revolver and fired, the shot taking affect in Fitzgerald's neck. The latter, it is said, turned and was running away when James fired a second shot, striking his victim just below the shoulder, the ball ranging downward, penetrating the liver and kidney. Fitzgerald fell and his slayer cooly walked to the city hall, gave himself up, and was locked in the city jail.

BULLETS EXTRACTED.

A number of people were soon at the scene and the wounded man was carried across the street to Dr. Donohue's office where Drs. Donohue and Wilson worked over the wounded man and rendered all the assistance possible. The bullets were extracted, after which the sufferer was removed to the Park City hotel and made as comfortable as possible. he died from his injuries at about 7 o'clock that evening.

COUNTY ATTORNEY SUMMONED.

County Attorney Callis was notified of the affair and came up Monday to investigate. A jury was impanaled and the remains were removed that afternoon.

THE INQUEST.

Tuesday afternoon the inquest was held before Justice Wilson by a jury composed of P. McPherson, Thomas Paull and Arthur Williams, who, after the examination of several witnesses returned a verdict that John Fitzgerald, the deceased, came to his death from bullets fired from a revolver in the hands of Frank James, with felonious intent.

TAKEN TO THE COUNTY JAIL.

Tuesday morning the prisoner was taken down to Coalville and placed in the county jail. Frank James is well known in Park City, and was for several years engaged in mining. A few months ago he purchased the Quinn interest in the livery firm of Quinn & McPolin, and since that time devoted his time to that business. Previous to this last scrape he has had several differences, but has in no way, we believe, been considered a dangerous man. From the facts, however, this far brought to light the slaying of Fitzgerald was certainly unwarranted, and the case savors strongly of hasty and cowardly action. While the provocation may have been great, it called for no such measures as were taken, which resulted in the taking of a life, and which will hang over the slayer for all time. However, there are usually two sides to all questions, and the facts will likely all be brought out in the trial, when a more impoartial judgment and verdict can be fomed. Judge O. W. Powers has been retained by James to defend him.

JOHN FITZGERALD.

The unfortunate victim of the sad affair, John Fitzgerald, is well known here, having resided in the Park for many years. He was probably his own worst enemy, and when not under the influence of drink was considered a good fellow and well liked. It is known that he was quick tempered, but he has never been considered vicious. When once a friend to a man, it is said he was always a good and faithful one. He was 44 years of age, and only a short time ago was an employee in the stable of the man who killed him. The funeral was held Tuesday afternoon from the Catholic church, and was well attended.

THE PRELIMINARY.

Frank James was brought up from Coalville yesterday and the preliminary hearing was begun before Justice Wilson this morning at 11 o'clock. The hearing was completed at 3 o'clock and the defendant was held to await the action of the Third District court on the charge of murder in the first degree. He will be returned to the county jail tomorrow.

(The Park Record, Park City, Utah; Issue for Saturday, August 31, 1901, page 2, column 2; University of Utah Library; copied 11/18/1978)

STATE OF UTAH
COUNTY OF SUMMIT SS. In the Justice's Court, Park City, Precinct, Utah
Before Geo. F. Wilson, Justice of the Peace.

THE STATE OF UTAH

vs. COMPLAINT.

Frank James, Defendant.

On this Thirtieth day of August, A.D. 1901, before me, Geo. F. Wilson. Justice of the Peace within and for Park City Precinct, Summit County, State of Utah, personally appeared ___*Frank Lake*___ who being duly sworn by me, on his oath did say that Frank James on the Twenty Fifth day of August, A.D. 1901, at Park City, County of Summit, State of Utah, did commit the crime of murder in the first degree, committed as follows:

That the said Frank James, on the said Twenty Fifth day of August A.D. 1901, at the County of Summit, State of Utah, upon one *John Fitzgerald*, unlawfully, wilfully, feloniously, deliberately, premeditatedly, of his malice aforethought and with the specific intent to take the life of him the said John Fitzgerald, an assault did make, with a certain gun, commonly called a revolver, which then and there was loaded with gun powder and leaden bullets, then and there by him the aid Frank James had and held in his hands, and then and there unlawfully, feloniously, deliberately, premeditatedly, of his malice aforethought, and with the specific intent to take the life of him the said *John Fitzgerald*, the said revolver so loaded as aforesaid, did shoot and discharge upon and against the body of him the said *John Fitzgerald*, thereby, and by thus striking the said *John Fitzgerald* with one of the said leaden bullets, inflicting upon and in the body of him the said *John Fitzgerald* one mortal wound from which mortal wound the said *John Fitzgerald* languished a short time and on the said Twenty Fifth day of August, A.D. 1901, he, the said *John Fitzgerald*, then and there died; and so the said Frank James, in the manner and form aforesaid unlawfully, wilfully, feloniously, deliberately, premeditatedly and of his malice aforethought, the said *John Fitzgerald* then and there did kill and murder; contrary to the form of the Statute in such cases made and provided and against the peace and dignity of the State of Utah.

Frank Lake

Subscribed and sworn to before me the day and year fist above written.

Geo. F. Wilson
Justice of the Peace.

THE PRELIMINARY HEARING

Perhaps the most interesting court document we located was the "Complaint," which charged Frank James with murder in the first degree. It was dated the 30th of August 1901 and left little doubt in the reader's mind as to what caused Jack's death. (see copy of Complaint which follows)

A "Warrant of Arrest" for Frank James was issued on the 30th of August 1901 by Justice of the Peace Geo. F. Wilson, and on the 31st of August 1901 C. W. Mair, the Sheriff of Summit County, Utah, certified that he had served the same "...by arresting the within named defendant Frank James, and bringing him into Court..." The following order was also signed by Justice Wilson on the 31st:

> "An order having been made by me that Frank James be held to answer upon a charge of murder in the first degree, said murder having been committed on the 25th day of August, A.D. 1901, at Park City, Summit County, Utah, you are hereby commanded to receive him into your custody, and retain him until he is legally discharged."

Frank James was brought into Justice Wilson's Court on the 31st of August 1901 and was informed of his rights under the law. The complaint was read to him and he entered a plea of "not guilty," after which he said he was ready for his preliminary examination.

The State of Utah was represented by a promising young Attorney named Charles A. Callis, who, interestingly enough, was of Irish extraction and was born in Dublin, Ireland. He had been a Constable, a member of the City Council of Coalville, a Representative to the Utah Legislature, a City Attorney of Coalville, and was then the County Attorney for Summit County. In 1933, he became a member of the Council of Twelve Apostles in the LDS Church and served an illustrious career with that organization. James engaged Judge Orlando Woodward Powers, a famous criminal lawyer of the day, for his defence. Judge Powers was a popular "Jurist-Politician" from Chicago, Illinois and was known to be an antagonist toward Mormon leadership at the time. He had been very successful as a criminal lawyer in California and other western states.

Thomas Malia, John B. Coughlin, Pat Heenan, John Shields, Pat Breen, John Rucker, and Doctors Donoher and LaCompte were all subpoenaed as witnesses for the preliminary hearing, and over fifty pages of testimony resulted.

Attorney Callis began the questioning of the subpoenaed witnesses, then Judge Powers cross examined. Judge Powers took a true "adversarial" position in his cross examination of each witness. If necessary, the cross examination was followed by questions on "redirect" where Callis might clarify or expand on a question asked or an answer given.

The hearing took place in the "Justice's Court of Park City Precinct, County of Summit, State of Utah" before George F. Wilson, Justice of the Peace. The State of Utah was listed as "Plaintiff" with Frank James shown as "Defendant."

Thomas Malia was the first to be sworn and testify and said he was a friend of Jack Fitzgerald's. He said that he lived on "Third street" in Park City and was a "miner" at the Silver King mine. He testified that he had been "taking a drink" in Ed Kelly's saloon, which was located on upper Main Street, and which was "not more than ten feet" from McPolin's livery stable. At about 2:00 o'clock Sunday morning, on the 25th of August 1901, he heard two shots coming from the stable, and after a short pause, he walked out to see what had taken place and met Frank James. Malia said James was standing on the sidewalk between the stable and the saloon, and "he had a gun in his hand." Attorney Callis asked Malia "What did he (James) say?" and Malia answered: "He said-I shot him, I shot him. We asked him who, and he says I shot the Son of a Bitch."

After that, Malia said he went to the door of the stable and saw "Fitzgerald staggering." Callis asked what Fitzgerald's first name was, and Malia answered: "John." Further questioning indicated Malia and Fitzgerald had been acquainted "for a year or more." Malia stated that he "run in and rung up Dr. Donoher's office," which was located "a short distance down the street," and then he "went up and got the Priest (Father Galligan)." Malia said Fitzgerald had a coat on when he was taken to Doctor Donoher's office, and that Frank James "seemed to be cool" and not excited when he was standing on the sidewalk with "a revolver in his hand." Malia testified that Fitzgerald did not have a revolver in his hands.

On cross examination, Attorney Powers had Malia repeat the fact that he was "Standing at the bar... drinking" when he heard the shots fired. Then he spent considerable time questioning Malia about the time interval between the two shots, eventually leaving the impression that Malia had no idea about the exact time interval between the two shots. He also tried to show that Callis had suggested a time interval for Malia to give, but Malia denied that. Powers also tried to show collusion between Malia and his friend Coughlin, but he couldn't make it stick, though he was able to show Malia hadn't been truthful about the number of drinks he had consumed up to the time of the shooting. Powers also asked Malia how long he had known Fitzgerald, and his answer was: "Ever since I can remember," but when asked if he was "Pretty friendly?" Malia said: "Just to speak as we pass." Powers showed that Malia and Fitzgerald had been drinking together in the saloon and that they were very friendly with each other but were not friendly with Frank James; they had both had previous disputes with him. Evidently Malia had rented a rig from James during the previous "4th of July" and had wrecked it without paying, but Malia denied that.

J. B. Coughlin was the second to testify, and he too was a miner in Park City, though he worked at the Quincy mine. Coughlin was "drinking a glass of beer" with "McDonald and Bennett" when he heard the two shots fired. He also went out and saw Frank James, opposite the saloon, with a "revolver in his hand." Because Coughlin helped Jack directly, I have copied several of the questions he was asked by Callis, and the answers given by Coughlin:

Q. Did you notice anything in James hands?
A. Yes, saw a revolver.
Q. In which hand?
A. I dont know
Q. Were you excited?
A. No sir.
Q. Did you feel alarmed about some one being shot?
A. No sir.
Q. Did you ask James anything?
A. No sir.
Q. Did you hear him state anything?
A. Heard him say "I shot him'.
Q. Did you address anything to him?
A. I just asked him who, and he said "I shot the Son of a Bitch".
Q. Where did you go then?
A. I went down street.
Q. Did he hand a gun to you?
A. No sir.
Q. Did he take it with him?
A. Yes sir.
Q. Where did you go then?
A. Down street.
Q. How far?
A. About twenty feet.

Q. Did you see anybody else on the side-walk but Fitzgerald?
A. No sir.
Q. Was he walking straight, or staggering?
A. He was walking pretty straight.
Q. Who was with him?
A. He was alone.
Q. Did you go up to him?
A. I went up and took hold of him.
Q. Did you speak to him?
A. Yes sir.
Q. Did he state who had shot him?
A. No sir.
Q. Did you help him down to the Doctor's office?
A. Yes sir.
Q. What did you do then?
A. Held him up for a few minutes, until the Priest came in.
Q. Did you notice how Fitzgerald was dressed?
A. He had on a black shirt, with stripes in it.
Q. Did he have a coat on?
A. Yes sir.
Q. Did you see any Revolver in Fitzgerald's hands?
A. No sir.
Q. Did you see any Revolver on the sidewalk?
A. No sir.
Q. When James stated that he had "shot the Son of a Bitch", did he appear to be excited?
A. Yes sir.
Q. Did you go into the barn?
A. No sir.
Q. Were you at the Doctor's office when Fitzgerald was undressed?
A. Yes sir.
Q. Did you notice any weapons in his clothes?
A. No sir.
Q. About how long was it, using your best judgment, after you heard the first shot, until you heard the second?
A. Ten or fifteen seconds, more or less.
Q. That would be your best judgement?
A. Yes sir.

Judge Powers then cross examined Coughlin and spent considerable time dealing with the time interval between the two shots. He tried to show Coughlin had been drinking excessively, but Coughlin insisted he was not drunk. Powers also tried to get Coughlin to agree that he and Malia had planned on what to say at the hearing, but he wasn't successful. He did get Coughlin to say that he and Malia had been drinking "more than just beer" and that they had frequented "sporting houses" earlier. Powers also got Coughlin confused in the number of drinks he had consumed, and pointed out that he was telling a "falsehood." He got Caughlin to say that he had been drinking since "eight or nine o'clock" that evening and that he and the others, including Fitzgerald, Malia, Bennett, and Durkins, had "kept it up until two o'clock in the morning." Caughlin had seen Fitzgerald in front of Ed Kelley's saloon before he was shot and again after he was shot, and he agreed that Fitzgerald was "Somewhat under the influence of liquor" at the time.

John Shields, a "Policeman in Park City," was the third to testify and said he was on duty when the Fitzgerald shooting took place. Among other things, he said:

> The first I saw of James he opened the door and came up; I was reading at the time, and he beckoned to me to come out. I called Breen who was going up stairs. I asked Frank if there was any trouble, and he said yes. I called my partner who was going up stairs, and I stepped out and asked Frank what was the matter. He said: "I shot Jack Fitz". I said Frank, you did'nt shoot him bad,--you did'nt kill him did you? He said "he was hit all right".

Shields testified that he and James "started up street" and "pretty soon Breen caught up with us, and we were talking about the shooting." James was evidently going back to the livery stable, but Shields thought he hadn't better go back up there and instructed Breen to stay with him while Shields went up to see what had happened. James told Shields to "find him a good man to look after the stables" and he sent for McPolin. When Shields arrived at Doctor Donoher's office, he found Fitzgerald undressed and lying on a table with "wounds on his back." Shields said that "After he got down to the Hotel I searched his pants" and found a "knife" which was closed. He was asked to identify the knife, which he did, so they had it at the preliminary hearing. Shields was also asked what else he had found in Fitzgerald's pockets, and he said: "Some tobacco, and a bill. We chewed the tobacco up, and there is the bill." He was also asked if he had found any jewelry, and he said: "No sir,-I believe there was a Handkerchief." He was then asked if he found a watch, and he said: "No, the watch was taken before I got to the Doctor's office." This is the first reference we find to Jack's watch, which ultimately found its way to New York.

Shields was next asked if he had searched Frank James and he responded:

> When I came back down here, James and Breen were going up street, and when I found that they were not in the office, I started up street after them, and I caught up with them about at Roy's, and I told Frank that we would have to take him down,--I says that man is dead. he says he is not dead, is he? I says yes, and I will have to take you down, and he says "all right".

Shields was then asked if he had examined the chambers of Frank's gun, but he said he didn't at the time because "...it was all excitement..." He was also asked if there were any empty shells and he said: "Yes sir, I saw there was some empty shells," but he "did'nt move the cylinder." When Shields was asked how many times James had shot Fitzgerald, he said he believed he was shot twice, but he couldn't recollect Frank's exact statement. Then Shields said:

> "O Yes, He said "He hit me in the mouth and I shot at him, and he came back at me again, and I fired again".

On cross examination, Judge Powers asked Shields if he had noticed James's mouth, and he said: "Yes, sir. His lips were bloody."

Patrick Breen, a partner of Shields and also a Park City Policeman, was the next to testify, and he said he saw James talking with Shields in front of the "old Park City Bank building" at about two o'clock in the morning on Sunday August 25th. When asked if he had talked with James, Breen answered in the affirmative and said:

> I asked him what was the matter of Fitzgerald, and he says "I shot him".

Breen testified that Shields took "A Gun and a Knife" from James, and that James told Breen "...He hit me in the mouth, and I fired at him". When asked if he (James) said anything else, Breen said: "Yes,--he says "he was coming for me again, and I gave him another one".

On cross examination, Judge Powers asked Breen if he had noticed James's mouth, and he said: "Yes, it had been bleeding and looked as though it had been hit with something." Breen said James's lip had been cut on the left side of the mouth. Judge Powers then asked Breen if Fitzgerald was a large sized man and he replied: "About five foot nine or ten" When asked if he was "Well proportioned" Breen said: "Yes, well proportioned. Dont think he would weigh over one hundred and forty five pounds." On further questioning, Breen agreed that Fitzgerald was "Quite a muscular man" and looked heavier than Judge Powers.

On redirect, Attorney Callis asked Breen how well he was acquainted with Fitzgerald, and he said: "I have known him since ninety." When asked if he had noticed any physical defects in Fitzgerald's form, he said Fitzgerald's right hand was crippled "So that he could'nt use a hammer." After that, Judge Powers cross examined again and suggested that Fitzgerald weighed over 175 pounds, but Breen wouldn't agree with it and said: "No sir; heard him say a month or so ago, that he did'nt weigh over one hundred and thirty three pounds." Judge Powers then said that a man would have to be pretty slim, five foot nine or ten high, that only weighted 140 pounds, but Breen wouldn't agree and the matter was dropped.

Pat Heenan was the next to testify and said he was a "Bar Tender" at Ed Kelly's saloon, which was located "On Upper Main street" in Park City, and he was on duty Sunday morning August 25th when he heard two shots coming from the livery stable. He testified that he had seen James and Fitzgerald pass by the side door, and he said that Fitzgerald had been drinking in the saloon that night. When asked if Fitzgerald was drunk, Heenan responded by saying: "Well, he had three or four in our place, and he was considerably under the influence of liquor."

Judge Powers started his cross examination of Heenan by suggesting that Fitzgerald was making trouble in his saloon that evening, but Heenan didn't agree. Powers said that "When Fitzgerald was drinking he was rather ugly was'nt he?" Heenan responded: "Could'nt say as he was; I saw him in trouble once before." Then Judge Powers said: "He was quite peaceable when not drinking, but when drinking was rather quarrelsome was'nt he? Heenan replied: "No, not as I know of." Following those remarks, Powers asked several questions about the time interval between the two shots and Callis followed on redirect by having Heenan say he "distinctly heard two shots, and there was a certain length of time between the two shots."

Doctor W. D. Donoher was the next to testify. He was the "County Physician" and his office was on Main Street, "about half way up," and it was "a Little above and across the street from McPolin's Livery Stable." He said he was asleep in his office on the morning of August 25th when he was aroused as follows:

> "I was called about two o'clock in the morning, and they brought in a man who was shot and asked me to take care of him, a man by the name of Fitzgerald."

Because of his personal involvement with Jack, I continue by giving Doctor Donoher's actual testimony. I have retained the original spelling and punctuation.

Q. Did you notice what condition Fitzgerald was In?
A. Yes, he was weak, nervous, and a little excited.
Q. Suffering from any gun shot wounds?
A. Yes sir.
Q. Please state the location of the wounds.
A. One wound through the neck--the fleshy part of the neck, another in his back, below the center of the back, in the spine.

Q. Did you say the bullet went through the spine?
A. Yes sir.
Q. Did it come out?
A. No sir.
Q. Did you make an incision to extract the bullet?
A. Yes sir, on the right side just about the point of the eleventh rib, near that region.
Q. Did you proceed, Doctor, to dress his wounds?
A. Yes sir.
Q. How was he dressed?
A. He had on an undershirt, a black overshirt and trowsers.
Q. Any coat?
A. Yes sir, I think he did.
Q. Would you know the coat if you saw it?
A. I think so.
Q. Did it have any holes through it?
A. Yes, a bullet hole in the collar.
Q. Any bullet holes in any other part of the coat?
A. Not that I noticed.
Q. Could you identify that, as the coat which Fitzgerald wore?
A. Yes sir, that's it.
Q. Where is the place through which the bullet passed?
A. That is it. (indicating)
Q. Which side of the neck did the bullet enter?
A. The left side.
Q. Then that would be the bullet hole?
A. Yes sir.
Q. Was that shot necessarily fatal?
A. No sir.
Q. Did you notice that hole through there-? (Pointing to hole in back of coat)
A. No sir.
Q. Would that have been the part of the back where the bullet entered?
A. Yes sir, right there some where.
Q. That would cover the region of the back where the bullet entered?
A. Yes Sir.
Q. Then that would be the bullet hole?
A. Yes sir.
Q. Was Fitzgerald's face powder-burned?
A. I could'nt say.
Q. Did'nt examine close enough?
A. No sir.
Q. Was the wound in the back, necessarily fatal?
A. Yes sir.
Q. Please state to the Court why, it would be necessarily fatal?
A. It went through the cavity of the abdomen, and they are usually fatal.
Q. And that then, was the wound that caused Fitzgerald's death?
A. Yes sir.
Q. Did you attend Fitzgerald at the time of his death?
A. I attended him until four o'clock in the afternoon.
Q. Where did you cause the patient to be removed to?
A. The Park City Hotel.

Q. How many times did you visit him during the day?
A. Four times.
Q. Was Fitzgerald suffering from any other physical ailment?
A. He had one crippled hand, think it was his right hand.
Q. Could you state how badly it was crippled.
A. No sir.
Q. Could you tell what caused it to be crippled?
A. No sir.
Q. Do you think it was a deformity?
A. Yes sir.
Q. Were you in the room when he was being questioned by the County Attorney?
A. Yes sir.
Q. Did you hear Fitzgerald state who shot him?
A. Yes sir.
Q. Who did he say shot him?
A. Frank James.
Q. Any other statement?
A. Yes sir.
Q. What did he state?
A. He said that he had gone to the barn to get a horse, words followed and James shot him.
Q. Did you hear him state the he started to run?
A. No sir.
Q. Did you hear him say that James ought to be prosecuted?
A. I dont remember.
Q. To the best of your recollection, what did you hear him state?
A. As I told you before, he went to the barn for a horse, and words followed, James shot him, and that is all I remember hearing him say.

CROSS EXAMINATION by Judge Powers.

Q. You say that this is about the place that the bullet would strike the coat?
A. Yes sir.
Q. You say that the bullet went through the spine?
A. Yes sir.
Q. The hole, even with the coat unbuttoned, would be four inches to the left of the spine?
A. Yes sir.
Q. And if the course of the bullet ranged from the left to the right, it would'nt hit the spine?
A. Yes, I think it might.
Q. Now what direction did the bullet take?
A. Straight through.
Q. So that it would be almost on a line with the seam of the coat?
A. Yes sir.
Q. Do you find it through on this side? It's just a worn hole, is'nt it?
A. It looks like a bullet hole.
Q. And that would hit the spinal column?
A. Yes sir.
Q. You tell me that the hole went directly in?
A. It did.
Q. What part of the spine was hit?
A. The base of the fourth lumbar vertebra.

Q. About the hip bone?
A. Yes sir.
Q. This hole I showed you last, would carry it below the hip bone, would'nt it?
A. Yes sir.
Q. Now what is you opinion?
A. I am supposed to state what I know.
Q. You are supposed to state your opinion?
A. I think it possible that the coat was twisted around.
Q. Did he have a vest on?
A. I dont remember of anything but his shirt.
Q. It would be possible of course, for the man to have had his coat off, been shot, and then put the coat back on would'nt it?
A. Yes sir.
Q. He was able to walk from the stable to your office?
A. I believe so.
Q. They said he walked; if he was able to do that, he would be able to put his coat on?
A. Possibly.
Q. Now there,--take the coat buttoned. Would'nt you say that it could'nt have gone through the spine?
A. No sir, not in that position.
Q. It dont seem to be the bullet hole, does it?
A. It is'nt in the place that it ought to be.
Q. If it went in there, it had to go through the coat?
A. I could'nt say.
Q. You observe where the hole is?
A. Yes sir.
Q. It passed about through there?
A. Yes sir.
Q. It never could have passed down and went through that place there--it dont look like a bullet hole does it? That would be going to the left.
A. Yes.
Q. According to your judgement as to the position, then, the bullet never passed through that place, did it?
A. I could'nt say.
Q. The man might have had his coat off?
A. Yes sir.
Q. That would'nt be near the spine, would it?
A. Now, I could'nt tell you.
Q. You said this hole here, was about in the region of the wound?
A. Yes sir.
Q. Do you say that this lower hole, would hit the spine?
A. It would go in the region of the spine.
Q. It would'nt hit the spine, would it?
A. Yes sir.
Q. Would you say they were bullet holes, or not?
A. They look like it.

I think Judge Powers was correct in trying to prove that the bullet didn't actually pass through the spinal column, but it is evident that Doctor Donoher was not going to concede the point. If the bullet had actually passed through the spinal cord, Jack certainly wouldn't have been able to walk the distance he did before being helped by Coughlin. The bullet probably passed near the spinal column but did not penetrate it.

Another interesting aspect of Jack's physical condition was his right hand, and we can only speculate about its true condition, as did the Doctor. Evidently his right hand had been injured previously and he was unable to grasp a hammer with it, but it was probably not a deformity from birth.

Following the testimony of Doctor Donoher, Doctor E. P. LeCompte was sworn and testified. He attended to Jack the following day, and his testimony helped clarify the question as to whether the spinal column had been penetrated by the bullet or not. When he was asked to describe the locality of the bullet hole, he said:

"It entered about the middle of the back, a little to the left of the back bone."

Doctor LeCompte also testified that Jack had a wound on the neck "...It entered the left side, and came out the right side of the neck..." When asked whether or not Jack was deformed, he said: "Yes, his right hand seemed to be drawn." He confirmed that the shot through Jack's back would have been the fatal one, and when asked whether he heard Jack say anything, he said: "I heard him state that he was shot up there in the stable," and that he was shot "Twice." Judge Powers then cross examined Doctor LeCompte and I have chosen to list the actual question asked and answers given.

Q. He said, did'nt he, that he had some difficulty up there in the stable with James about a horse?
A. Yes sir.
Q. And that he hit James in the face, or mouth, slapped him--then James shot him?
A. Yes sir.
Q. Did you see James after that?
A. Yes sir.
Q. State to the court what you found?
A. I found that on the right side of his lip it was cut considerable.
Q. Been produced by a blow?
A. Yes sir.
Q. What is your idea as to what caused the deformity of Fitzgeralds hand?
A. I heard that it had been done some years ago.
Q. Did you hear it was hurt in a fight?
A. Yes.
Q. Could the deformity have been caused by a man striking a blow with his fist?
A. That's hard to say, suppose it might.
Q. Did it appear to be an inherited deformity?
A. It's hard to tell, just what caused it, it was certainly a deformity.
Q. There are various ways in which it could have been produced?
A. Yes sir.

John Rooker was the next to testify and he gave the following interesting statments:

Q. Mr. Rooker what is your name?
A. John Rooker.
Q. Where do you reside?
A. In Park City.
Q. What is you business?
A. I am a laborer.

Q. What was you doing on August 25th, all day?
A. From eight o'clock A M until seven thirty P M, I was with Fitzgerald the wounded man.
Q. Did you stay with him until he died?
A. Yes sir.
Q. Did you see him die?
A. Yes sir.

C. W. Mair, the Sheriff of Summit County was the last to testify at the preliminary hearing and his testimony follows:

Q. What is your name please?
A. C W Mair.
Q. Where do you reside?
A. In Park City.
Q. What is your present business?
A. Sheriff of Summit County.
Q. Were you acquainted with Fitzgerald?
A. Yes sir.
Q. Were you in the room where Fitzgerald was, when Fitzgerald was being questioned by the County Attorney?
A. Yes sir.
Q. Did you hear Fitzgerald state who shot him?
A. Yes sir.
Q. Who did he say shot him?
A. Frank James.
Q. Did you hear him state how many times James shot him?
A. I could'nt say.
Q. Did you hear him make any statement as to the shooting?
A. Yes, he said he went after a horse, and James would'nt give him one. It appears that another man went in and got a horse, and Fitzgerald said to James-"you can give every one a horse but me", and then he slapped James in the mouth, and James shot him.
Q. Did he state whether he started to run or not?
A. No sir.
Q. Did he say anything about James being prosecuted?
A. He said that James had no right to shoot him, and that he should be prosecuted.
Q. Was that testimony taken down in writing?
A. Yes sir, I believe it was.

Following the Sheriff's testimony, there was a certification signed by L. Learn and notarized by James M Lockham, Notary Public, as follows:

> L. Learn, being first duly sworn, deposes and says: That the above and foregoing is a full, true and correct transcript of all the testimony taken at the Preliminary Examination of Frank James, on the 31st, day of August 1901, at Park City, Summit County, Utah, in the case of State of Utah --vs--Frank James.
>
> SUBSCRIBED AND SWORN to before me, this 9th day of September A D 1901. James M. Lockham Notary Public.

After arguments of counsel were completed, Justice Wilson signed the following order:

> "...It appearing to me that the offense of murder in the first degree has been committed and that there is sufficient cause to believe the said Frank James guilty thereof, I order that he be held to answer for the same to the Third District Court, and that he is hereby committed to the sheriff of Summit County, Utah."

At the conclusion of the preliminary hearing, Frank James was lodged in the Summit County jail at Coalville, Utah, and counsels for the Prosecution and Defence began to prepare their cases for trial. The State was represented by District Attorney Dennis C. Eichnor and County Attorney Charles A. Callis while the defence was conducted by Judge Orlando W. Powers and Henry Shields. James was released on bond, pending the trial, which didn't begin until the 24th of March 1902; a second complaint was filed which reduced the charge from "Murder in the First Degree" to "Murder in the Second Degree."

There is evidence to show that Jack's relatives in New York were notified shortly after the killing, and there is evidence to show that Homer Clapp (a brother-in-law of Jack), and perhaps others, came west shortly after the killing and took charge of Jack's personal affairs. They may or may not have arranged for his funeral and burial, which took place on the 27th of August 1901, but they certainly obtained his personal affects, some of which were later determined to be in possession of the family in New York.

The trial was conducted at Coalville, Utah in the Third Judicial District Court, beginning on Monday the 24th of March 1902, and a verdict of "Not Guilty" was returned by the jury on Wednesday the 26th of March 1902, acquitting Frank James of the murder. As mentioned above, I was unable to obtain copies of the actual trail proceedings, but I did get a copy of the Judge's instructions to the jury. They reveal many things which were brought out in the trial and should be read in their entirety to get a clear picture of what was actually presented during the trial.

THIRD JUDICIAL DISTRICT FOR THE STATE OF UTAH
IN AND FOR THE COUNTY OF SUMMIT

THE STATE OF UTAH vs FRANK JAMES Defendant	INSTRUCTIONS TO JURY

Gentlemen of the Jury:- -

The defendant, Frank James, is accused by the information of the crime of Murder in the Second degree, in that the said Frank James, on the 25th day of August, A.D. 1901, at Park City, Summit County, State of Utah, upon one John Fitzgerald, unlawfully, wilfully, feloniously and of his malice aforethought, and with an assault did make with a certain gun, commonly called a revolver, which then and there was loaded with gunpowder and leaden bullets, then and there by him, the said Frank James, had and held in his hands, and then and there unlawfully, feloniously and of his malice aforethought, and with the specific intent to take the life of the said John Fitzgerald, the said revolver so loaded as aforesaid, did shoot at and discharge upon and against the body of him, the said John Fitzgerald, thereby and by thus striking the said John Fitzgerald, with one of the said leaden bullets, inflicting upon and in the body of him, the said John Fitzgerald, one mortal wound, from which mortal wound the said John Fitzgerald languished for a short time, and on the said 25th day of August, A.D. 1901, at Park City, Summit County, State of Utah, died; and so the said Frank James, in the manner and form aforesaid, unlawfully, wilfully, feloniously and of his malice aforethought, the said John Fitzgerald then and there did kill and murder, contrary to the statutes, etc.

(Paragraph 2)

To this charge the defendant has interposed a plea of "Not Guilty," and you are instructed that such plea puts in issue every essential fact constituting the crime of murder in the second degree, and casts upon the State the burden of proving every such fact constituting the crime charged, to your satisfaction beyond a reasonable doubt.

(Paragraph 3)

Murder, as defined by the statutes of our State, is the unlawful killing of a human being with malice aforethought. Such malice may be express or implied. It is express when there is manifested a deliberate intention unlawfully to take away the life of a fellow creature. It is implied when no considerable provocation appears, or when the circumstances attending the killing, show an abandoned or malignant heart.

(Paragraph 4)

Murder in the second degree is the unlawful killing of a human being with malice, but without any admixture of deliberation or premeditation. The term malice means a wish to vex, annoy, or trouble, or injure another person.

(Paragraph 5)

Manslaughter is the unlawful killing of a human being without malice. It is of two kinds,

1. Voluntary, upon a sudden quarrel or heat of passion.
2. Involuntary, in the commission of an unlawful act, not accounting to felony, or in the commission of a lawful act which might produce death in an unlawful manner, or without due caution and circumspection.

(Paragraph 6)

The burden of proof is on the prosecution to prove all the essential facts constituting the offense charged, to your satisfaction beyond a reasonable doubt. The intent or intention with

which an act is done is shown by the circumstances connected with the act done, and the sound mind and discretion of the accused.

(Paragraph 7)

In determining whether the defendant acted with malice and with the specific intent to kill, charged in the information, you must take into consideration all that he may have said, or may have done (so far as the evidence may show, he did say or do anything) and from it all determine whether he did in fact kill the deceased with the malice and the specific intent to kill, as charged in the information.

(Paragraph 8)

If you believe from the evidence given before you in this case, beyond a reasonable doubt, that the defendant, Frank James, on the 25th day of August, A.D. 1901, at the County of Summit, State of Utah, shot John Fitzgerald with a pistol, and thereby inflicted on him a mortal wound of which he there died, and that there was no considerable provocation therefor, and that such killing was done with malice and with a specific intent to kill, and on that alone you should find him guilty as charged in the information.

(Paragraph 9)

You are further instructed that the offense of manslaughter is necessarily included in the offense which is charged in this information; and under our law a defendant may be convicted of the offense so included, and if in this case it shall appear to you that the defendant has committed a public offense, and there is to your minds a reasonable ground to doubt in which of two or more degrees he is guilty, you can convict him of the lowest of such degrees only.

(Paragraph 10)

You are further instructed that the statutes of this State provide that upon a trial for murder, the commission of the homicide by the defendant being proved, the burden of proving circumstances of mitigation, or that justify or excuse it, shall devolve upon him, unless the proof on the part of the prosecution tends to show that the crime committed amounted only to manslaughter, or that the defendant was justifiable or excusable.

(Paragraph 11)

In this case the defendant admits that he shot and killed the deceased, but he asserts that in so doing he was justifiable, and that he did it in necessary self defense.

(Paragraph 12)

You are instructed that section 4168 of the Revised Statutes of this State specifies the cases in which homicide is justifiable, and in subdivision Two and Three thereof it is provided that homicide is justifiable, "when committed in defense of habitation, property or person against one who manifestly intends or endeavors, by violence or surprise to commit a felony; or against one who manifestly intends and endeavors in a violent, riotous or tumultuous manner to enter the habitation of another, for the purpose of offering violence to any person therein, or when committed in the lawful defence of such person, or of a wife, husband, parent, child, master, mistress, or servant of such person, where there is a reasonable ground to apprehend a design to commit a felony or to do some great bodily injury, and there is imminent danger of such design being accomplished; but such person, or the person in whose behalf the defense was made, if he was the assailant, or engaged in mortal combat, must really and in good faith have endeavored to decline any further struggle before the homicide was committed."

(Paragraph 13)

A bare fear of the commission of any of the offenses mentioned in subdivisions Two and Three above set out, to prevent which homicide may be lawfully committed, is not sufficient to justify it. But the circumstances must be sufficient to excite the fears of a reasonable person, and the party killing must have acted wholly under the influence of such fears.

(Paragraph 14)

Under these statutes, and by the common law of the land, one who is without fault himself, when attacked by another, may kill his assailant, if the circumstances be such as to furnish reasonable ground for apprehending a design to take away his life or to do him some great bodily harm, and there is reasonable ground for believing the danger imminent that such design will be accomplished; although it may afterwards turn out, that the appearance was false, and there was in fact no such design, nor any danger that it would be accomplished; but this principle will not justify one in returning blows with a dangerous weapon, when he is struck with the naked hand, when there is no reason to apprehend a design to do him great bodily harm.

(Paragraph 15)

You are further instructed that if you shall believe from the evidence given before you in this case, that the defendant was in his place of business, at the time of the killing, the defendant has a legal right to be and remain there, and if the deceased advanced upon the defendant in a threatening manner, and if the accused did not provoke the assault, and had at the time reasonable ground to believe, and did in good faith believe, that the deceased intended to take his life, or to do him great bodily harm, he had the legal right to stand his ground, and meet any attack made upon him, in such way and with such force as, under all the circumstances, he at the moment honestly believed, and had reasonable grounds to believe, was necessary to save his own life, or to protect himself from great bodily injury.

(Paragraph 16 was missing from the courthouse file)

(Paragraph 17)

You are instructed that when one is attacked in such a manner and under such circumstances as to furnish him at the time with reasonable ground for apprehending a design upon the part of the deceased to take his life, or to do some great bodily harm, he may act upon appearance and kill his assailant, if it seems to him necessary in order to avoid the apprehended danger, and the killing will be justifiable although it may afterwards turn out that the appearances were false, and there was not in fact any design to do him injury nor any danger that it would be done. He must decide at his peril under the circumstances in which he is placed, but he will not act at the peril of making that guilt, if the appearances prove false, which would be innocent had they proved true.

(Paragraph 18)

If the jury believe from the evidence that the defendant was assaulted by Fitzgerald in such a way as to induce in the defendant a reasonable belief that he was actually in danger of great bodily harm, then he was justified in defending himself, whether the danger was real or apparent. Actual or positive danger is not indispensable to justify self defense. The law considers that men, when threatened with danger, are obliged to judge from appearances and to determine therefrom as to the actual state of things surrounding them; and in such cases, if persons act from honest convictions, induced by reasonable evidence, they will not be held responsible criminally, for a mistake as to the extent of the actual danger. In other words, a person need not be in actual, imminent peril of his life, or of great bodily harm, before he may slay his assailant. It is sufficient if, in good faith, he believes and has a right as a reasonable man, to believe from the facts as they appear to him at the time, that he is in imminent peril.

(Paragraph 19)

The jury are instructed that, if from the evidence there is reasonable doubt whether the defendant himself, at the time of the killing, was under reasonable apprehension and honest fear that Fitzgerald intended and was about to inflict upon him great bodily harm and that the defendant fired and shot under that belief, then the verdict of the jury must be Not Guilty.

(Paragraph 20)

Where one without fault is placed under circumstances sufficient to excite the fears of a reasonable person that another designed to commit a felony or some great bodily injury upon him, and to afford grounds for reasonable belief that there is imminent danger of the accomplishment of this design, he may, acting under those fears alone, slay his assailant and be justified by the appearances. And where the attack is sudden, and the danger imminent, he may increase his peril by retreat; so situated he may stand his ground, that becoming his "wall", and slay his aggressor even if it be proved that he might more easily have gained his safety by flight.

And in this case you are instructed that the defendant had a right to be in the stable, and if while peaceably there the deceased provoked a quarrel and followed it in so violent a manner as to excite the fear of a reasonable man that he was in danger of great bodily harm and the fear of defendant being thus excited, and acting solely from such fear, and believing from appearances that he was in imminent danger of great bodily harm he shot and killed deceased, the verdict must be Not Guilty.

(Paragraph 21)

Persons, when threatened with danger, must determine from the state of things surrounding them, as to the necessity of resorting to self defense; and if they act from reasonable and honest convictions, they will not be held responsible criminally for a mistake in the extent of the actual danger, where other judicious men would have been alike mistaken.

(Paragraph 22)

The facts show that the defendant was where he had the lawful right to be, and if it appear from the evidence that the deceased advanced upon him in a threatening and violent manner for the apparent purpose of doing him great bodily harm, and if defendant did not provoke the assault, and at the time reasonable ground to believe, and in good faith believed, that the deceased intended to take his life or to do him great bodily harm, the defendant was not obliged to retreat nor to consider whether he could safely retreat, but was entitled to stand his ground and meet any attack made upon him in such way and with such force, as, under all the circumstances, he, at the moment, honestly believed, and had reasonable grounds to believe, was necessary to save his own life or to protect himself from great bodily harm.

(Paragraph 23)

The law at the outset clothes the defendant in a criminal case involving the charge of murder, with the presumption of innocence; and when the proof tends to overthrow this presumption and to fix upon such defendant the presumption of such a crime, the latter is permitted to support the original presumption of innocence by proof of good character for peace and quietness. Such good character, when proven, is a circumstance tending, in a greater or less degree, to establish his innocence. It is of value not only in doubtful cases, but also when the testimony tends very strongly to establish the guilt of the accused. When proven, it is itself a fact in the case; and it is not to be put aside by the jury in order to ascertain if the other facts and circumstances, considered in themselves, do not establish defendant's guilt beyond a reasonable doubt; but also when the testimony tends very strongly to establish the guilt of the accused. When proven, it is itself a fact in the case; and it is not to be put aside by the jury in order to ascertain if the other facts and circumstances, considered in themselves, do not establish defendant's guilt beyond a reasonable doubt; but such good character, if proven, should be considered by the jury in connection with all the other testimony in the case and not independently thereof, and the guilt or innocence of the defendant determined from all the testimony in the case. And when so considered, no matter how conclusive the other evidence in the case, considered by itself, may point to the guilt of the defendant, such good character, if proven, may be sufficient to create a reasonable doubt of the defendant's guilt, and, to, where such doubt would not otherwise exist but for such good character, and it may lead the jury to believe, in view of the probabilities, that a person of such good character would not be guilty of the offense charged, and that the other evidence in the case is not true or that the witnesses, in some way, may be mistaken therein.

(Paragraph 24)

If it has been proved that the deceased was a man of high temper and had a bad reputation for peace and quietude, and defendant knew the character of deceased in that regard, it is an important matter for the consideration of the jury. for the knowledge or belief of the defendant, that the person assaulting him, if you find he was so assaulted, was a man of high temper and quarrelsome disposition, was a most important circumstance from which he could estimate the probability and character of the attack, and what course of contact he had reason to expect from the deceased, as well as the means which at the moment, he deemed necessary to guard himself from the threatening danger.

(Paragraph 25)

The jury are instructed to entitle one to defend himself against a violent assault by another, he is not required to first call upon the officers of the law for protection, neither is he required to wait until he is actually injured by his assailant. If one is assaulted by another in a manner calculated to excite the fears of a reasonable person that he is in imminent danger of great bodily harm, he may stand his ground and kill his assailant if that seems to him necessary, in order to avoid the apprehended danger. He may do this though officers of the law are present and are endeavoring to quell the disturbance. And he may act upon appearances--upon the condition of things as they present themselves to his mind at the time, provided that the circumstances were sufficient to excite the fears of a reasonable person and the party killing acts wholly under the influence of such fears.

(Paragraph 26)

The jury are instructed that the fact that the defendant was arrested, examined and held for trial, and that he has been informed against and charged with killing John Fitzgerald cannot be considered as indicating the guilt of defendant. He is presumed by the law to be innocent and this presumption attached through all the various steps in the case until it is completely overborne by evidence of such weight and character that it excludes every reasonable doubt from the mind of each juror. And, notwithstanding the fact that the defendant stands charged with the crime unless the jury is satisfied that every essential fact and material element going
to make up the offense charged, had been proven beyond a reasonable doubt, the verdict must be Not Guilty.

FRANK JAMES "ACQUITTED"

According to the Coalville Times (Issue for March 28, 1902, page 1, column 4) the verdict was rendered by the jury on Wednesday Evening the 26th of March 1902, and I quote from the article as follows:

> **FRANK JAMES ACQUITTED**
>
> **Verdict Rendered by the Jury Wednesday Evening**
>
> Frank James, charged with murder in the second degree, was acquitted Wednesday evening by a jury of his peers, after a trial lasting three days.
>
> District Attorney Eichnor and County Attorney Callis prosecuted and the defendant was represented by Judge Powers and Judge Shields.
>
> One the 25th day of August last year Frank James, who owned a half interest in the Park City livery stable, killed John Fitzgerald by shooting him with a revolver. The killing took place in the stable at two o'clock on the morning of the 25th. James claimed that Fitzgerald assaulted him and that he shot the latter in self defense. Fitzgerald was shot twice, one of the bullets entering the neck and the other striking him in the center of the back passing through the spine. This was the shot that proved fatal. The wounded man lived about fifteen hours after he was shot and an hour or two before he died he stated to the county attorney that he struck James whereupon James shot him in the neck and as he (Fitzgerald) was running away, shot him in the back.
>
> On the trial James swore that he acted in self defense. Prominent citizens of Park City testified to the good reputation of James and the bad reputation of Fitzgerald.
>
> Throughout the trail the conduct of the attorneys on both sides towards each other was courteous and gentlemanly. The opening argument for the prosecution was made by County Attorney Callis and Judge Shields performed a like service for the defense. He was followed by Judge Powers and the district attorney closed for the State. The judge then delivered his charge to the jury. The charge strongly favored the defendant.
>
> The jury was composed of the following named citizens: Samuel Brinton, Thomas Davis, Heber C. Richins, Geo. Beckstead, Ole Olsen, William Richins, Thomas Richins and Thomas Beard.

In my opinion, the Prosecution didn't have a chance. Jack Fitzgerald had three strikes against him before the case was ever brought to trial, and there was no way in the world a jury would find Frank James guilty, even though he did in fact murder Jack in cold blood. At that time, Utah Code gave a person the right to take "any action he deemed necessary" to prevent another person from entering his property and "doing him possible bodily harm." Jack had certainly entered James' property, and it was clearly evident that he had attempted bodily harm, so Frank James was justified in killing him, according to Utah law. Also, character was a strong determining factor in a man's innocence or guilt at the time, and the Defence was able to paint an excellent picture of Frank James' character; and at the same time, they were able to paint a very poor picture of Jack Fitzgerald's character, because of his excessive drinking and his bad temper. Frank James had a family and was well respected in the community, but Jack had no family and a bad reputation.

After carefully examining the court documents relating to the Frank James case, I give my version of what I think actually happened at the time of Jack's death. I must agree that

I am prejudiced against Frank James and feel that he really "got away with murder." Also, most of my information comes from the preliminary hearing and the Judge's instruction to the jury; not from the actual trial.

On Saturday evening between 8:00 and 9:00 o'clock, the 24th of August 1901, Jack (John) Fitzgerald and some of his friends; Malia, Coughlin, Bennett, Durkins, and others, were drinking in Ed Kelly's saloon, which was located on upper Main Street in Park City, Utah. Jack would be going to work at the Silver King Mine much before daylight Sunday morning, the 25th of August, and he would need to rent a horse to ride up to the mine which was some distance further up the canyon; renting a horse to ride up the canyon to work was evidently a common practice with local miners. It was also the practice of some miners to have a few drinks before going to work; that took the edge off the drudgery and hard physical work in the mine where many of them were "muckers' (persons who dug and shoveled the ore). This being Saturday and the weekend, Jack probably drank a little more than usual, and he may have visited other establishments in the City before stopping at Kelly's saloon.

Jack was well known in Park City and had been a resident there for more than ten years. He had several personal friends who considered his friendship strong and firm, and he was a likeable person when one got to know him, but he also had a few enemies in town. He was known to be short tempered, particularly after he had been drinking, and he had engaged in skirmishes and scuffles on more than one occasion. It was said that he had injured his right hand severely while engaging in such a conflict, and the hand appeared to be deformed.

At about 2:00 o'clock Sunday morning, the 25th of August, Jack left Ed Kelly's saloon through the side door and walked a short distance to the McPolin and James Livery Stable, where he attempted to rent a horse for his proposed ride up the canyon to work. Frank James, a part owner of the stables, was on duty at the time and knew Jack personally. Jack had actually worked for James previously, and they had argued with one another on more than one occasion. Frank didn't really believe that Jack had the money to rent a horse when he entered the stable and asked for one. As a consequence, Frank told Jack that he didn't have a horse available at the time, whereupon Jack turned around and left the stable, realizing he would have to make other arrangements to get to work. At that very moment, another person evidently entered the stable and asked for a horse, and Frank agreed to rent him one. Upon hearing that exchange, Jack turned around and walked briskly up to Frank, saying: 'You can rent anyone a horse but me, can't you!" and either slapped James across the face or actually hit him in the mouth with his fist.

Park City must have been a real "Wild West Town" at the time, because Frank James pulled a loaded revolver from its holster and fired a shot at Jack, who was evidently facing him; the shot passing through the collar of his coat, hitting the fleshy part of the neck, and at the same time wheeling him around. At that point, Frank fired another shot at Jack, which hit him in the back just missing the spinal column and lodging in his abdomen. Jack did not fall to the ground but staggered to the door and stood there, where his friend Coughlin found him when he came out the side-door of the saloon to see what the shooting was about. Coughlin then assisted Jack to Doctor Doneher's office, which was across the street and down from the livery stable.

Frank James said that Fitzgerald "came after him again" so he shot him a second time, but I can't believe that scenario. If Jack had been coming at him, the second shot would have entered from the front, but that was not the case. Jack was shot first in the side of the neck, which wheeled him around, then James shot him a second time in the back. Judge Powers tried to show that Jack was trying to run away from James when he was shot in the back, but that doesn't fit either; Jack simply staggered to the door of the livery stable after he had been shot and was assisted to Doctor Doneher's office by Coughlin.

One thing in the testimony which really bothered me was the fact that another person came into the livery stable to rent a horse after Jack tried to rent one, and he was given a horse. That person was never identified and didn't give any testimony. It would seem that his testimony would have been essential and would have been very relevant. Perhaps he had already gone with his horse when Jack came back and slapped James in the mouth, but it would seem that he could have been identified and could have given good testimony.

At any rate, James followed Jack to the door of the livery stable, after the shots were fired, and was standing there when Coughlin came out of Ed Kelly's saloon to investigate. James told Coughlin that he had shot Fitzgerald and was simply standing outside the livery stable with his revolver in hand. In the mean time, Malia had come out of the saloon to see what had happened and had run back in the saloon to call the doctor. After that, he "went up" and got the Catholic priest.

After Coughlin helped Jack to the doctor's office, Frank James evidently walked up to the police station and turned himself in to Shields and Breen. James was kept at the station by Breen while Shields went down to investigate the shooting. Shields testified that he checked the personal belongings of Jack; finding some money, some chewing tobacco, a pocket knife, and a handkerchief--but no watch. There had been a watch, but it had been taken by someone else previously. Perhaps Doctor Donoher removed it while Jack was in his office, or perhaps Coughlin had taken it, but it did finally turn up and was taken by Jack's relatives who came west at the time of his funeral.

There was a bit of humor and irony in the searching of Jack's person at the time. In spite of the fact James thought Jack didn't have money to rent a horse, he did have money, and it is interesting that Shields (a policeman) and others "chewed up" the tobacco which was in Jack's pockets. Fortunately, all of his personal belongings were identified and later used at the preliminary hearing and trial.

It appears that Doctor Donohue operated on Jack right in his office, then Jack was taken down to the Park City Hotel where he languished all day Sunday (25 August 1901) and finally passed away at about 7:30 o'clock that evening. Doctor LaComte cared for Jack while he was at the Hotel, and John Rooker watched at Jack's bedside from about 8:00 o'clock in the morning until Jack died that evening.

County Attorney Charles A. Callis came all the way from Coalville, about fifty miles to the east as the crow flies, and personally interviewed Jack on Sunday before he died, but I was unable to find a record of the actual testimony in the court files. During the preliminary hearing, Sheriff C. W. Mair gave his version of what was said (see Mair's testimony above), and he stated it had been had been recorded. It would have been helpful to have the actual record.

Another bit of irony comes from our finding that Attorney Callis actually interviewed Jack Fitzgerald before he died. On the 4th of September 1941, Clyde Martin Lunceford and Thelda Moss were married in the Salt Lake LDS Temple by Apostle Charles A. Callis. At the time, Apostle Callis had no idea that Clyde Lunceford was a grandson of Jack Fitzgerald, and Clyde had no idea that Charles A. Callis had personally interviewed his grandfather Jack Fitzgerald before his death. Had President Lunceford known that, he could have learned much more about his grandfather through the personal knowledge of Attorney Callis. Was it fate, a coincidence, or just chance that brought these two Irishmen together some forty years later? Perhaps someday they may speak with Jack about it.

Jack's funeral was conducted from the Catholic church in Park City at 4:30 p.m. on the 27th of August 1901, and his remains were interred in the city cemetery. According to the newpapers, his family in Gouverneur, New York were notified of the death, but it is highly unlikely that any of them were able to attend the funeral--transportation being what it was then--but they evidently arrived in Utah to take possession of what few personal belongings Jack had, and to talk with a few local people about the tragedy.

I have a special respect and warm feeling for Jack Fitzgerald, eventhough I am not related to him and have no real connection to his family. I also have a great love and respect for the Lunceford family; especially for Clyde and his lovely wife, Thelda (Moss) Lunceford and their children. Unfortunately, Thelda passed away on the 16th of October 1979 in the

Utah Valley Hospital after an extended illness. It was she who first got the ball rolling on the Jack Fitzgerald quest, and we can only hope that she has been pleased with the progress.

POSTSCRIPT

After completing my writing of this book, and to satisfy my own curiosity, I checked the 1900 Federal U.S. census for Park City, Utah in an effort to locate Jack (John) Fitzgerald the year before he was murdered, but I couldn't locate him. I searched the enumeration for Park Precinct twice and the entire Summit County district without finding a single person who met his description. There was a "John J. Fitzgerald" living in the McFadden Boarding House in Park City, but he was only 19 years of age and was born in July of 1880. He and both of his parents were born in the State of New York according to the record, but he couldn't be our Jack.

I was able to locate a Frank James, however, and a few of the other people directly involved with Jack's murder. Frank was identified as a 39 year old "Miner of Silver and Lead," who was born in December of 1860 in Germany; both of his parents were likewise listed as born in Germany, and the record indicated he emigrated to the United States in 1877, having been 23 years in this country. "Rose K. James," aged 37 years, born November 1862 in Switzerland, was shown as his wife, and the record stated they had been married four years; her parents were also listed as born in Switzerland. "Rose Noble," aged 18 years and single, born December 1881 in Utah, was shown as a "Step Daughter" to Frank. She was the only child listed in the household.

John J. Malia, who considered himself a friend of Jack's and who testified at the Preliminary Hearing was living in a boarding house in the City. He was born April 1876 in Pennsylvania, but his parents were both born in Ireland, according to the record. He was identified as a "Clerk-Miner Silver/Lead."

A "Murty McPolin" was identified as a 50 year old "Capitalist" who had been married for only 8 years. He and both of his parents were born in Ireland, and the record said he emigrated to this country in 1873. Could he have been part owner of the "McPolin and James Livery Stable" in 1901? I think not, because of the following entry.

"Patrick Heenan," the bartender at Ed Kelly's Bar the night Jack was shot, was identified in household 114/117 as a "Bartender," who was born September 1863 in Ireland and whose parents were both born in Ireland. He was listed as 36 years of age and the record said he had been married "14" years. In this same household, "Frank McPolin" was listed as "Brother-in-law" whose occupation was "Livery Stable Keeper." This McPolin was shown to be born in June of 1863 and was 36 years of age. He had been married only one year and was born in Ireland, as were both of his parents. The record indicated he (McPolin) had emigrated to the United States in 1887. Patrick Heenan emigrated in 1895 and had been in the States only five years.

"Patrick Breen," the Park City policeman who was on duty with John Shields the night of the shooting, was enumerated in household 117/121 at Park City. He was listed as "Head" of the household and was 41 years of age, having been born February 1859 in the State of New York. His parents were both born in Ireland, and the record indicated he had been married for twelve years.

"Charles Ford," Jack's old-time buddy from 1880, was head of household 334/340 of the City and had been married for eighteen years. He was 41 years of age and was born in the State of Illinois, according to the record. Both of his parents were shown as born in Massachusetts, but in the 1880 census, they were supposedly born in New Hampshire.

There were undoubtedly others whom I missed, but it was interesting to see some of the participants in Jack's murder in their domicile settings. Jack should have been enumerated with them, but perhaps he was in another county at the time. There is a "Soundex" to the 1900

Federal U.S. census, and I searched it very carefully, but there is not a person shown who fits the description of our Jack; perhaps he was taken before his time!

There are still many things which might be done to enlarge upon and add to the information presented in this work, but I will have to end my involvement for now and move to other personal matters. Perhaps a family member will find interest in the Jack Fitzgerald line and continue the work. I will forever remain a friend of the family and a staunch supporter of Jack--"I like the guy!" He may have had a hot temper, but what Irishman doesn't; he may have been a little abusive, but what Irishman hasn't; he may have drunk a little whiskey, but few Irishman haven't; but he may have been a little repentant, and what Irishman can fault that?

The Lord will forgive whom he will forgive, but of us it is required to forgive all men. Jack and his family, and all of his friends and associates, did nothing bad toward me, but I forgive them and ask the same for me. To those of you who were offended by Jack or any member of his family, or by any of his friends and associates, please forgive them and you will be a happy soul!

THE END

FITZGERALD CENSUS EXTRACTS

1880 Census of Summit County, Utah (BYUF#1338)

#94/111 - Park City ED74 Page 10

Fitzgerald, John 22 WM Miner N.Y. Eng. Ire.

Ford, Charles 21 WM Miner Ill. N.H. N.H.

1850 Census of Franklin County, New York (GSF#3988 pt 35)

#1405/1438 - Bombay		
James Fitzgerald	50 M Farmer	Ireland
Mary	52 F	Ireland
Dewitt	25 M Wheelwright	Ireland
David	22 M Laborer	Ireland
Dennis	20 M Laborer	Ireland
William	16 M Laborer	New York
Margaret	18 F	New York
Mary	17 F	New York
Bridget	14 F	New York
Eliza	12 F	New York
John	10 M	New York
Francis	11 M	New York
James	8 M	New York
#1419/1454 - Bombay		
Lary Fitzgerald	60 M Farmer	Ireland
#1420/1454 - Bombay		
John Fitzgerald	40 M Farmer	Ireland
Catherine	40 F	Ireland
Ellin	16 F	New York
Mary	11 F	New York
Michael	9 M	New York
Catherine	7 F	New York
Ann	4 F	New York
John	2 M	New York
#188/210 - Burke		
Patrick Fitzgerald	12 M	Ireland
#201/224 - Burke		
Patrick Fitzgerald	45 M Laborer	Ireland
#375/401 - Chateaugay		
Richard Fitzgerald	30 M Laborer	Ireland
#442/470 - Chateaugay		
David Fitzgerald	22 M Laborer	Ireland
Margaret	40 F	Ireland
Mary	20 F	Ireland
Thomas	18 M	Ireland
John	17 M	Ireland
Ellen	14 F	Ireland
Daniel	11 M	Ireland
#485/513 - Chateaugay		
Ellen Fitzgerald	14 F	Ireland
#993/1026 - Fort Covington		
Margaret Fitzgerald	17 F	New York

#1297/1327 - Fort Covington		
James Gillon	**40 M Farmer**	**Ireland**
Mary	**40 F**	**Ireland**
Michael	**16 M Laborer**	**Ireland**
Patrick	**14 M**	**Ireland**
Catherine	**13 F**	**Ireland**
James	**11 M**	**New York**
Sarah	**4 F**	**New York**
#601/622 - Malone		
Hannah Fitzgerald	**29 F**	**Ireland**

1860 Census of Franklin County, New York (GSF#803,754)

#170-/170 - Malone		
Patrick Fitzgerald	**57 M Laborer**	**Ireland**
#243/242 - Malone		
Mary Fitzgerald	**18 F Servant**	**Canada**
#302/300 - Malone		
Ellen Fitzgerald	**48 F Washerwoman**	**Ireland**
Thomas	**13 M**	**Ireland**
#1113/1115 - Malone		
M. Fitzgerald	**35 M Laborer**	**Ireland**
Rose	**29 F**	**Ireland**
Mary	**4 F**	**New York**
Cathrine	**3 F**	**New York**
Morris	**1 M**	**New York**
Roscan	**2/12 F**	**New York**
#196/200 - Bombay		
James Fitzgerald	**65 M Farmer**	**Ireland**
Mary	**62 F**	**Ireland**
Bridget	**22 F**	**New York**
Elisa	**20 F**	**New York**
John	**18 M**	**New York**
James	**16 M**	**New York**
#200/204 - Bombay		
Lawrence Fitzgerald	**60 M Farmer**	**Ireland**
#808/807 - Bangor		
William Gillan	**24 M Section Hand**	**Ireland**
Rosina	**23 F**	**Ireland**
#520/520 - Westville		
Julia Fitzgeralds	**20 F Servant**	**Vermont**
#534/534 - Westville		
Mary Fitzgeralds	**22 F**	**Ireland**
Ann	**20 F**	**Ireland**
Michael	**24 M Farmer**	**Ireland**
#757/757 - Westville		
Mary Fitzgeralds	**20 F Servant**	**Vermont**
#795/795 - Westville		
Thos. Fitzgeralds	**60 M Farmer**	**Ireland**
Julia	**64 F**	**Ireland**
Mary	**21 F**	**Vermont**
Julia	**19 F**	**Vermont**
Edward	**12 M**	**Vermont**

#2284/2272 - Leyden		
Hannah Fitzgerald	17 F	New York
#3275/3253 - Highmarket		
Timothy Fitzgerald	60 M Farmer	Ireland
Ellen	35 F	Ireland
Mary	18 F	New York
Hannah	16 F	New York
Edward	14 M	New York
Timothy	12 M	New York
John	6 M	New York
#4354/4323 - Diana		
John Gillmon	48 M Laborer	Canada
#4380/4347 - Diana		
Morris Fitzgerald	55 M Farmer	Ireland
Mary	55 F	Ireland
Morris	23 M	New York
Mary	27 F	New York
Michael	21 M	New York
Elisabeth	19 F	New York
Theophilus	17 M	New York

<u>1850 Census of Herkimer County, New York (GSF#3988 pt 42)</u>

#61/61 - Fairfield		
John Fitzgerald	19 M Laborer	Ireland
#52/58 - Frankfort		
Mary A. Fitzgerald	23 F	Ireland
#412/428 - Frankfort		
Alexander Gillon	40 M Laborer	Scotland
#287/294 - Little Falls		
John Fitzgerald	27 M Laborer	Ireland
#726/771 - Little Falls		
Mary Fitzgerald	20 F	Ireland
#727/772 - Little Falls		
Catharine Fitzgerald	22 F	Ireland
#247/256 - Russia		
William Fitzgeralds	26 M Farmer	New York
Mary	20 F	England
Stephen	24 M Laborer	New York
#20/21 - Wilmurth		
James Fitzgerald	31 M Farmer	New York
Martha	22 F	New York
Richard	5 M	New York
Esther	4 F	New York

1860 Census of Herkimer County, New York (GSF#803,759)

#311/328 - Manheim		
Michael Fitzgerald	71 M Day Laborer	Ireland
John	41 M Day Laborer	Ireland
Catharine	38 F	Ireland
Michael	8 M	New York
Bridget	5 F	New York
Thomas	2/12 M	New York
Mary	35 F Servant	New York
Bridget	21 F Servant	New York
#328/345 - Manheim		
James Fitzgerald	51 M Laborer	Ireland
Mary	31 F	Ireland
#475/450 - Schuyler		
Thomas Fitzgerald	30 M Farm Laborer	Ireland
#496/468 - Schuyler		
William Fitzgerald	40 M Laborer	Ireland
Margaret	30 F	Ireland
William	4 M	New York
Catherine	3 F	New York
Edward	1 M	New York
#662/610 - Schuyler		
Michael Fitzgerald	25 M Farm Laborer	Ireland
#665/613 - Schuyler		
Henry Gillon	19 M Farm Laborer	Ireland
#927/854 - Russia		
James Fitzgeralds	40 M Laborer	New York
Martha	36 F	New York
Richard	15 M	New York
Ester	14 F	New York
Henry	5 M	New York
Matilda	6 F	New York
#931/857 - Russia		
Michael Fitzgerald	25 M Farm Laborer	New York
#1005/925 - Russia		
Thomas Fitzgerald	31 M Laborer	Ireland
Rose	36 F	Ireland
Mary	11 F	New York
Timothy	8 M	New York
#348/344 - Little Falls		
Patrick Fitzgeralds	19 M Farm Laborer	Ireland
#432/440 - Little Falls		
Mary Fitzgerald	30 F	Ireland
John	3 M	New York
#918/903 - Little Falls		
John Fitzgerald	75 M Day Laborer	Ireland
Margaret	72 F	Ireland
#950/935 - Little Falls		
John Fitzgeralds	23 M Factory Hand	Ireland
Sarah	22 F	Ireland
Thomas	2 M	New York
John	2/12 M	New York

#1318/1293 - Little Falls		
Catharine Fitzgeralds	18 F Domestic	Ireland
#1397/1367 - Little Falls		
Bridget Fitzgeralds	23 F Domestic	Ireland

1850 Census of Jefferson County, New York (BYU F#514)

#138/156 - Watertown		
Michael Fitzgerald	20 M Tailor	Ireland
Mary A.	30 F	Ireland
#471/471 - Clayton		
Barrington Fitzgerald	26 M Farmer	Ireland
Michael	56 M Laborer	Ireland
Hannah	56 F	Ireland
Peter	19 M Laborer	New York
John	28 M Farmer	New York

1880 Census of Jefferson County, New York

#172/189 - Antwerp	
Fitzgerald, Lawrence	45 WM Miner Ire. Ire. Ire.
Maggie	35 WF Wife Ont. Ire. Ire.
William	18 WM Son N.Y. Ire. Ont.
Edward	16 WM Son N.Y. Ire. Ont.
Michael	14 WM Son N.Y. Ire. Ont.
Lawrence	12 WM Son N.Y. Ire. Ont.
John	9 WM Son N.Y. Ire. Ont.
Charles	6 WM Son N.Y. Ire. Ont.
Thomas	2 WM Son N.Y. Ire. Ont.
Mary	1 WF Dau. N.Y. Ire. Ont.
#176/201 - Antwerp	
Fitzgerald, John	60 WM Miner Ire. Ire. Ire.
Mary	55 WF Wife Ire. Ire. Ire.
Maggie	20 WF Dau. Ont. Ire. Ire.
Mary	14 WF Dau. N.Y. Ire. Ire.
Michael	11 WM Son N.Y. Ire. Ire.
James	9 WM Son N.Y. Ire. Ire.
Tina	6 WF Dau. N.Y. Ire. Ire.
Letia	4 WF Dau. N.Y. Ire. Ire.

1850 Census of Lewis County, New York (GSF#3988 pt 53)

#1630/1665 - Denmark		
David Fitzgerald	20 M Farmer	New York
#2408/2443 - Diana		
Morris Fitzgerald	50 M Farmer	Ireland
Mary	45 F	Ireland
Mary	17 F	New York
Morris	14 M	New York
Michael	12 M	New York
Betsey	9 F	New York
Theophilus	7 M	New York
Elizabeth	5 F	New York
Susan	4 F	New York

#540/551 - West Turin		
Timothy Fitzgeralds	**36 M Farmer**	**Ireland**
Ellen	**30 F**	**Ireland**
Mary	**9 F**	**New York**
Joanna	**7 F**	**New York**
Edward	**5 M**	**New York**
Timothy	**1 M**	**New York**

1860 Census of Lewis County, New York (GSF#803,777)

#4380/4347 - Diana		
Morris Fitzgerald	**55 M Farmer**	**Ireland**
Mary	**55 F**	**Ireland**
Morris	**23 M**	**New York**
Mary	**27 F**	**New York**
Michael	**21 M**	**New York**
Elizabeth	**19 F**	**New York**
Theophilus	**17 M**	**New York**
#3275/3253 - Highmarket		
Timothy Fitzgerald	**40 M Farmer**	**Ireland**
Ellen	**35 F**	**Ireland**
Mary	**18 F**	**New York**
Hannah	**16 F**	**New York**
Edward	**14 M**	**New York**
Timothy	**12 M**	**New York**
John	**6 M**	**New York**
#2284/2272 - Leyden		
Hannah Fitzgerald	**17 F**	**New York**

1850 Census of St. Lawrence County, New York (BYU F#589)

#394/401 - Gouverneur		
Patrick Fitzgerald	**17 M Shoemaker**	**Ireland**
#203/212 - Brasher		
Michael Gillen	**34 M Farm Hand**	**Ireland**
Lucy	**34 F**	**Ireland**
Thomas	**12 M**	**Vermont**
Betsy	**9 F**	**New York**
Michael Jr.	**8 M**	**New York**
John	**5 M**	**New York**
James	**5 M**	**New York**
George	**4 M**	**New York**
Lucy Ann	**1 F**	**New York**
Mary	**1 F**	**New York**
Catherine	**2/12 F**	**New York**
#204/213 - Brasher		
Michael Gillen	**20 M Laborer**	**Ireland**
#185/193 - Canton		
John Fitzgerald	**35 M Laborer**	**Ireland**
Mary	**25 F**	**Ireland**

#7/7 - Lorraine Twp.		
Henry Fitzgerald	30 M Farmer	Ireland
Rosie	28 F	Ireland
William	6 M	New York
John	4 M	New York
#2136/2164 - Lorraine Twp.		
John Fitzgerald	28 M Farmer	Ireland
Mary A.	28 F	Ireland
James	1 M	Ireland
#2389/2389 - Lorraine Twp.		
James Fitzgerald	24 M Farmer	Ireland
#6/6 - Louisville		
John Fitzgerald	40 M Farmer	Ireland
Mary A.	31 F	Ireland
Michael	20 M	New York
Mary	8 F	New York
Ellen	6 F	New York
Catherine	3 F	New York
#689/731 - Potsdam		
Thomas Fitzgerald	48 M Laborer	Ireland
Catherine	41 F	Ireland
Edward	16 M Laborer	Ireland
Ellen	13 F	Ireland
Dennis	10 M	Ireland
Timothy Malory	45 M Laborer	Ireland
Timothy Lines	45 M Laborer	Ireland

1860 Census of St. Lawrence County, New York (GSF#4014 pt 35)

Page 29 - Rossie		
John Gillon	30 M Laborer	Ireland
Margaret	20 F	Ireland
Michael	2 M	New York

1870 Census of St. Lawrence County, New York (GSF#552,598)

#17/17 - Rossie		
Gillin, Grace	36 F Keeps House	Ireland
Rosannah	10 F	New York
Daniel	6 M	New York
William	3 M	New York
#94/89 - Rossie		
Fitzgerald, John	50 M WorksOreBed	Canada
Margaret	40 F Keeps House	Canada
Anna	18 F At Home	New York
John	10 M	New York
Maggie	9 F	New York
Catherine	8 F	New York
Amy	4 F	New York
Michael	2 M	New York

#95/90 - Rossie		
Pound, John	45 M Day Laborer	Irland
Mary	40 F Keeps House	Ireland
John	15 M WorksOreBed	Ireland
Ann	13 F At Home	Ireland
Patrick	11 M	New York
Julia	9 F	New York
William	7 M	New York
James	5 M	New York
Peter	3 M	New York
Edward	3 M	New York
#128/118 - Rossie		
Pound, Patrick	48 M Farmer	Ireland
Teressa	32 F Keeps House	Switzerland
Thomas	15 M Works on Farm	New York
Peter	14 M	New York
William	**12 M**	**New York**
Edward	11 M	New York
Mary A.	9 F	New York
Francis	8 M	New York
Teressa	6 F	New York
Julia	4 F	New York
Hannah	3 F	New York
Catherine	1 F	New York
Thomas	**70 M Day Laborer**	**Ireland**
#185/185 - Gouverneur		
Clapp, Thos. C.	35 M Cabinet Maker	Canada
Frances	33 F Keeps House	Canada
Fred	11 M	Canada
Allen	8 M	Canada
Homer	**6 M**	**Canada**
Aleda	3 F	New York
#388/402 - Gouverneur		
Fitzgerald, David	28 M Farmer	Ireland
Ellen	25 F Keeps House	New York
James	6 M	New York
Edwin	3 M	New York
Mary	1 F	New York
#653/653 - Gouverneur		
Fitzgerald, William	23 M Teamster	Ireland
Mary	24 F Keeps House	Canada
Mary L.	6 F	New York
Maggie E.	3 F	New York
William H.	1 M	New York
#106/106 - Hopkinton Township		
Gillin, John	25 M Stone Jobber	New York
Nora	23 F Keeps House	Ireland
Allen	2 M	New York
Lucy	7/12 F	New York

#368/368 - Hopinton Township

Gillin, Michael	55 M Farmer	Ireland
Julia	40 F Keeps House	Canada
Mary A.	10 F At School	New York
Edwin	6 M	New York

1880 Census of St. Lawrence County, New York (GSF#43984 pt 231)

#163/172 - Rossie (Page 18)

Gillin, Grace	46 WF Widow Ire. Ire. Ire.
Rosanna	20 WF Dau. N.Y. Ire. Ire.
Daniel	16 WM Son N.Y. Ire. Ire.

#35/36 - Gouverneur (Page 4)

Fitzgerald, David	43 WM Farmer Ire. Ire. Ire.
Ellen	35 WF Wife Ire. Ire. Ire.
Edwin	13 WM Son N.Y. Ire. Ire.
Mary A.	11 WF Dau. N.Y. Ire. Ire.
Nora	7 WF Dau. N.Y. Ire. Ire.
Rose	3 WF Dau. N.Y. Ire. Ire.
Ellen	3/12 WF Dau. N.Y. Ire. Ire.

1900 Census of St. Lawrence County, New York (FHL F#1,241,156)

#10/12 -Gouverneur

Fitzgerald, Tinnie 18 **Servant; Single; born Jan 1882**
born New York; parents born Ireland
(In household of Andrew Irving; age 60; born Canada)

#46/50 - Gouverneur

Fitzgerald, Margaret 67 **WF Widow; born Aug 1832**
mother of 11 children; 8 living; to U.S. 1860
born Ireland; parents born Ireland

Fitzgerald, James 26 **WM Son; single; born Apr 1874**
born New York; parent born Ireland

#248/254 - Gouverneur

Fitzgerald, Margaret 59 WF Married; born Oct 1840
mother of 8 children; 8 living; born Canada
parents born Canada; 1870; 30

Fitzgerald, Charles 36 WM Son; born Jan 1874; single
born New York; father born Ireland; mother born Canada

Fitzgerald, John 32 WM Son; born Dec 1877; single

Fitzgerald, Thomas 28 WM Son; born Aug 1871; single

Fitzgerald, May 21 WF Dau; born May 1879; single
(birth for John, Thomas, May same as for Charles)

#402/410 - Gouverneur
Fitzgerald, Michael 31 WM Laborer; born July 1868
married 7 years; born New York; parents born Ireland
Fitzgerald, Margaret 34 WF Wife; born Feb 1866
married 7 years; mother of 3; 3 living
born New York; father born Ireland; mother born N.Y.
Fitzgerald, Charlie 6 WM Son; born Feb 1894; single
born New York; father and mother born New York
Fitzgerald, Clarence 4 WM Son; born Oct 1895; single
born new York; father and mother born New York
Fitzgerald, Stanley 2 WM Son; born March 1898; single
born New York; father and mother born New York

1905 Census of St. Lawrence County, New York (State) GSF#885,346)

John Street - Gouverneur
Clapp, Allen 42 WM Cabinet Maker born U.S.
Tilla 35 WF Wife born U.S.
Orra 14 WF Dau. born U.S.
Carl 14 WM Son born U.S.
Ray 9 WM Son born U.S.
Parker Street - Gouverneur
Orford, William F. 28 WM Marble Quarry born U.S.
Nellie N. (Millie) 34 WF Wife born U.S.
Fitzgerald, Harry 14 WM Stepson born U.S.
Gouverneur
Fitzgerald, Margaret 63 WF Irish; Canada; 42 yrs U.S.
John 33 WM Blksmth born U.S.
Charles J. 30 WM Marble Worker born U.S.
Thomas 26 WM Engineer born U.S.
Mary A. 25 WF Lace Mill Worker born U.S.
#10 Wall Street - Gouverneur (Page 28)
Fitzgerald, Margaret 72 WF born Ire; 65 yrs in U.S.
James 33 WM Son Night Watchman b. U.S.
Grove Street - Gouverneur (Page 3)
Fitzgerald, Tinney 29 WF Servant; born U.S.
(in household of Andrew Irvin 55 born Canada)
Town of Rossie (Page 10)
Fitzgerald, Michael 35 WM Bartender born U.S.
(in household of Vivian Whitney Hotel Keeper)
Town of Rossie
Pound, Mary J. 46 WF Dressmaker born U.S.
Leo 15 WM Grandson born U.S.
Pound, Patrick 79 WM born Ire; 56 yrs in U.S.
Mary A. 44 WF Dau. born U.S.
Pound, James 29 WF Farmer; born U.S.
Rose Ann 25 WF Wife; born U.S.

1925 State Census of St. Lawrence County, New York (FHL F#532,414)

Wall Street #35 1/2 - Gouverneur
Fitzgerald, James 52 WM Repairman; born U.S. citizen
Fitzgerald, Tinnie 50 WF Sister; born U.S. citizen
Fitzgerald, Stanley 26 WM Brother; born U.S. citizen

Hailesboro #9 - Gouverneur		
Fitzgerald, Charles J.	50 WM Head; born U.S. citizen	
Fitzgerald, Thomas E.	48 WM Brother; born U.S. citizen	
Fitzgerald, Mae A.	46 WF Sister; born U.S. citizen	

1851 Census of Grenville County, Ontario, Canada (GSF#349.210)

Page 27 - Wolford Township		
James Fitzgerald	M 34-1852 Farmer	Ireland
Agnes	F 22-1852	Ireland
Edward	M 3-1852	Canada
James	M 2-1852	Canada
Page 92-Wolford Township		
William Fitzgerald	M 14-1852	Canada
George	M 9-1852	Canada
Page 94 - Wolford Township		
Betsey Fitzgerald	F 56-1852	Ireland

1861 Census of Grenville County, Ontario, Canada (GSF#349,269)

Page 14 - Merrickville		
Helen Fitzgerald	F 18-1861	Canada West
Page 13 - Prescott		
Michael Fitzgerald	M 35-1861 Labourer	Ireland
Mary	F 30-1861	Ireland
Bridget	F 4-1861	Upper Canada
Allace	F 2-1861	Upper Canada
Page 18 - Wolford Township		
James Fitzgerald	M 40-1861 Yeoman	Ireland
Agnes	F 29-1861	Ireland
Edward	M 12-1861	Canada West
James	M 11-1861	Canada West
Mary	F 9-1861	Canada West
Cathrine	F 7-1861	Canada West
Samuel	M 5-1861	Canada West
Sarah	F 2-1861	Canada West
Martha	F 1-1861	Canada West
Page 39 - Wolford Township		
Bridget Fitzgerald	F 17-1861 Servant	Upper Canada
Page 44 - Wolford Township		
Ann Fitzgerald	F 17-1861 Servant	Upper Canada
Page 49 - Wolford Township		
John Fitzgerald	**M 47-1861 Labourer**	**Ireland**
Margaret	**F 45-1861 Wife**	**Ireland**
Ann	**F 6-1861 Dau.**	**U.S.**
John	**M 3-1861 Son**	**U.S.**
Margret	**F 1-1861**	**U.S.**
Page 66 - Augusta Township		
James Fitzgerald	M 27-1861 Laborer	Ireland
Mary	F 26-1861	Ireland
John	M 5-1861	Upper Canada
Michael	M 3-1861	Upper Canada
Rosa Anna	F 1-1861	Upper Canada

Page 116 - Augusta Township		
John Fitzgerald	**M 40-1861 Farmer**	**Ireland**
Edward	**M 16-1861 Farmer**	**Upper Canada**
Joseph	**M 15-1861 Farmer**	**Upper Canada**
Cathrine	**F 13-1861**	**Upper Canada**
Mary	**F 8-1861**	**Upper Canada**
Cathrine	**F 80-1861**	**Ireland**

<u>1861 Census of Leeds County, Ontario, Canada (GSF#349,289)</u>

Page 12 - Brockville		
Edward Fitzgerald	**M 80-1861**	**Ireland**
Page 29 - Kitley Township		
Michael Fitzgerald	**M 71-1861 Farmer**	**Ireland**
Mary	**F 30-1861**	**Ireland**
Ellen	**F 19-1861**	**Upper Canada**
Bridget	**F 18-1861**	**Upper Canada**
Ann	**F 17-1861**	**Upper Canada**
Mary	**F 15-1861**	**Upper Canada**
Michael	**M 12-1861**	**Upper Canada**
John	**M 10-1861**	**Upper Canada**
Agnes J.	**F 8-1861**	**Upper Canada**
Peter	**M 6-1861**	**Upper Canada**
Thos.	**M 4-1861**	**Upper Canada**
Page 41 - Kitley Township		
Margaret Fitzgerald	**F 36-1861 Farmer**	**Ireland**
Ellen	**F 60-1861**	**Ireland**
John	**M 17-1861 Labourer**	**Upper Canada**
Daniel	**M 14-1861 Labourer**	**Upper Canada**
Patt	**M 13-1861 Labourer**	**Upper Canada**
Mary	**F 11-1861**	**Upper Canada**
Thomas	**M 6-1861**	**Upper Canada**
Bridget	**F 4-1861**	**Upper Canada**
Margaret	**F 2-1861**	**Upper Canada**
Page 44 - Kitley Township (Wm P. age 1 also below)		
Thomas Fitzgerald	**M 80-1861 Farmer**	**Ireland**
Mary	**F 43-1861**	**Ireland**
John	**M 23-1861**	**Upper Canada**
Patrick	**M 20-1861**	**Upper Canada**
Peter	**M 18-1861**	**Upper Canada**
Thomas	**M 16-1861**	**Upper Canada**
James	**M 14-1861**	**Upper Canada**
Michael	**M 12-1861**	**Upper Canada**
Lenora	**F 9-1861**	**Upper Canada**
William H.	**M 7-1861**	**Upper Canada**
Mary A.	**F 5-1861**	**Upper Canada**
Edward	**M 3-1861**	**Upper Canada**
Jerold	**M 1-1861**	**Upper Canada**

Page 61 - Leeds Township
James Gillon M 26-1861 Blksmth Ireland
Page 71 - Yonge Township
John Gillan (or Gilland) M 47-1861 Farmer Ireland
Charlotte F 43-1861 Upper Canada
Joseph M 26-1861 Labourer Upper Canada
Amelia F 20-1861 Upper Canada
Adaline F 16-1861 Upper Canada
John W. M 13-1861 Upper Canada
Louisa F 10-1861 Upper Canada

<u>1900 Census of Grant County, New Mexico (FHL F#1,241,000)</u>
#20 - Pinos Altos
Robinson, Lewis (Head) 41 WM Doctor of M.; born Sep 1858
married 9 years; born Pa; parents born Pa.
Robinson, Katie 31 WF Wife; born Jan 1869 New York
married 9 years; mother of 5; 4 living
father born Ireland; mother born Switzerland
Robinson, Shelburn 6 WM; Son; born May 1894; New Mexico
Robinson, Edgar J. 4 WM; Son; born Dec 1895; New Mexico
Robinson, Lewis S. 2 WM; Son; born Mar 1898; New Mexico
Robinson, Mary E. 1/12 WF; Dau; born Apr 1900; New Mexico
Pound, Hannah 33 WF; D-in-law; born Jan 1867 New York
father born Ireland; mother born Switzerland
#39 - Pinos Altos
Pound, William (Head) 42 WM Gold Miner; born Oct 1857
married 19 years; born New York
father born Ireland; mother born Switzerland
Pound, Maggie 38 WF Wife; born April 1862
married 19 years; mother of 6; 4 living
born Canada; parents born ireland; 1867; 33
Pound, Fred 14 WM Son; born May 1886; single
Pound, Marie 12 WF Dau; born Feb 1888; single
Pound, Roy (data unreadable)
Pound, Charles A. (data unreadable)

INDEX

www.ingramcontent.com/pod-product-compliance
Lightning Source LLC
Chambersburg PA
CBHW080423270326
41929CB00018B/3142